TEACHING LITERATURE IN VIRTUAL WORLDS

What are the realities and possibilities of utilizing online virtual worlds as teaching tools for specific literary works?

Through engaging and surprising stories from secondary and college classrooms where virtual worlds are in use, this book invites readers to understand and participate in this emerging and valuable pedagogy. It examines the experience of high school and college literature teachers involved in a pioneering project to develop virtual worlds for literary study, detailing how they created, utilized, and researched different immersive and interactive virtual reality environments to support the teaching of a wide range of literary works from Anglo-Saxon poetry and Shakespeare plays, to eighteenth-century novels, commonly taught modern works, and young adult fiction.

Readers see close-up how, in these online environments, students role-play as literary characters, extending and altering character conduct in purposeful ways, and how they explore online, interactive literature maps, museums, archives, and game worlds to analyze the impact of historical and cultural setting, language, and dialogue on literary characters and events. These virtual worlds, which have been visited by students from around the globe, have been created in at least seven distinct online forms: intertextual map, virtual tour, role-play stage, alternative reality game, second world, textual riff, and virtual museum. Elaborating this typology itself makes an important contribution to the literature on online learning.

Within education, the use of virtual worlds is growing exponentially. The Literary Worlds Project from which this book emerges has served as a laboratory for research into the utilization of virtual spaces in the teaching of literature. This book breaks exciting ground, offering insights and pedagogical suggestions, and inviting readers to consider the future of this innovative approach to teaching literary texts—one that is sure to engage both the brightest and the most reluctant reader in the classroom.

Allen Webb is Professor of English Education and Postcolonial Studies at Western Michigan University.

TEACHING LITERATURE IN VIRTUAL WORLDS

Immersive Learning in English Studies

Edited by
Allen Webb

Routledge
Taylor & Francis Group

NEW YORK AND LONDON

First published 2012
by Routledge
711 Third Avenue, New York, NY 10017

Simultaneously published in the UK
by Routledge
2 Park Square, Milton Park, Abingdon, Oxon OX14 4RN

Routledge is an imprint of the Taylor & Francis Group, an informa business

Library of Congress Cataloging in Publication Data
Teaching literature in virtual worlds: immersive learning in English
    studies / edited by Allen Webb.
    p. cm.
    Includes bibliographical references and index.
    1. Educational technology. 2. Literature—Study and teaching—
    Technological innovations. 3. Web-based instruction. 4. Immersion
    method (Language teaching) I. Webb, Allen.
    LB1028.3.T3864 2011
    371.33–dc23   2011017810

ISBN: 978–0–415–88628–4 (hbk)
ISBN: 978–0–415–88629–1 (pbk)
ISBN: 978–0–203–83647–7 (ebk)

Typeset in Bembo
by Florence Production Ltd, Stoodleigh, Devon

Printed and bound in the United States of America on acid-free paper
by Walsworth Publishing Company, Marceline, MO

SUSTAINABLE
FORESTRY
INITIATIVE

Certified Sourcing
www.sfiprogram.org
SFI-00555
The SFI label applies to the text stock.

CONTENTS

PREFACE

Teaching Literature in Virtual Worlds: Immersive Learning in English Studies explores the possibilities for literary virtual worlds as pedagogical tools for middle school, high school, and college teaching. Specific chapters report on teachers and students using virtual worlds to better understand Shakespeare plays, popular novels like *Of Mice and Men, The Great Gatsby, Lord of the Flies, Things Fall Apart, Brave New World*, and works by Daniel Defoe, Virginia Woolf, Tony Kushner, Anglo-Saxon poets, and others.

This book invites teachers to participate in the use and development of an emerging pedagogical approach likely to be of increasing importance in all disciplines, not only in the teaching of literature. Chapters report on middle school, high school, and college teachers developing literary virtual worlds, students experiencing them, and our research on the learning that results.

There are a variety of ways that virtual worlds can support and extend the reading of literary works. Depending on the source text and the goals of the virtual world builder there are even different types of literary virtual worlds that can be created. Because virtual worlds draw on immersive, technology-enhanced multimedia, and interactive approaches, they engage students and create new and interesting opportunities for learning. How and what students learn in a literary virtual world depends on the way that world interprets literary settings and cultural and historical contexts and how it calls for student interaction, dialogue, and writing. Writing in a virtual world can range from casual book-group conversation to careful literary criticism and historical analysis, from lively role-play to creative and sophisticated extensions of source materials. Integrating virtual worlds into literary study is not a matter of simply setting students at computers and dropping them off in virtual space. The teacher needs to think carefully about his or her goals and approaches, including preparing students for specific virtual world experiences, thoughtfully supporting their participation, and creating opportunities for in-depth reflection on their learning. This book illustrates that while virtual worlds are an enjoyable and interesting diversion from the traditional classroom, they also can be a rich resource for enhancing education.

Overview

In Chapter 1, Allen Webb explains how literary virtual worlds bring together pedagogical, content, and technological knowledge to create engaging environments for reading and responding to literature. Constructivism, discovery and problem-posing learning, ensemble production, and new media literacy offer important theoretical frameworks for understanding learning in virtual worlds. Well-designed literary virtual worlds are deeply connected to their source texts and offer diverse ways to respond to and extend literary reading. The chapter describes the enCore interface used by the Literary Worlds Project and identifies a typology for literary virtual worlds including role-play stage, alternative reality game, second world, textual riff, intertextual map, virtual tour, and virtual museum.

Chapter 2, "A Virtual World for *Lord of the Flies*: Engaging Students and Meeting Common Core Standards," by Cara Arver, describes the experience of a high school teacher designing and using a virtual world to teach William Golding's novel *Lord of the Flies*. Arver draws on transcripts of student activities in the virtual world as they develop and role-play characters on the island; she also discusses how student dialogue as virtual characters allows them to address specific Common Core Standards for the teaching of reading and writing.

In Chapter 3, "*Midsummer Madness* and *The Virtual Tempest*: Shakespeare as Foolish Role-play Game," Joseph Haughey and Jennifer Barns describe virtual worlds for Shakespeare's plays *A Midsummer Night's Dream* and *The Tempest*. Building on performance approaches for teaching Shakespeare and scholarship on the spontaneity of Shakespeare's stage, the chapter argues that virtual worlds can effectively introduce students to Shakespeare and deepen their understanding of his works including language, characters, setting, and action. The virtual worlds described are in the form on online role-playing games and the chapter draws on the theory of James Gee while inviting other teachers of Shakespeare to develop additional virtual worlds.

Chapter 4, "From Migrant Labor to High Society: *Of Mice and Men* and *The Great Gatsby* in Virtual Worlds," by Gretchen Rumohr-Voskuil and Meghan Dykema, describes virtual worlds for teaching two of the most commonly taught works of American literature, *Of Mice and Men* and *The Great Gatsby*. Both worlds allow students to role-play characters from the novels in an online virtual environment. The *Of Mice and Men* world focuses on the portrayal of migrant labor and the process of unionization. It connects Steinbeck's novel to the Mexican American work, *And the Earth Did Not Devour Him* by Tomas Rivera and draws on themes also found in *The Grapes of Wrath* and *In Dubious Battle*, and on images and films about migrant workers and unionization. *The Great Gatsby* world emphasizes jazz music and the "roaring 20s" and many of the images used in this world come from contemporary New York City postcards.

In Chapter 5, "Teaching *Things Fall Apart* in *The Village of Umuofia*," Cheryl Taliaferro, a high school teacher, describes teaching students about the novel *Things Fall Apart* by using the virtual world called *The Village of Umuofia*. Her 9th grade students do background research on Africa, write responses to images found in the virtual world, and practice assuming the perspective of characters during the reading of the novel by journaling from their point of view. Then her students engage in a virtual role-play where they "wake up" in the virtual world as characters from the novel including Igbo citizens, missionaries, and British colonizers.

Chapter 6, "Content Learning in Literary Virtual Worlds: *The Village of Umuofia*," by Allen Webb, is a close examination of student learning about the culture, history, characters, and themes of *Things Fall Apart* from their experience in a virtual-world role-play. Drawing on the thinking of Franco Moretti, Tzvetan Todorov, and Roland Barthes, the chapter shows how a literary virtual world can be understood as an interpretation as well as an extension of its source text. *The Village of Umuofia* maps *Things Fall Apart*, creates an immersive experience through West African music and a visual gallery of historically related black and white photographs. In this virtual world, as in the novel, students confront and respond to representations of "the Other." The virtual role-play allows students to extend the source text by entering into dialogue in action from the point of view of characters. An analysis of a virtual world transcript illustrates student in-depth knowledge, and ability to extend the source text.

In Chapter 7, "Building a Secondary *Brave New World*," Robert Rozema, a 12th grade high school teacher, reports on his students joining him in building a virtual world for teaching Aldous Huxley's novel *Brave New World*. Students used the *Brave New World* virtual space to talk about the major ideas of the novel, including its critiques of consumerism, technology, and the culture of recreation. Drawing on reader-response theory, Rozema describes how an experiential model of reading underlies the experience of a literary virtual world. Students describe and develop their own characters and create a wide variety of spaces that closely relate to yet extend Huxley's vision in the novel.

Chapter 8, "Riffing on the Pied Piper: Combining Research and Creativity," by Linda Dick explores how students can become virtual world builders and, along with their professor, gather historical, cultural, literary, and interpretative texts and images that respond, in this case, to the legend of "The Pied Piper of Hamelin." The chapter describes an approach to literary virtual world design called a "textual riff," an inviting and open form that invites student research and creativity in an immersive, ever-growing environment. Drawing on Rob Pope's idea of textual intervention, students connect research on history of the Middle

Ages to elaborate aspects of the legend, including adding creative writing from the point of view of characters, creating maps or images related to the story, analyzing the story from a feminist perspective, learning specific medieval vocabulary, and connecting the legend to other popular stories and fairy tales.

In Chapter 9, "Virtual *Flanerie*: Strolling through *Mrs. Dalloway's London*," Todd Kuchta explains how a virtual world based on early twentieth-century photographs of London allows students to closely follow two walking trips that the main characters in Virginia Woolf's *Mrs. Dalloway* take through the city and to consider the connection between their inner thoughts and the urban geographical landmarks in the novel. This virtual world also allows students to explore Woolf's approach to modernist writing, particularly the experimental, stream-of-consciousness technique she called "tunneling." Space-based literary critics Henri Lefebvre, Mikhail Bakhtin, and Franco Moretti provide theoretical justification for the pedagogical value of literary mapping. The virtual world includes extensive period maps, and textual selections from the novel paired with E. O. Hoppe's photographic images from the period of locations or objects described in the novel. The chapter includes an appendix of discussion questions relating the novel to the London setting.

Chapter 10, "Virtual Museums: British Literary Works in Historical and Cultural Context," by Christopher Nagle, Ilse Schweitzer VanDonkelaar and Cynthia Klekar, describes three different virtual world museums the authors created to inform student reading of British literary works from the Anglo-Saxon period (*Beowulf* and Anglo-Saxon poetry from the Exeter manuscript) to the eighteenth and nineteenth centuries. The Anglo-Saxon world includes images from recent archaeological finds and illuminated gospels to create both an interior and exterior world. The world for Daniel Defoe's *Moll Flanders* draws students' attention to the complex relationship between text, history, and culture and addresses topics such as female education, marriage laws, the city and country, charitable institutions, fashion, architecture, manners, and trade. The world for Sydney Owenson's novel *The Wild Irish Girl* includes audio clips of authentic Irish harp performance from the period, background on Irish Catholic religious contexts, information on sensibility and allusions to other literary works (the novels of Richardson and Sterne, the poetry of Collins and Goldsmith), images of the original manuscript, and historical maps of Dublin and the environs of the novel.

Chapter 11, "'The Kindness of Strangers:' *Angels in America* in a Virtual World," by Steve Feffer, considers the possibilities and problems in using a literary virtual world as a form of production dramaturgy to augment the reader's experience of Tony Kushner's play *Angels in America*. The virtual world maps the physical spaces contemporary to the play's setting as well as historical (the Reagan White House, the Rosenbergs) and imaginary settings (Kushner's image of heaven, Harper's drug-induced image of Antarctica) relevant to its content. This virtual world draws students into exploring "The Theatre of Fabulousness" and its relationship to Bertolt Brecht, Walter Benjamin's theory of history, and Paul Klee's painting.

Chapter 12, "From MUDs to Metaverses: The Past and Future of Immersive Literary Worlds," by Robert Rozema, describes a variety of moments in the development of virtual worlds for literary study, and offers some ideas about the future of this approach. Early multiplayer environments, MUDS and MOOs based in part on *Dungeons and Dragons* allowed the development of MUD1 and *Zork*, and in the late 1980s and early 1990s, TinyMUD, LambdaMOO, and LinguaMOO, all based in Multi-user Domain, Object Oriented programming. The debut of enCore in 1998, created by Cynthia Haynes and Jan Rune Holmevik, brought a split-screen interface and command bars providing a more visual, intuitive MOO environment that capitalizes on the resources of the web. Villa Diodata and cmc MOO were early literary MOOs. *Second Life*, brought online by Linden Labs in 2003, includes the New Media Consortium (NMC) Campus. Never fully executed, *Arden: The World of William Shakespeare* was designed in 2006 by Edward Castronova. Next was the rise of massively multiplayer online games (MMOGs) including *EverQuest*, *World of Warcraft*, *Grand Theft Auto*.

Chapter 13, "On the Building of Worlds," by Kevin Jepson, supports teachers or others who want to build new literary virtual worlds, providing extensive information about how to conceive such a project, and specific steps to take to build in enCore, either through Literary Worlds or on your own. This chapter explains how to build, embellish, and connect rooms, use the Xpress Object Editor, insert images and media files, develop a classroom, use the transcript system, create players, and basic object programming. Accessing additional information and technical support is also a theme of the chapter.

ACKNOWLEDGMENTS

This book would not have been possible without the collegial support and close faculty/student relationships of the English Department at Western Michigan University (WMU). The department embodies a synergistic collaboration between faculty and students in literary studies, creative writing, and English education. For many years one of the largest English teacher education programs in the United States, WMU's English Department is one of only a handful that grant Ph.D.s concentrated in English education. Research into the teaching of English carried out in English departments facilitates a deep exploration of humanities pedagogy, amply demonstrated by this volume. Funded by a 2006 WMU Presidential Innovation grant, the Literary Worlds Project has involved cutting-edge classroom experimentation, teamwork across areas and academic levels, scholarly research and publication, and the development of meaningful friendships.

Credits

1

INTRODUCTION

Allen Webb

A literary virtual world is a computer-based simulated environment interpreting a literary source text or texts. Drawing on the Literary Worlds Project, *Teaching Literature in Virtual Worlds: Immersive Learning in English Studies* explores the possibilities for literary virtual worlds as pedagogical tools. This book invites teachers to participate in the use and development of an emerging pedagogical approach likely to be of increasing importance in all disciplines, not only in the teaching of literature. Chapters report on middle school, high school, and college teachers developing literary virtual worlds, students experiencing them, and our research on the learning that results.

Virtual worlds differ significantly one to another in terms of their pedagogical demands and strategies, but they all draw on immersive, constructivist, multimedia, and technology-enhanced approaches. We have found literary virtual worlds to facilitate learning in diverse ways depending on their integration of textual geographies, visual images, sound effects, student/avatar interaction and discussion, textual language, narrative structures, historical and cultural contexts, and analytical, creative, and perspectival writing. Student dialogue and writing in a virtual world takes place in a technology-based performance space created by virtual world builders working within the possibilities and constraints of particular software platforms. Entering an imaginative world based on a literary work and created by a teacher-builder, students engage in and, at times, modify, that world based on their reading of the literary text, their learning from writing, dialog, and class instruction, their previous reading and life experiences, as well as their observation, interaction, and participation in the virtual world itself. The powerful textual, visual, aural, and participatory immersion of virtual world experiences combined with knowledge from the careful reading of literary works helps students develop increasingly complex and contextualized comprehension of the source texts. And, not only that, but literary virtual worlds are fun!

While the experiments reported in *Teaching Literature in Virtual Worlds* have broad possibilities and implications for learning in the twenty-first century, this book comes out of a specific undertaking. Between 2005 and 2010 seventeen different literary worlds were created and implemented by the Literary Worlds Project, a grant-funded, non-profit activity in the English Department at Western Michigan University. Western Michigan University supports one of the largest teacher training programs in the United States and this pioneering project has provided a laboratory for research into the development and utilization of virtual spaces in teaching at the secondary and college levels.

All of the worlds we have created are free and openly available online from literaryworlds.org. While the worlds are interesting in themselves, they can be easily integrated with traditional classroom instruction. At the user end, they require no special software beyond a web browser. Literature students, teachers, and scholars—readers of this book—are invited to visit and experiment with these worlds, to imagine and create new ones, and to draw on them to think about twenty-first-century learning. Our team of teachers and scholars created virtual reality environments to support reading and writing about a wide range of literary works from Anglo-Saxon poetry and Shakespeare plays, to eighteenth-century novels, to commonly taught modern works such as *Lord of the Flies*, *The Great Gatsby*, *Of Mice and Men*, and *Things Fall Apart*. In these worlds, secondary and university English students role-play as literary characters extending and altering character conduct in purposeful ways, and they explore online, interactive literature maps, museums, archives, and game worlds to analyze the impact of historical and cultural setting, language, and dialogue on literary characters and events.

Literary virtual worlds bring together pedagogical, content, and technological knowledge to create engaging environments for reading and responding to literature. Punya Mishra argues that:

> Effective technology integration for pedagogy around specific subject matter requires developing sensitivity to the dynamic, transactional relationship between all three components. A teacher capable of negotiating these relationships represents a form of expertise different from, and greater than, the knowledge of a disciplinary expert (say a mathematician or a historian), a technology expert (a computer scientist) and a pedagogical expert (an experienced educator).

This chapter explores these three kinds of knowledge. Subsequent chapters shed light on the diversity of literary virtual worlds—as I describe at the end of this chapter illuminating a typology of forms for instructional virtual worlds.

Pedagogical Knowledge

While teaching in virtual worlds is certainly innovative, this "learning by doing" approach draws on well-established educational theory and methods including constructivism, discovery, and problem-based learning advocated by leading educational theorists such as Dewey, Piaget, Bruner, and Vgotsky. Constructivist learning theory argues that students are not blank slates, but that they build new knowledge based on the knowledge they already possess. Thus students learn best when they are allowed to construct personal understandings based on experience and reflection. Prior knowledge and social interaction shape the way new experiences are assimilated to existing knowledge frameworks— or new experiences interrupt those frameworks and call for their evolution. From a constructivist perspective the goal of the teacher is to foster interactive, immersive, and student-centered learning. Wesley Hoover (Hoover, 1996) describes constructivist learning theory in a way that captures student experience in Literary Worlds activities,

> Learners remain active throughout this process: they apply current understandings, note relevant elements in new learning experiences, judge the consistency of prior and emerging knowledge, and based on that judgment, they can modify knowledge.

Discovery and problem-based learning are teaching methodologies consistent with constructivist learning theory. Discovery methods emphasize engaged, inquiry-based instruction including interacting with new objects and information, participation in simulation activities, and exploring complex questions. The idea is that by immersion in new challenges and environments students solve problems and acquire knowledge and skills in a way that is transferable and long lasting. Problem-based teaching emphasizes students collaboratively solving challenging, open-ended, loosely structured problems and reflecting on their experiences. In a problem-based approach students generally work in collaborative groups as teachers take on the role of facilitators.

These approaches emphasize the activity of the learner and the development of motivation, independence, and autonomy. They move away from top-down, teacher-delivered knowledge, and toward student exploration, simulation, interaction, and independence—precisely what happens in virtual world learning.

Games provide another model for theories of immersive learning in virtual spaces. There are at least thirty-six different principles that video/computer games draw on to provide the gamers with the complex skills and information they need to become successful (Gee, 2003). These games, where players act as characters, invite analysis of identity and social relationships.

> They situate meaning in a multimodal space through embodied experiences to solve problems and reflect on the intricacies of the design of imagined

worlds and the design of both real and imagined social relationships and identities in the modern world.

(Gee, 2003, 48)

Some virtual worlds, like many video/computer games, are designed for, or allow, participation by individuals acting alone. In these settings the builder is responsible for creating the options that construct learning for the student. Andrew Burn (2005) argues:

Narrative in games oscillates between offering information and demanding action, triggering a cycle in which the player acts, which functions as a demand to the game (what next?), which replies with more information and demands, and so on.

(Burn, 52)

While all of the literary virtual worlds described in this book allow group interaction, several are explicitly designed as Alternative Reality Game (ARG) activities (*Thoughtcrime, Midsummer Madness, The Virtual Tempest*). Other worlds (*The Village of Umuofia, Mice, Men, and Migrant Labor, Gatsby's American Dream*) could be described as virtual Live Action Role Plays (LARPs), activities typically prepared by a "gamemaster," in this case the virtual world builder. In role-playing games the players participate in the imaginary world through their characters, but they are not necessarily absorbed into a role and may retain a level of judgment and connection to the world outside the game that allows them to think critically about the experience (Lancaster, 40).

Participation in virtual worlds offers a form of identity experimentation important for learning and ethical understanding. Beach et al. (2008) argue "adolescents construct their identities through their participation in social worlds, including [imaginative] participation in worlds portrayed in multicultural literature" (ibid., 6). Critical to a pedagogy based in exploring and examining different social worlds is a student's consideration of how characters perceive their actions, each other, and the institutions they inhabit (ibid., 279). This examination can take place through drama activities where students create monologues from the point of view of characters or place characters in real world situations and ask them to respond (ibid., 127–128). When students enter into a virtual world, they may be extending the plot, action, and dialogue beyond the source text. Indeed, since the activities in virtual worlds occur collaboratively, one of the best pedagogical models for instruction in virtual worlds is ensemble theater. In this sense, student activity and interaction in virtual worlds creates a "devised work."

"Devising" is a word applied at various times to any process of collaborative creation, or ensemble-created pieces, or even to what Joan Schirle terms "making it up ourselves." The term, even in its loose application, has provided an umbrella for the contemporary re-blossoming of alternative artistic methodologies and has facilitated a sense of community that encourages dialogue among those whose current work challenges traditional models (Herrington in Feffer, 46–47).

In a literary virtual world participation and performance takes place in a highly technologically mediated environment.

Indeed, there has been a great deal of interest in computer-assisted learning, new technologies, software, and Internet resources. If in the twenty-first century computers and the Internet are a necessary part of education, access is not a sufficient condition for meaningful learning. Technology must be closely integrated in content- and discipline-specific ways. The New Media Literacies Project (www.newmedialiteracies.org) argues that while building on traditional reading, writing, research, and critical analysis, there are now new literacies needed by students and that these literacies constitute core cultural competencies in our technologically mediated, participatory culture:

- *Play*: the capacity to experiment with one's surroundings as a form of problem-solving.
- *Performance*: the ability to adopt alternative identities for the purpose of improvisation and discovery.
- *Simulation*: the ability to interpret and construct dynamic models of real-world processes.
- *Appropriation*: the ability to meaningfully sample and remix media content.
- *Multitasking*: the ability to scan one's environment and shift focus as needed to salient details.
- *Distributed Cognition*: the ability to interact meaningfully with tools that expand mental capacities.
- *Collective Intelligence*: the ability to pool knowledge and compare notes with others toward a common goal.
- *Judgment*: the ability to evaluate the reliability and credibility of different information sources.
- *Transmedia Navigation*: the ability to follow the flow of stories and information across multiple media.
- *Networking*: the ability to search for, synthesize, and disseminate information.
- *Negotiation*: the ability to travel across diverse communities, discerning and respecting multiple perspectives, and grasping and following alternative norms.
- *Visualization*: the ability to translate information into visual models and understand the information visual models are communicating.

Clearly virtual world pedagogy holds out the potential to experience and develop many of these twenty-first-century literacies. In virtual worlds constructivist, discovery-based, problem-solving models developed in a prior century can be brought forward to address the technology- and media-infused skills utilized in contemporary society.

Content Knowledge

Literature invites readers into an imaginative second world in their own heads. A good writer helps us "see" from the point of view of characters, and discover new interpersonal, historical, cultural, and geographic spaces through a "willing suspension of disbelief." This is the very power of literature. In this sense a literary work is itself already a kind of virtual world. Given the power of the human imagination, the book is almost always better than the movie. Yet films or virtual worlds that interpret or supplement literary texts can add much to our understanding. This may be especially true of literary virtual worlds as they create an active environment where the reader/player builds on and extends the experience of literary reading.

The kind of reading experiences we are creating in the Literary Worlds Project were first described as a theoretical possibility in MIT professor Janet Murray's *Hamlet on the Holodeck: The Future of Narrative in Cyberspace* (1997). To some degree "choose your own adventure" books or hypertext fiction of the 1990s, such as *Patchwork Girl* by Shelly Jackson, offer a reading experience that prefigures literary virtual worlds. As our worlds are inspired by and deeply engaged with the language, setting, characters, and context of literature, reader participation in the virtual world participates in interpreting the source text. In the virtual world readers may become not only scholars and critics, but also writers themselves, imaginative re-shapers of their reading, moving from a consumption model to an approach based in activity and production.

Reader-response theory helps us think about the way literary works are read and can help us understand the experience of a literary virtual world. Reader-response focuses on the reader's experience of a literary work rather than on the author, form, or content. According to Louise Rosenblatt, meaning is found not in the text itself, but in the transaction, "live circuit," between reader and text. The prior experiences and knowledge that the reader brings to the literary work shape its meaning. Rosenblatt argues that:

> Every time a reader experiences a work of art, it is in a sense created anew. *Fundamentally, the process of understanding a work implies a re-creation of it, an attempt to grasp completely the structured sensations and concepts through which the author seeks to convey the quality of his sense of life.*
>
> (Rosenblatt, 113, emphasis in original)

A literary virtual world is one kind of reading, one kind of re-creation of a literary work, that begets other readings based on what the participant brings to it. One strand of reader response emphasizes experiential knowledge, especially appropriate to thinking about the possibilities of literary virtual worlds:

> Experiential reader-response theory seeks to identify and describe the strategies readers employ—for example, how they identify with a character, visualize the setting, draw connections to their own lives, and detach themselves from the story in making a critique.
>
> *(Rozema, 2004, 93)*

Jeff Wilhelm has argued that many teenage readers have difficulty entering imaginatively into the story world of literary works and that teachers should utilize visualization and role-play experiences to develop teenagers' imaginative skills. Teaching literature in virtual worlds supports students entering the second world of literature, developing new meanings and interpretations. Drawing on student prior knowledge, on close and careful reading, literary virtual worlds extend, rewrite, and re-envision literary works in ways that enrich students' reading comprehension of the source text.

Thus one of the questions that builders of these worlds wrestle with is how can we create online virtual environments where students will have significant freedom to make choices about their activities or the roles they play, and still maintain fidelity to the imaginative literary text on which the world is based?

We believe that crucial to the development of any of the virtual worlds we have made is a deep engagement, "transaction" as Rosenblatt calls it, with the content and form of the literary source. We have created virtual world projects based on novels, plays, short story and poetry collections, legends, and epics from many historical and cultural periods. The teachers and scholars designing these literary worlds include experts in Anglo-Saxon, Renaissance, Early Modern and contemporary British literature, and in American, postcolonial, and children's literature. No virtual world is a replica of any other because the specific themes, character interactions, settings, and language of the literary source profoundly shape the look, form, agenda, and activity that takes place in the corresponding virtual world. An important dimension of this new medium is the possibility it creates for exploring the time period and setting of literary works, settings perhaps far from the experience of student readers. In this sense, these worlds open up possibilities for engaging historical, multicultural, and cultural studies teaching as will be illustrated by each chapter in *Teaching Literature in Virtual Worlds: Immersive Learning in English Studies.*

Finally, despite the possibilities for greater content understanding, students need to evaluate both the affordances and the limitations of virtual experiences. Neither reading literature nor participating in a virtual world is the same thing as real-world, experiential knowledge. The historical and cultural gaps bridged by literary works and literary virtual worlds may be enormous. Builders of literary virtual worlds are not simply reproducing an already imagined reality, but are creating their own interpretation of the source text. Students may role-play characters from different cultural backgrounds and historical periods. Virtual worlds and performance inside them may lay claims on authenticity, but are simultaneously what Gyatri Spivak (1990) calls a "worlding:"

> the notion of texuality should be related to the notion of the worlding of the world on an uninscribed territory . . . basically about the imperialist project which had to assume that the earth that it territorialized was in fact previously uninscribed.
>
> *(Spivak, 1)*

Care must be taken by teachers and students alike to recognize how virtual worlds, devised productions, and live action role-plays create knowledge always in some measure unfinished. The relationship between a literary virtual world, its source imaginative text, and real-world experiences are important topics for ongoing analysis and study.

Technology

A variety of technologies have emerged that can facilitate the development of literary virtual worlds. The technology framework we have used to build virtual worlds is enCore 4, an open-source software package released in 2004. This software emerged from text-based multi-user domain technology designed for educational use. Built on LambdaMOO (a Multi-user Domain, Object Oriented) with a built-in server-side client called Xpress, enCore allows builders to create online learning environments featuring visual images, easy navigation between rooms, static avatars, synchronous participant communication, textual activities, the incorporation and complex utilization of a wide range of objects including textual, visual, audio, and video files, maintenance of running records of actions and speech, the incorporation of "bots" (virtual characters with a pre-programmed speaking repertoire), and a wide range of programmable options. EnCore is not three dimensional, but it is an immersive, self-contained multi-user virtual environment (MUVE) that is easy to access, use, and build in.

The prototype enCore literary virtual world was created by Robert Rozema and his students for studying Aldous Huxley's *Brave New World*. At the time a high school English teacher working part-time on a doctoral degree under my direction, Rozema developed this significant innovation that became, in part, the focus of his doctoral dissertation. Rozema's 2003 NCTE presentation about his experience teaching secondary students using the virtual world he developed was recognized by his winning the National Technology Leadership Award, and he went on to author an article in the *English Journal* (Rozema, 2003). Additional worlds created by Rozema (*Thoughtcrime*), Joe Haughey (*Midsummer Madness*), Cara Arver (*Lord of the Flies*), and myself (*The Village of Umuofia*) became the models

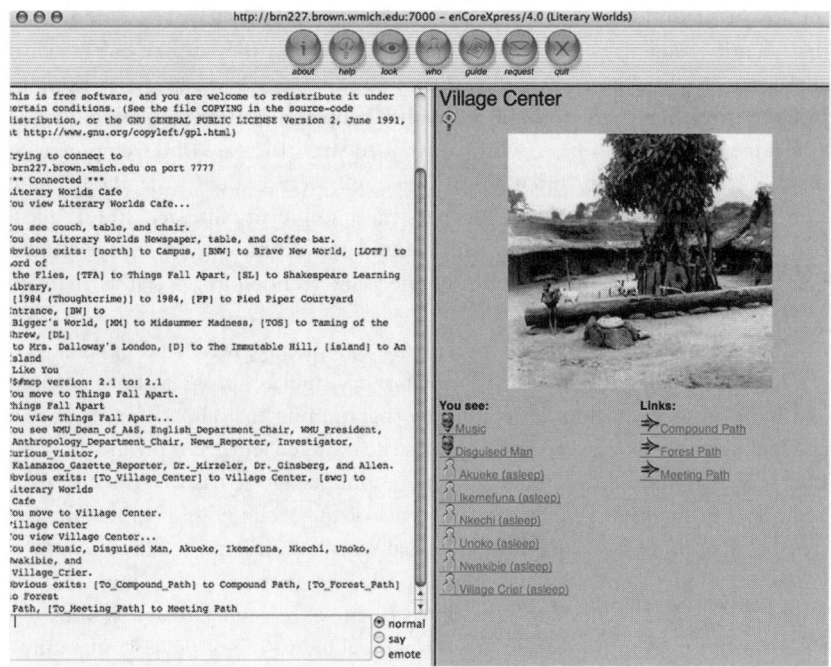

FIGURE 1.1 EnCore Literary Worlds User Interface

for a Western Michigan University Presidential Innovation Grant ($118,000) that funded the Literary Worlds Project.

Maintained on a dedicated server at Western Michigan University, enCore software has proven to be a rich and flexible tool. Looking at Figure 1.1 taken from *The Village of Umuofia*, the enCore Literary Worlds user/player interface shows: a touch button control bar along the top; a running record of places visited, actions taken, and conversation transcript in the left hand box; a dialogue box where participants can input commands, speech, and actions on the lower left-hand side; and the room name, image, clickable objects ("Music," "Disguised Man"), character avatars, and links to connected rooms on the right. Sound and video files can be cued to play when characters enter the "room."

Technology interfaces are crucial to their function (Johnson), and we have been able to invent a range of ways that this interface can be utilized for the development of literary virtual worlds. While the enCore interface does not offer the same sensory experience as contemporary video games or more sophisticated virtual worlds, such as *Second Life*, its simplicity has advantages. The enCore platform does not require any special software downloaded onto computers that access it, and enCore can work well on a wide range of machines, including those with slower processors. All that is needed is web access and a standard browser set to "accept popups." Worlds can be created where use or participation is so intuitive that students need little time to master them. Avatars are static images that identify student locations to other participants but they can be enhanced, if appropriate to the activity, by giving them names, images, and textual descriptions. EnCore is relatively easy to build in; with a couple of hours of guided assistance a beginner can create a basic world. I want to stress the ease of development of these worlds; the worlds discussed in this book were created by undergraduate students, employed secondary teachers, and university literary and English education scholars. Though we had a wonderful technology specialist (Kevin Jepson) as a resource, none of the builders are technology specialists or even technology geeks.

The enCore program is also potentially complex; experienced builders can create objects that participants can move or manipulate, program bots to speak and respond to cues, develop complex programming that allows for characters (student participants/players) and objects to be changed and given diverse abilities. Our specialized focus on literature content and pedagogy has led us to develop additional programming and enhancements of the technology platform for the specific creation of literature-related virtual worlds. While more fully immersive video game environments have their appeal, they cost tens, even hundreds, of millions of dollars to develop. EnCore is open source and Literary Worlds is a free, non-profit educational activity. Those seeking to use or develop literature-related projects are welcome to access our virtual worlds and develop their own. (For a review of the history and speculation about the future of literary virtual worlds see Chapter 12. For information on building your own enCore world see Chapter 13.)

One of the goals for the creation of virtual worlds in the Literary Worlds Project is that they are easy to use by teachers, and enCore meets that requirement. The worlds we have made fit easily into existing literature and language arts courses and are used by students in public schools and universities across the United States and around the world. In addition to developing practical instructional formats, builders have also been encouraged to focus on texts that are frequently taught. (Not all builders followed that recommendation, but all projects have been used for instructional purposes.) The worlds are designed so that students can participate in them easily, during a small number of visits arranged during a class period where all the students have or share computers (in a lab or with laptops) or from home as a "homework assignment." The transcript feature we developed (not used in all worlds) allows the teacher to monitor and evaluate student behavior in the virtual world. The issue of control is important in virtual world development (Osberg) and we have found the transcript feature a useful component in maintaining on-task behavior. The transcript also provides a total number of words entered into conversation and this number can be used, along with an analysis of the content of student comments, to assess student performance, learning, and assign grades, if desired. Teachers may have specific roles to play in certain worlds and may be able to open or lock "doors" to specific rooms or areas. These literary virtual worlds are not places where teachers simply "drop off" students—instead they are spaces that invite teachers to develop academically meaningful activities tied to curriculum.

Typology of Virtual Worlds for Literary Study

Literary virtual worlds are diverse, deeply connected to their source text, and used in a variety of ways. We have created literary virtual worlds in at least seven distinct forms:

1. *Role-play Stage*: The virtual world provides a geographical, visual, and auditory environment; avatars are based on characters from source texts; multiple participants engage in dialog in character. For example: *The Village of Umuofia* based on *Things Fall Apart* (Chapters 5 and 6); *Lord of the Flies Virtual Island* —a series of characters based on the text recreate life on the island (Chapter 2); *Mice, Men, and Migrant Labor*—characters from the 1930s novel about migrant labor in California (*Of Mice and Men*) and a 1960s novel about migrant Mexican Americans in the Midwest (*The Earth Did Not Devour Him*) first meet in their own worlds, then a door is opened and they enter into dialog with each other (Chapter 4); *Gatsby's American Dream*—five characters from the novel explore/return to the locations of the novel as their former selves and discuss events from the text (Chapter 4).

2. *Alternative Reality Game*: On a role-play stage, participants as avatars engage in activities with specific goals and follow rules based on principles or objectives from the source text. For example: *Midsummer Madness*, after reading the first act of the play students enter an enormous virtual world based on the play, all have separate entrances and assigned, interrelated goals activities based upon roles in the play; *The Tempest Virtual Island*, similar to *Midsummer Madness* (both described in Chapter 3); and *Thoughtcrime* where characters assume roles from Orwell's *1984* of outer party, inner party, and thought police and engage in a high stakes detective game (Rozema, 2008).

3. *Second World*: Students become builders and design a virtual world that parallels the world of the novel. For example: *Brave New World MOO*. Based on the Huxley novel, students designed a world that not only included buildings and spaces mentioned in the novel, but additional spaces that were conceivable based on the novel. This world also functioned as a Role-play Stage—students designed their own character as well—and as a virtual classroom where students could discuss the novel and related topics (Chapter 7).

4. *Textual Riff*: Students become builders and, along with the professor, gather historical, cultural, literary, and interpretative texts and images that respond to the source text. For example: *Pied Piper* based on the medieval legend (Chapter 8); *Island Barrio* based on Judith Ortiz Cofer's *An Island Like You*.

5. *Intertextual Map*: As themselves, participants follow a virtual path through the setting of a literary work. For example: *Woolf's London* based on early twentieth-century photographs of the city closely follows two walking trips that the main characters in Virginia Woolf's *Mrs. Dalloway* take through downtown London. Participants explore the connection between character inner thoughts and the urban geographical landmarks in the novel. The world includes extensive period maps and textual selections from the novel paired with images of actual locations or objects described (Chapter 9). *Bigger's World* provides a similar resource in the 1930s Chicago African American neighborhood of Richard Wright's novel *Native Son*.

6. *Virtual Tour*: Participants, individually or in groups, enter as themselves and explore and interact in a world based on literary sources. For example: *Dickens' London*—in a nineteenth-century version of London based on three Dickens novels, students encounter a complex city of images, textual fragments, and literary characters (as bots) that they can speak with.

7. *Virtual Museum*: An archive of image, sound, and cultural materials as a supplement to a specific literary work, can be entered by individuals or groups who may then engage in conversation. For example: *Anglo-Saxon Mead-Hall* based on Anglo-Saxon poetry and epic (Chapter 10); *Moll's World* based on *Moll Flanders* (Chapter 10); *Inismore* based on *Wild Irish Girl* (Chapter 10); *Angel's Space* based on Tony Kushner's play *Angels in America* (Chapter 11); *The Immutable Hill*, set primarily in Hawaii, also involves scenes in California and South East Asia and refers to a wide spectrum of international events during the Vietnam and Cold War based on Joan Didion's novel *Democracy*.

New Technologies, Evolving Pedagogies

A literary virtual world is both a technology-enhanced interpretation of the source text and a pedagogical tool. Mastering the technology to build a virtual space in enCore is not so difficult, but designing virtual spaces that will be truly engaging for students while creating significant content-based learning constitutes a challenge. To develop a successful virtual world learning activity requires *projective skill* at working together content, pedagogy, and technology. As virtual world developers, teachers need to imaginatively put themselves into the position of students experiencing the virtual world they intend to create, and, then, as classroom facilitators, teachers must adequately prepare students to enter into a virtual world learning experience by developing necessary prior knowledge and preparation. In Literary Worlds that typically, but not always, means that students have carefully read the literary work and engaged in activities specifically designed to ready them for the virtual world event. Teachers versed in discovery, problem-posing, and reader-response pedagogies have an important advantage in designing virtual worlds over colleagues who have an "information transfer" model of learning. One experience of the Literary Worlds Project was that the literary scholars designing these worlds, excellent teachers themselves, tended to think of learning as closely examining textual passages or acquiring additional information relevant to understanding the literary work. It was easier for some virtual world builders to imagine virtual museum spaces rather than interactive role-play, gaming, or building environments. Certainly the enCore platform allows museum or gallery-like spaces to be rich and contextual and, just as modern museums do, to permit interactivity and collaborative learning. When carefully developed and well integrated into classroom learning, all forms of virtual worlds have significant potential to enhance student learning.

Teaching with virtual worlds is new to teachers, likely something they themselves did not experience in school. Knowledge of how best to manage virtual world experiences and weave them effectively into existing curriculum and instruction is developed by repeated use and experimentation. Increasing familiarity with the technology reduces problems and generates new strategies. Experience observing and assessing student learning in virtual worlds leads, with repeated practice, to clearer and better focus on content learning. We have found that discussion and writing related to the virtual activities is important both before and after participation. Teachers may have mixed feelings or even disappointment with their first attempt at utilizing virtual worlds, but increased experience will improve outcomes. *Teaching Literature in Virtual Worlds* offers examples and explanation that teachers can learn from, and plenty of evidence of the effectiveness, and intellectual and academic value of virtual world teaching.

2

A VIRTUAL WORLD FOR
LORD OF THE FLIES

Engaging Students and Meeting Common Core Standards

Cara Arver

Terms such as virtual reality and virtual worlds are getting more and more attention, both from players of the new video games and from serious learning activities pioneered in graduate studies at major universities such as MIT and Harvard. Unfortunately, many of these virtual experiences, while of great potential interest to secondary students, are still unavailable to them. As much as they love video games and computer simulations, secondary and college students typically have had few opportunities to participate in virtual worlds with research or academic purposes. In addition, many school computers are unable to handle the complex technical demands of the advanced new programming. However, using literaryworlds.org, it has been possible, indeed valuable, for my secondary students to become engaged in virtual worlds as they study literature.

I worked with a group of university literature professors to design a collection of free, open-source, virtual worlds for literary study at the secondary and college level. These virtual worlds use an older technology that is more accessible in schools and yet prefigures emerging possibilities. Robert Rozema describes this technology as a "text-based virtual environment, a sort of sophisticated chat room complete with its own architecture and interconnected rooms, stockpile of manipulable objects, and cast of interesting characters" (Rozema, 2003, 33). The virtual worlds we designed have strong visual elements that are historically and culturally related to specific literary texts from Shakespeare and Dickens to Virginia Woolf and Chinua Achebe. They can incorporate sound and video files to create museum and role-play environments.

I was skeptical the first time I ventured into a virtual world, but I was intrigued enough to take a closer look. I consider myself a technologically backward English teacher, but in a graduate English education methods class, I learned more about literature and technology and how to integrate it into a secondary classroom. In this class, we discussed, used, and created literature archives, online journals, and Webquests, and I developed a teaching web site. All of this helped me become more proficient in the world of technology. Then, during one class period, Robert Rozema, one of Professor Allen Webb's former students, joined us in the virtual world that he created for his students to experience Aldous Huxley's *Brave New World*. My classmates, all experienced literature teachers, had a blast exploring his literature-oriented world where players ventured into different rooms that Rozema had created, based on the rich details Huxley offers in the first three chapters of the novel (ibid., 34). We had character names and identities; ate too much soma, "the wonder drug of the World State" (ibid., 35); and were denied access to restricted areas because of our identities. One of the remarkable things about the visit our graduate class made to the *Brave New World* virtual world was that there were four young people who just happened to be actively participating in the world that evening. These were Rozema's former high school students who had learned about the world as part of a class project—*and they were still role-playing characters from* Brave New World *on their own, a full year later.* What does that have to say about the allure of this kind of learning?

Even with this stimulating exposure to the possibilities of a literary virtual world, I was still doubtful about this kind of experience in the secondary English classroom. How would I be able to use a virtual world and what benefits would it provide? My 9th graders showed me the answers. This was a class of loud, belligerent, unmotivated, funny young men and a smattering of shy girls. I needed to focus their abundant energy, and I was also concerned with the achievement level of the boys in my English classes—our state testing scores showed that the boys were lagging behind in language arts. Armed with my brief experience in a literary virtual world, I began an independent study with Webb and Rozema to create a virtual world. I hoped to use students' interest in technology to inspire them to delve into the literature that we were reading. I wanted students to get "stuck in the middle of a tale" (ibid., 33). I wanted to help them hone their skills in reading, writing, speaking, thinking, and sharing. A technologically enhanced interactive setting appealed to the active young men in the classroom, and I hoped it could encourage even resistant 9th graders to move beyond traditional interactions with the literature they read. I came to realize that participating in a virtual world activity draws on a range of learning styles and comprehension skills and also creates opportunities for students to develop meaningful curricular connections.

Building an Online Literary World

I began teaching myself to build a virtual world by reading chapters from *High Wired: On the Design, Use, and Theory of Educational MOOs* (Haynes and Holmevik, 2001). The most useful chapter, "MOO Educational Tools," helped me work through various tasks: making "rooms," creating objects, writing on the virtual blackboard, modifying my online virtual-reality environment, accessing the Internet from the virtual world, and creating "bots," interactive robot characters within the environment. I learned to program the bots to respond to keywords and correspond with the other "inhabitants" of the virtual world. (See Box 2.1 for explanations and definitions of some of these objects, commands, and navigational systems.)

I called my homepage within this virtual world "Mrs. Arver's Classroom." Within the classroom, default "furniture" appeared: a desk, table, and blackboard. Other objects, including multimedia educational objects, such as a web projector, rewritable note, and slide projector, can be added to the environment as well (see Box 2.1). My favorite object was the virtual blackboard. A participant or visitor can read and write on the blackboard within a classroom, and this is where I posted most of my assignments. A few keystrokes and mouse clicks lets me build the additional rooms and links I want.

There are several things to consider when creating a virtual environment around a piece of literature. A strong setting is one of the most important considerations. The world I created was based on William Golding's *Lord of the Flies*—the setting of this novel is clearly integral to the plot, fostering and sustaining the conflicts in the story. The island has vivid features such as ethereal beaches, steamy jungles, and a broad mountain top, and these varied environments helped me envision a diversity of "rooms" for the virtual environment.

The setting isn't the only important part of the novel. The boys are thousands of miles from a civilization that may no longer exist, and there is no adult or authority figure to tell them how to behave. As in the popular television series *Lost*, the characters sense civilization slipping away and civility is affected by time, distance, and the cruel realities of survival. I wanted discussion of these issues to come about naturally as the students entered the virtual-reality setting online.

Another reason I chose *Lord of the Flies* was that the characters are appealing. Every reader can either feel sympathy for Piggy, pride in Ralph for his determination, harmony with Simon's spirituality, or anger toward Jack and his heavy-handed ways. I could easily see students in this group of 9th graders "becoming" one boy or another on the island in a virtual-reality world. They could maintain individuality but would still have restrictions placed on their interactions based on their characters, circumstances, and setting.

I linked the *Lord of the Flies* room to "Mrs. Arver's Classroom." From there, I created additional rooms for students and experimented with placing images, such as one I chose for the island itself, "roughly boat-shaped: humped near this end with behind them the jumbled descent to the shore" (Golding, 29). I spent hours getting images to become visible and trying to program my bots to "talk." I wanted students to be able to "eat" from the fruit bowl I created, but that was a technological feat I couldn't achieve. I also linked resources from the World Wide Web to the rooms. For example, I connected a "generic thing" named

Box 2.1

When you become a virtual-world creator, you are essentially the manager of your online world. Entering through the literary worlds portal, you see a split screen. The left side is a dialogue box as you would see in any chat room. It describes the room you are in and what the participants are saying and doing. On the right, you see two columns. Below "You see" you have a list of participants that are in the room and objects that have been created. "Links" gives you portals to the different places you can visit within this virtual world. At the top, you have a toolbar with buttons that help you manage your site.

- **About** tells you the important information about this literary virtual world (license information, server, and so on).
- **Look** shows you where you can go within this virtual world. The left-hand side of the screen also provides a brief description of the different rooms and areas.
- **Who** tells you who has logged on, where they are, and for how long. This is an important tool to help teachers keep track of where the students are.
- **My Stuff** shows builders of all the objects you have created, what actions you can take with each, and how much space you have used (your quota).
- **Mail** gives you a way to communicate within the virtual world.
- **Objects** leads builders to the Xpress Object Editor, where you can create new objects, such as rooms, slide projectors, bots, handouts, and links to the Internet. It also shows you what objects you have already created and how to edit them. Some of the options include renaming the objects, sharing them, and editing a description. For example, my object "Author William Golding" had a bad URL, an easy fix within the Xpress Objects Editor.

Some of these buttons are available to guests and to students when they log in. Students/players are not given the same rights as the builders or wizards of a virtual world, but they still have a split screen and can move around within the virtual world and interact with the objects, furniture, and bots.

Additional Information

Bots are virtual characters. They can be easily programmed with the "Objects" button on the toolbar to respond to other characters. This can be fun, especially if the bots you create are important characters and if they have strong personalities. Bots can be easily "activated" and "hushed."

The furniture within a room adds authenticity to the different parts of your virtual world.

If you click on the "light bulb" icon, standard in each of the rooms and for each of the objects, it tells you, "Here are some of the things you can do with

> this object. Type the obvious verbs shown here into the Xpress talk area. The word 'anything' should be substituted for a valid object name."
>
> If you click on any object or participant's icon on the right side of the screen under "You see," you will get a description of that participant/object or a link to its web site.

"Author William Golding" to a web address where students could read information about the author. Many other objects are available within the virtual world, and I hope to integrate them into my site as my designing skills develop.

At points frustrated and overwhelmed, there were times when I felt like giving up. I recommend that teachers who seek to create literary virtual environments for their students do their homework and talk to other teachers who have developed and used one. Through these frustrating times, Robert Rozema was supportive. He was there the first time I used the virtual world in my classroom and students enjoyed "meeting" him in virtual space. He had ideas to support the concept of the *Lord of the Flies* virtual environment, helped me come up with meaningful assignments, and develop my online classroom management skills.

Inside the Virtual World

Rozema helped me create enough student characters for every student in my class. Each student needed a user/login name and password to enter. Once in, they changed their login name, became a character from the novel (a new "named" boy on the island), and began to develop descriptions for their characters/avatars. They created their own names and descriptions, but they all had to be English schoolboys, ranging from five to thirteen years old. They interacted with each other within the virtual environment, as they would in a chat room. Some of their character descriptions include the following:

> A brown haired, medium height boy—can be quiet sometimes. His name is Logan. He doesn't get any attention or respected for anything. Most people, when they hear of Logan, they don't know anything about him. He doesn't get counted to do anything—he is pretty much an outsider.
>
> Jacob is short, strong, very fast, good at building huts, and good at inventing new and better designs for huts.

To further organize our entry into the virtual world, I divided the class into five groups of three or four students: Hut Builders, Fire Builders, Hunters, Littleuns, and Food/Fruit Finders. I grouped the students with at least one member who would act as leader. Together they created a description of their meeting place, relevant and appropriate to their assigned character. This encouraged students to think about the island, its appearance, and their roles. The group interactions fostered both independence and group cooperation. Students became participants in creating the virtual-reality environment where they would role-play and discuss the events of the novel. The following are some of the meeting-place descriptions they created:

> The location of the hut builder's meeting place is next to the woods so we can get lumber easily. We build the huts on the beach. The materials we use are dead trees. We also use the creepers to keep the wood together as we build it. Moss is also good to fill in some of the cracks to keep the wind out. We can only build one hut a day because it takes a long time to collect the supplies.

> We meet at the top of the mountain by the fire. There are a lot of logs piled up on both sides of the fire. Piggy's glasses will be laying to the left of the fire (when he's not using them). There is a coconut full of water on each side of the fire just in case.

Their rooms became their home base, and students met there with their cohorts to decide on a plan of action, including how to complete specific tasks that I assigned. In these meetings they discussed in role the realities faced by the boys in the novel, how to obtain resources, and, thus, engaged in problem solving.

When we entered the *Lord of the Flies* virtual world, I had specific goals and outcomes in mind. If I wanted students to practice vocabulary, for example, I made sure they had time to have conversations within their groups using the vocabulary words correctly. Group meetings allowed students to share information and establish positive group dynamics. After the students had acclimatized themselves to the virtual environment, created their personas, and bonded as a group, they found their assignments on the blackboard in my virtual classroom.

One day the students had a conversation assignment in which they had to remain in character, using the weekly vocabulary words from the novel. Next, they were asked to write poems about the characters and events on the island. Students created personal "Notebooks" where they could write and then post their poems in the virtual world. After they created their notebooks, they "dropped" them into a "Box" in "Mrs. Arver's Classroom." This assignment worked well; students enjoyed the creativity of the notebooks and used their knowledge of the characters to craft poetic homage to them. The notebooks also allowed them to experiment with the tools in the virtual world. Visitors to the world can read some of the students' poetry in the "Box" in my virtual room. (To visit the world, go to literary.worlds.org, go to "Enter," go to "Direct Portal Entrance," log in as a "guest"—no password needed—and from "Literary Worlds Welcome Center" go to *Lord of the Flies*).

Rozema stated that when he began he had to be the "police officer" within his virtual world (Rozema, 2003, 36). I had the same problem. Rozema and I herded wayward students who strayed from "Mrs. Arver's Classroom" and the *Lord of the Flies* virtual space back to their assigned rooms. Sometimes we found students in the Literary Worlds café drinking coffee concoctions and eating sandwiches. After we realized what we were up against, Rozema redirected the group members into their specific meeting rooms and "locked" the doors behind them to discourage those who were curious and wandering. When students realized that the *Lord of the Flies* virtual world wasn't just for play most of them settled down and worked together. A development at Literary Worlds makes possible the emailing of transcripts of student activities and conversations to themselves and their teacher. Some virtual-world designers report that this feature has reduced goofing around.

During this *Lord of the Flies* unit, practically every student came into my classroom asking, "Do we get the computers today? Are we going to the virtual world?" I had never seen these students so excited about class work. Many of the less vocal students, those who rarely contributed during class discussion, were less intimidated within this online environment. Once in character it seemed they were more comfortable being open with their opinions and reflections.

Evaluating the Experience

After we finished *Lord of the Flies*, students reflected on the activity in their journals. One student stated:

> It was cool. I was a hut builder and our group really got along well. We had some good ideas on how to build the huts. While in our room we talked about what was going on in the book and why the people were doing what they were doing. We didn't like Piggy, but respected him and we liked Ralph and hated Jack. We also talked about what makes a good leader and discussed why we would make good leaders.

Another student said:

> I've never done anything like this before . . . I was excited to come to class to see what else we could do in the virtual world. It was really confusing at first but it's just like a chat room but for books. I liked pretending to be a boy on a deserted island and figuring out how to survive and deal with problems.

So what does a virtual environment allow that traditional role-playing does not? It has several advantages. My students dug deeply into the novel in memorable ways, more than if we just had discussions, questions, and vocabulary in a conventional fashion. The experience enhanced student comfort and skill in online environments without exposing them to violence or predators. The virtual world opened up new ways to work together as a class and a team. Students communicated without being nervous or intimidated by face-to-face contact, and those who are reserved may break out of their normal boundaries and interact differently. Inevitably, students drew connections between their lives and those of the characters they read about.

A virtual-world activity combines writing and role-play in a visually rich, text-based environment that leads to higher-order thinking and new perspectives. An online virtual world allows students to go beyond writing essays; they enter imaginatively into the characters. Rozema called these virtual worlds an "electronic book club that meets with the story world of the book itself and invites all to participate on equal footing" (Rozema, 2003, 38). My students experienced our virtual world as a forum to connect with the story on their level.

I had some false starts when building my virtual world, and there are several things that I want to do to make it more enjoyable in the future. Technology can be overwhelming, but I learned that we needn't be intimidated by it. It's easy to say, "I don't know how to do that" or "There are just too many options," but if we don't start learning now, we'll be left behind. I'm a perfect example of this timidity when it comes to technology; I am still surprised when I manage not to fry the computers or, in this case, crash the entire Literary Worlds site. I overcame my fears and apprehension, one step at a time.

In September 2007 I published an article about the virtual world in the *English Journal*, and I received feedback from many readers. Indeed, I got so many emails that my technology gurus in the virtual world, Tim Heacock and Jennifer Barnes (then undergraduate students at Western Michigan University), created a generic list of login names for teachers who wanted to use the resource. Even three years later, I am still receiving inquiries about the site and how I used it. No matter how many requests I get, it has never became a burden to send anyone the information or offer guidance.

I wanted to continue to use my *Lord of the Flies* virtual world myself, but the novel became part of the junior curriculum and I was still teaching freshmen. Finally, as I became head of the department, my teaching assignment changed. During the fall of 2010, I used the *Lord of the Flies* virtual world with a class of 11th graders. Before entering into the world again with my students, I updated the site, reacquainted myself with the technology, and contacted a technology support person, Kevin Jepson (a contributor to this volume). I planned to use the virtual world within the first couple of weeks of class. But after our annual days of professional development at the beginning of the school year, I became a little nervous. We were told that, as a staff, one of our goals for the year was to realign our units and assessments with the new national Race to the Top Common Core Standards (CCS) for English Language Arts.

Literary Virtual Worlds and the Common Core Standards

The new standards focus of our curriculum meant that I had to make sure that everything I was doing in my thematic units linked up somehow with a standard-based lesson. I carefully examined the standards, and the assignments I had used previously with the *Lord of the Flies* virtual world. With a few tweaks here and there, I found that I could link the vocabulary exercise to the Language standards, and the writing/conversation assignments would work well with the Reading and Writing standards. At the very minimum, to be able to interact successfully within the virtual world, the students would have to read this complex text, and complex texts are strongly encouraged in the CCS. It would be difficult for them to fake their way through a conversation as a boy on the island without having the background knowledge of the story and the characters.

For one early assignment, after they had created their character, all of the students had to go to their meeting rooms and have a conversation in role. I suggested they introduce themselves to each other and greet everyone who entered their room. Each group then was to have an in-depth problem-solving conversation. In the Common Core Language Standards, under Vocabulary Acquisition and Use, students must "Determine or clarify the meaning of unknown and multiple-meaning words and phrases based on grades 11–12 reading and content, choosing flexibly from a range of strategies." (CCS, 55) In class we had discussed vocabulary words as they came up in the text, and linked them to the different characters. Thus, each "boy" had a list of character-specific vocabulary words they had to use correctly in the online conversation (words such as "gesticulate," "vex," "indignant," etc.). One of the strategies that worked well with this virtual world assignment was that students "use[d] context (e.g. the overall meaning of a sentence, paragraph, or text; a word's position or function in a sentence) as a clue to the meaning of a word or phrase" (ibid., 55). So they addressed the problems on the island and, at the same time, developed skills in the use of vocabulary in a specific language context. A partial conversation from the transcript of their visit indicates both how students in role addressed problems on the island and used new vocabulary words:

> Ralph says, "The huts that are falling down!"
> Hut Builder 4 says, "What are we going to do about the huts that are supposedly falling down? It's mortifying!"
> Hut Builder 2 says, "So we are going to build it out of trees and put rocks around the bottom so it helps support the trees and not fall."
> Hut Builder 5 says, "Yes."
> Hut Builder 4 says, "I assent to the rocks."
> Simon says, "I assent to the rocks, too."
> Hut Builder 2 says, "I think that if we use the rocks then it will make the huts more steadfast."

> Hut Builder 2 says, "Some of these people are starting to vex me."
> Hut Builder 5 says, "This whole situation is vexing me."

While the virtual world did create a setting for the integration of vocabulary words into active vocabulary in the context of a "real" (well, "virtual") conversational context, the conversation lost some of its naturalness, as students were no longer speaking purely in the voice of the young boy characters on the island. The students may have been troubled by the use of this vocabulary in this context, though it is not clear from the conversation if the "vexation" is with the huts or the discussion! Problems of usage are typical in vocabulary instruction, so I consider the use of the virtual world to address the Common Core standard at least a partial success.

I like how these problem-solving conversations required the students to use their knowledge of the text while at the same time requiring the characters to interact successfully. For example, the Fire Builders had this task: "The Beast is by the fire on the mountain. The fire won't start and keep going on the beach. What's your solution?" They had to know who the beast is and then analyze why the fire won't keep going on the beach and use textual evidence to help solve the problem. This assignment fits in well with Common Core Reading Standard RL11–12.1: "Cite strong and thorough textual evidence to support analysis of what the text says explicitly as well as inferences drawn from the text, including determining where the text leaves matters uncertain" (CCS, 38).

Indeed, by immersing themselves into the world of the novel, "becoming" a boy, and using the text to solve problems and understand character motivations on the virtual island, the students are covering several of the important Reading Literature standards, including RL11–12.10: "By the end of grade 11, read and comprehend literature, including stories, dramas, and poems" and RL11–12.3: "Analyze the impact of choices regarding how to develop and relate elements of a story or drama (e.g. where a story is set, how the action is ordered, how the characters are introduced and developed)."

As the students interact within the virtual world and support the actions of their characters, they are again "citing strong and thorough textual evidence to support analysis" (RL11–12.1). This standard is also covered in the final assessment for the reading and virtual world activity for which I had the students write an essay from the point of view of the character they had become. For this essay, they had to think like their character and assess what he would feel *after* the novel was completed.

My last Common Core assignment for the virtual world was a short writing assignment addressing argumentative text, which links up with the Writing Standard W11–12.1: "Write arguments to support claims in an analysis of substantive topics or texts, using valid reasoning and relevant and sufficient evidence" (CCS, 45). The students were to write, in character, about who they believed was truly responsible for the death of either Piggy or Simon. I had them do the writing as an ACT practice essay, but it would be easy enough to create a "Box" in the virtual world and have them drop their short essays into it for me to evaluate.

Nowadays, I am conscientious about linking all assessments and activities to the Common Core Standards. The assignments that I created in the virtual world were no exception. I am glad that I was able to link such a rich literary experience to the standards that I am required to cover. I knew what we were doing in the virtual world was valuable, but now, with links to national standards, I could point curious administrators to official validation. And beyond the standards, I have found the virtual activity relevant to my students' understanding of literature; I really think the students connected better with the characters after "becoming" one of them, even for a brief time.

The Teacher's Perspective

It was a lot of fun to watch my students' interactions and their intense concentration within this online world. It got to the point where every single student on every single computer in the lab was logged on to a room in the *Lord of the Flies* virtual world. I walked from student to student, beaming, commenting, and laughing at their interactions. I had forgotten what a rush it was to see the students so engaged, and thoroughly enjoying the literary virtual world I had made. I sent a student down to get the yearbook camera. I had to catch this on film!

After class, I checked my email and there were twenty-nine messages, all conversations from my students from their meeting rooms sent to me from the virtual world. I printed out one from each meeting room and sat down to see what they had said and how they interacted. The transcript feature counts the words each character says, and monitors the comings and goings of the students. Even though I was in the virtual world with them, I couldn't be in each meeting room all the time and thus was not able to overhear much of their conversation. The transcript is a wonderful addition for the teacher to assess group and individual learning.

Based on my study of the transcript, the students seemed to take seriously the interaction, and kept with the intensity on the island. At one point, students in the role of hut builders yelled at Jack and a Hunter when they wandered into their space—it was obvious they were not welcome.

> Jack arrives from the *Lord of the Flies* Crash Site.
> Hunter 3 arrives from the *Lord of the Flies* Crash Site.
> Ralph says, "Go away Jack."
> Jack says, "Hey."
> Hunter 3 says, "Hi, everybody."
> Hunter 3 leaves for the *Lord of the Flies* Crash Site.
> Hut Builder 5 says, "Hi."
> Ralph says, "We don't need u."

> Hut Builder 4 says, "Go away. You're not hut builders."
> Ralph says, "Yea."
> Hut Builder 2 says, "Yeah GO AWAY."
> Jack leaves for the *Lord of the Flies* Crash Site.

The Fire Builders stayed in character and picked on Piggy, and Piggy was even able to show his response to the abuse, using the "emote" commands in the chat room.

> Fire Builder 3 says, "Shut up FATTY!"
> Fire Builder 3 says, "FAT FAT FAT FAT FAT"
> Piggy is crying.

Given the emotional intensity of role-playing in *Lord of the Flies*, it was not always easy to keep time in proper sequence.

> Ralph says, "Simon? Next chapter u die . . ."
> Simon says, "Oi."
> Ralph says, "HA, HA."

Even when the conversation was morbid, the virtual world allowed the possibility of humor.

From the transcript I could see that some of the character/students and groups were more productive than others, giving me guidance for working with this group the next day. The transcript also let me see which of the vocabulary words we needed to review—for example, some of the students had a hard time with using "tenacity" and "conspiratorial" correctly. The transcript gave us a text with the vocabulary words students had used in context that I could project for the whole class to examine.

I plan to continue to experiment with additional assignments in the virtual world. I want students to have more, and more intellectually demanding, conversations. Just as with the crazy goings-on of the characters in the later years of the television series *Lost*, it might be interesting to have students meet in character both before and/or after the events in the novel take place. This kind of out-of-time sequence event is possible in a virtual world. I want the students to have to "update the status" of their character—tell me what each of their characters is doing now that they have been rescued (this could include even Simon and Piggy—beyond the grave). These assignments would get the students thinking about the deep themes we discussed, the lack of adult supervision, the consequences of deteriorating civilization, and questions about the basic dimensions of human nature. This kind of meta-reflective, post- or pre-activity assignment could be effective in virtual worlds for many different literary works. Every time I teach within the virtual world, I think of ideas for virtual worlds for other books I teach, and wish I had thirty hours in a day so that I could create them all.

3

MIDSUMMER MADNESS AND THE VIRTUAL TEMPEST

Shakespeare as Foolish Role-play Game

Joseph Haughey and Jennifer Barns

> "Far more good has come from foolishly playing Shakespeare than learnedly parsing him."
>
> *Henry Norman Hudson (1881)*

Shakespeare can be intimidating. Students encounter unfamiliar, apparently unintelligible language and too quickly convince themselves that they cannot understand or connect to the story. For more than the one hundred years that Shakespeare has served as a school subject, teachers introducing his works have seen panic, even despair, on students' faces. Since Henry Norman Hudson's day good teachers have also reminded us that successful teaching requires easing these tensions and helping students develop a genuine interest and appreciation for Shakespeare. Through a variety of teaching experiments from middle school to college we have discovered that online virtual role-play games can create fun and engaging opportunities to both introduce students to Shakespeare and deepen their understanding of his works.

This approach is in the tradition of performance-based teaching that encourages students to think about Shakespeare from the perspective of actors and directors, and invites them to be intimately involved with the text as they study plays as scripts and assume and interpret character roles. Through active learning students understand language, motives, relationships, and events. There are a wide variety of performance-based methods. In the introduction to *Teaching Shakespeare Through Performance*, Milla Cozart Riggio points out that, "performance pedagogy —more than simply an approach or option—provides a holistic frame with a broad range of options and implications" (Riggio, 1999, 1). Our innovation is to involve students in Shakespeare through virtual-world role-play gaming.

Of course, students are naturally attracted to games, and in the twenty-first century computer gaming is enormously popular. When students play certain types of video games, they are taking on the role of a character and in the course of the game either create or discover more about that character. This differs from reading a story or watching a movie because unlike the reader or viewer, the player actually acts and interacts as the virtual character, projecting their identity and making decisions, and taking actions. James Gee argues that this connection to characters is powerful because:

> it is both active (the player actively does things) and reflexive, in the sense that once the player has made some choices about the virtual character, the virtual character is now developed in a way that sets certain parameters about what the player can do.
>
> *(Gee, 2003, 58)*

Given their interactive appeal perhaps it is not surprising that our students are more eager to develop characters in games such as *World of Warcraft*, *Second Life*, *The Sims*, and *Diablo* than to write character analysis papers on Prospero, Puck, or Polonius. So how do we channel the appeal and engagement of gaming role-play to our students studying Shakespeare?

We are the creators of virtual worlds for two of what we consider to be Shakespeare's most magical and entertaining plays: *A Midsummer Night's Dream* and *The Tempest*. The worlds were created to allow students, using specific user-names and passwords, to "wake up" as a character in the play, interact with other characters, and participate in a complex gaming experience closely related to the action of the source text in a visually rich and highly complex virtual environment. OK, we admit, our virtual worlds are not as technologically or visually astounding, nor have the same level of suspense or fast action as the massively multiplayer online role-playing games (MMORPG) that some students may be familiar with. It is also the case that successful MMORPGs cost at least ten million dollars to develop, and we created our worlds at no cost in our spare time as graduate (Joseph—*Midsummer Madness*) and undergraduate (Jennifer—*The Virtual Tempest*) students at Western Michigan University.

In a graduate class in the spring of 2005, perhaps ironically titled "Literature on the Web," Dr. Webb introduced me (Joseph) to the idea of virtual worlds dedicated to literary works. Students in that class took those ideas and immediately began work in many different directions, transforming favorite pieces of literature into online virtual spaces. Initially, the idea of using such a space for Shakespeare seemed out of place, and I admit that I scoffed (to myself) at the idea of reducing Shakespeare's rich language into a container as limiting as the virtual worlds that I had envisioned up until that point. Would Shakespearean passages simply be torn apart and rewritten in each of these virtual rooms for students to read as they wandered aimlessly through the space? Yet, as I began thinking about the nature of Shakespeare's stage, a different vision of a potential virtual space emerged. I considered how Shakespeare comes alive when actors embody characters, and I began to think about the abundant scholarship on teaching Shakespeare through performance that had convinced me that the best way to teach Shakespeare was to allow students to become characters in the way that actors do. If students could become actors in a virtual space, even if only an actor armed with little more than a description of the character they were to become, and then wander through a stage devised to introduce them to the rich language, settings, props, and characters of the play, then they would, like the professional actor, have had a genuine theatrical experience that could introduce them to Shakespeare. *Midsummer Madness* was born.

I worked fervently and designed a massive and complex space that I hoped would capture some of Shakespeare's magic though a medium that would engage students otherwise hesitant with Shakespeare. I shared the virtual space with my own students the following semester in a Shakespeare class I was teaching as a graduate student. I was excited to try out the virtual stage with a group of real students. A few were hesitant, but most were engaged. There were bugs to be worked out, and the game's first run was rough. Not everything worked quite the way I had envisioned. A group of my undergraduates volunteered to try the game a second time. So, with the help of those undergraduates, I set out to fix the bugs. Several undergraduates were excited by the space and chose, as a final project for the course, to create their own virtual world inspired from one of the plays studied in the class.

This is how *The Virtual Tempest* creator Jennifer Barns became involved. As an undergraduate student in my Shakespeare course she, and several other students, created a virtual environment for *The Tempest*. As Jennifer progressed through this project, she realized she needed to have a depth of knowledge about the play's plot, language, themes, character relationships, and even do research on the play's background theories. After a classroom visit from Dr. Webb, Jennifer was challenged to consider the many, and sometimes contradicting, visual depictions of Prospero's island. Just like the students who chose to write a traditional research paper, Jennifer found herself working with and through the intricacies of Shakespeare's language and working in the library looking for scholarly sources to help explain the complex geography present in *The Tempest*. Also, as a student progressing toward a teaching degree, she saw the possibilities this technology offered for classroom instruction. Even after the class ended, she continued to develop *The Virtual Tempest* space and joined together with myself and a group of Western Michigan University students and professors as they worked on the Literary Worlds Project.

Despite their relative simplicity, middle school, high school, and college students have found the worlds we created highly engaging. We believe they offer inspiring models of a gaming approach to virtual worlds for literature instruction, not only for Shakespeare, but potentially for many other works. (In Literary Worlds,

Thoughtcrime, created by Robert Rozema and based on George Orwell's novel *1984*, is another game-styled literary virtual world.) *Midsummer Madness* and *The Virtual Tempest* allow students to take on and make decisions for virtual characters from the corresponding Shakespeare play in order to achieve a desired outcome based on that character's plot function in the source text. Students become more connected to the plays by their experiences, thinking from the perspective of their character. Just like an actor, they take an internal view of Shakespeare's language and characters. The action does not happen in front of them as a passive audience, but instead happens because they make it happen. In this way they better understand plot, character motives and relationships, and are better able to analyze major themes. Virtual gaming is an unconventional yet exciting way to teach Shakespeare and in this chapter we explain in detail how this approach can work as a component of classroom instruction.

Midsummer Madness

Midsummer Madness is an interactive, multiplayer game, in which participants take on a role from the play *A Midsummer Night's Dream*, and together with other students, explore Shakespeare's magical Athenian world. Through their immersion in the virtual world, participants become familiar with Shakespeare's characters, settings, objects, and themes, and develop a stronger understanding of the elements of Shakespeare's drama. But, even more importantly, through their "play," they create their own unique variation of the drama, a loose translation of Shakespeare's story, created by the student/character's novel interplay, a performance that has never been played before nor will ever be played again. Though the product of their "play" will resemble Shakespeare's story, the performance they create is also entirely their own, much as actors make a stage performance their own. Thus, the true value of the virtual world stems from this playful interaction—immersion in the virtual world inevitably leads to participants' more profound engagement with the actual play.

Think of *Midsummer Madness* as a collection of "rooms" attached to one another. Characters click on green arrow links, located at the bottom of the right half of the screen, to move from room to room. Some links work like one-way doors; once you pass through to another room, you will not be able to return. Often there are multiple links within a single room, and characters will have a choice of which room to go to next. There may also be links that are locked to certain characters or guests; these are represented by a small red arrow (instead of a green arrow). In this case, you will be able to see the link but not use it. The geography of *Midsummer Madness*, like Shakespeare's actual play, is divided in half: a city and also a surrounding forest. The rooms of the first half of *Midsummer Madness* are laid out in typical orderly Elizabethan fashion. Everything is logical and where it should be. Symmetrically centered around a city path are six shops: Bottom's Weaver Shop, Snug's Joiner Shop, Snout's Tinker Shop, Starveling's Tailor Shop, Flute's Bellows Shop, and Quince's Carpenter Shop. The basic geography of the virtual space reads like a dramatis personae at the beginning of the play. At the end of that path sits the Royal Palace, where Theseus and Hippolyta are wed at the end of the play.

On the other side of Athens' Gates, though, in the rooms of the other half of *Midsummer Madness*, things are not quite so civilized. Northrup Frye, a renowned Shakespearean critic, writes of the "drama of the green world" and a "rhythmic movement from normal world to green world and back again" in Shakespeare's comedies (Frye, 182). For Frye, this green world is a confusing, but cleansing place, a place that "collides with the stumbling and blinded follies of the world of experience, of Theseus' Athens and its idiotic marriage law" (ibid., 183–184). As Frye suggests, *Midsummer Madness*, on the other side of Athens' Gates, is a chaotic place, yet navigating this space is the only way for the game's human characters to find success, just as Shakespeare's actual characters must navigate their own version of the green space in Shakespeare's original plot. This other half of *Midsummer Madness* is a maze of twenty-nine rooms, all interconnected, but daunting to find your way through. If you stay near the forest path, then you will likely not lose your way, but venture a few steps away and even those who have previously played the game are quickly lost. At one end of the forest corner lies Titania's bower, and at the other end, Oberon's. The maze, though, feels less like a maze to Titania and Oberon than for the human players because they can easily use their "magic" to return to their bower or a familiar place in the forest. Oberon, for example, simply needs to type "home" and he finds himself back in his bower. Titania, Puck, and the other fairies have similar magic. For the fairy characters, unlike for the human characters, the forest is home.

Up to twenty students can play *Midsummer Madness* at one time. It is possible for a group from one school to play alongside a group from another school, even if the schools are thousands of miles away from one another. In cases where there are more than twenty students, two can be assigned to one computer and work together as a single character. When a student takes on a role in *Midsummer Madness*, he or she, like an actor, is expected to become that character. Boys can easily play girls and girls can easily play boys because, once inside the world, nobody knows who is playing whom. When a character logs in, he/she suddenly finds himself/herself in a staging room, waiting for the "doors" to unlock so they can make their entrance. Each character has a separate entrance. The "rude mechanicals," Bottom, Quince, Snug, Starveling, Snout, and Flute, each enter through their own respective living quarters located above their shops. The other characters enter from different places in the virtual world: the other Athenians from different spots in the Royal Palace, and the fairies into either Oberon's or Titania's bower.

I like to use this virtual world before students have read the play or at least before they have finished reading the second act. Thus, as they enter the virtual world, most students are unfamiliar with most of Shakespeare's actual play, and may know little more than the bits of background information provided in the game just before they start. Upon entering, each character learns that he or she has a simple goal to accomplish, but they have scarce information about how to go about attaining that goal. Over the course of the game, students need to navigate the space and find for themselves a solution to the problem with which they have been presented. In some sense, this is not unlike the experience of an Elizabethan actor receiving his script. Tiffany Stern explains that Elizabethan actors were given a "part [that] contained his own lines and the one, two, three or (occasionally) four words that preceded each of his speeches" and that "the part contains no indication to whom any speech is directed, nor does it give the name of the speaker of the cue" (Stern, 61). Stern goes on to add that Elizabethan actors spent relatively little time rehearsing, and suggests that "performances were rehearsals" in which actors learned their parts (ibid., 122). In many ways, actors just simply got up on stage and simply did the scene. In this sense, *Midsummer Madness* mimics this original stage practice. Students do not study the text extensively first, but instead jump right into the stage, into the world of Shakespeare, and begin to "play" and successfully meet the goal given to them.

Consider, for example, Puck's goal in *Midsummer Madness*:

> You are a fairy of no common rate, and perhaps the most mischievous fairy in all of the Athenian wood. You delight in the peril of others, and get great satisfaction from their blundering. You must commit three mischievous acts with your magic in order to succeed. The first (50 percent) is defined for you—you have just stolen six scripts from Peter Quince, an Athenian playwright. (You can see them in your inventory by using the inventory command; simply type "inventory" to see the objects that you are carrying.) He needs to distribute the scripts to his acting company to prepare a performance for the upcoming wedding of the Duke of Athens— Theseus. As soon as you enter the game, scatter the scripts throughout the Athenian forest so that he and his friends must search for them. Use the "drop" command to put each in a different forest room—but do not place any in Oberon's bower, as this is a sacred place and would upset Oberon greatly. Next, find Peter Quince, or any of the other rustic actors, tell them what you have done and laugh at them heartily.
>
> The other two mischievous acts (each worth 25 percent) are up to you; simply finish them before the end of the game. Your only hindrance might be your service to Oberon—you must obey him in everything he says. Should you disobey him, you will automatically fail in your other goals; in fact, if he even says at the end of the game that he is dissatisfied with your performance, then you have failed. You can oftentimes use his instructions, though, to fulfill your own mischievous motives; take advantage of his requests and create your own mischief as you obey him. Use the magical

charms hidden throughout the forest to accomplish your goals. Beware, though, of Titania and her attendants—Cobweb, Peaseblossom, Moth, and Mustardseed—they have access to the same magical charms that you do and have their own goals to accomplish, namely to protect a young human child that Titania has recently adopted. Oberon is extremely jealous of the attention Titania pays to this child and desires to make the child his own servant. Be certain Oberon will employ you in winning the child, and that Titania and her fairies will work hard to prevent you from winning the child. Remember, though, your first goal is to scatter Peter Quince's scripts throughout the forest! Accomplish this quickly before worrying about Oberon's troubles!

In *Midsummer Madness* not all characters will be successful in their goals. In fact, it is impossible for everybody to be successful because some characters are pitted against one another. Hermia, for example, must marry Lysander by the end of the play, but so must Helena. As in the play, both women chase the same man. Goals also can change, however, as the game progresses. The fairies, just as in Shakespeare's original, have powerful magic, and that magic can be used to affect the game play for the human characters. Puck can transform other human characters in the play to animal forms. Just as Bottom is transformed into a donkey in Shakespeare's original, human characters can be changed at the whim of a mischievous fairy. And how will Helena ever convince Lysander to marry her if she has been transformed into a rabbit?! (It is possible, by the way, and has been done before in game play; other fairies have the power, though, to help out and restore a transformed character back to his or her original shape). Also, flowers can be used to alter another character's goals. Love-in-idleness flowers, for example, can make any human, when applied by a fairy, fall madly in love with another character.

The purpose here is not to re-create Shakespeare's play inside the game space. It may happen that Bottom is never turned into a donkey in the course of the game play. It may instead be that Helena, as mentioned previously, is instead transformed into a rabbit. The purpose is to awaken in students an interest in learning more. Once students have seen some of what is possible in the magical world of *Midsummer Madness*, foolishly playing with some of his lines upon a virtual stage, they can then proceed to Shakespeare texts excited and ready to learn more about Shakespeare's original. Most students come to Shakespeare with trepidation; they've learned from parents and even other students that Shakespeare is to be revered, respected, and most of all, feared. The purpose of this virtual world is, instead, to create an unexpected and enjoyable introduction to *A Midsummer Night's Dream*. If they play *Midsummer Madness*, then by the time they begin reading they'll have already seen some of its language—it is scattered throughout the game space—and they'll have met many of the play's characters and seen some of its settings. They'll know that the forest is chaotic and filled with magic. They'll have a basic framework in place to speculate about what could take place in the play before they have read it.

The Virtual Tempest

The Virtual Tempest shares attributes with *Midsummer Madness*, but also differs in significant ways. Based on a careful reading of clues from Shakespeare's play, *The Virtual Tempest* includes more than sixty "rooms" clustered and separated into different, interconnected landscapes to form the island setting. Shakespeare's characters refer to a harsh, confusing, and disorienting environment and offer surprisingly contradictory descriptions. Gonzalo proclaims, "How lush and lusty the grass looks! How green!" While Antonio and Sebastian assert that Gonzalo mistakes the truth and the island is, in fact, "tawny" (yellowish brown). Adrian says, "this island seem to be desert." Caliban describes "fresh springs, brine-pits, barren place and fertile." Matching these diverse descriptions *The Virtual Tempest* includes images of desert, forests, beaches, mountainous areas, and swamps, accompanied by quotations from the play. This combination of images with text is one step toward making the language of the play accessible. Ten rooms together make up a forest, and Prospero's hut contains many rooms, including his fully stocked library. The complex virtual island is, in fact, difficult to navigate without a map—in the game the only characters who have access to a map are those with knowledge of the island: Prospero, Miranda, Caliban, and the fairies. The castaways just arrived on the island, much like the rude mechanicals first venturing into the forest of *Midsummer Madness*, must find their way through the island labyrinth.

As a role-playing game *The Virtual Tempest* can accommodate eleven to twenty players. It is recommended to have students keep the character they are playing secret until the end of the activity—it is entertaining when they discover afterwards who was playing whom. While the game needs at least eleven players, additional characters from the royal party and fairies can be added to accommodate more students, up to twenty. With a class of more than twenty, students can pair up to play at one computer and they both discuss where their character should move, what to say, and what actions they should undertake to achieve their character's specific goals. (Playing in pairs is recommended for younger students, especially those playing the larger roles.) In the virtual world, characters must achieve goals based on their role and circumstance in the Shakespeare source text. For instance, Ariel helps Prospero with his goals, to disorient, awe, separate, and stage manage the royal party, tricking them with different commands or "spells." Ariel also helps Prospero arrange meetings between Miranda and Ferdinand. Students discover the goals for their character when they sign into the game, using their character's username and password, and look in their character's "inventory." Students can view their character's goals at any point by using the "view" command. (There are a number of simple commands that the students use to take full advantage of the environment—it is helpful to orient students to the world before engaging in game play, and to print out the commands for students for easy reference.)

As in *Midsummer Madness*, when students are assigned their character they receive a brief summary of who they are, their background and motivations, and a list of goals they need to accomplish in the role-play game. For example, the student playing the character of Prospero is informed:

> You are the ruler of an enchanted island. Twelve years ago you were the Duke of Milan, but your brother greedily stole your position and exiled you and your young daughter from your home. After coming upon the island, you made the island native Caliban your slave after he showed you the secrets of the land. You also freed a fairy named Ariel from a tree and made her your servant with the promise of one day granting her freedom, and built yourself a new home. You also assumed control over several other fairy servants that obey what you and Ariel ask. It is now twelve years after your exile, and you have learned that a ship holding the royal party (including your brother and the King of Naples, Alonso) is close by the island. Your servant Ariel's magic makes the royal party believe they were shipwrecked due to a violent storm and flee the boat for the island. Now your goal is to get your revenge on your brother, regain your position as Duke of Milan, and set up Miranda and the king's son Ferdinand, so that she will be the future Queen of Naples.
>
> Your goals:
>
> 1. In your inventory you have a map. The only other people that have maps are those who have lived on the island with you all these years (the fairies, Miranda, and Caliban). Type "look map" to see where you are and where you need to be. Once you encounter Ferdinand, convince him to ask Miranda to marry him. Once he agrees, give him a test to prove he truly loves her. Tell him to find the Dead Forest and collect three items that could be used to create a fire. Tell him to take Miranda with him for she knows her way around the island (her map) and can lead the way.
>
> 2. As your revenge on those who have wronged you, you will play a trick on the royal party. Have your fairies coax the king and the men he is with into the Grove of Linden Trees. They will be trapped in here until you unlock the circle in the sand, which will allow them to come into your lagoon. While trapped in the forest, the fairies will transform into random objects and knock down members of the party with gusts of wind.
>
> 3. Unlock Circle in the Sand after Ferdinand has completed his tasks you gave to him that prove his love for your daughter Miranda. When the royal party enters the lagoon via the Circle in the Sand, you will inform them

that the prince Ferdinand is alive and well. Then convince Alonso to allow his son and your daughter to marry, and to give back your position as the Duke of Milan.

4. If he does this, then unlock Deep Nook, which will reveal the royal party's boat looking unharmed. Inform them that the original storm was a trick conjured by you in order for you to regain what was rightfully yours.

The goals for each character are unique. Some goals are actions that can be undertaken throughout the activity, and others occur as a sequence of events, depending on the actions of other characters. A goal for the fairies, for example, it to use their special commands, such as the "transformation" command (transform into an object like a tree or scorpion), or "knock down" command (virtually push other characters), in order to trick the royal party and further disorient them. These actions are performed throughout the activity and do not require achieving a prior goal. An example of sequential goals: Prospero is to have the fairies play these tricks on the royal party to eventually lead them into a maze; next, Prospero needs to unlock a room at a certain point, when all other goals have been completed, and allow the royal party to leave the maze.

Prior to starting the activity, it is helpful if students have time to look closely at their story and description. This can be done in the last minutes of the previous class or assigned as homework. The more information students have prior to participation in the activity, the smoother it will run. Students will be reminded of their goals in the first few minutes of game play again, as they wait in their own staging area when they first sign in to *The Virtual Tempest*.

While the goals of the characters reflect the events that occur in the play, the dialogue between characters, where characters go and their actions, and how they attempt to achieve their goals allow the story of this world to be different every time it is played. Students have significant ownership of what they do in *The Virtual Tempest*, and this creates a connection between the student and the virtual character they perform. Through the developing relationships and interactions between characters, the students learn more about their character. Thinking through the play from the point of view of one character illustrates the richness of a performance-based approach, especially when students engage in discussion and writing after their performance experience.

We have found that these virtual game environments work best when experienced either before or at the beginning of reading. The activity then exposes students to the characters, plot, environment, and some language before tackling the text. When *The Virtual Tempest* was used with college freshmen in an introductory literature course at Western Michigan University, students were enthusiastic:

"The activity put me inside the plot."

"Interactive . . . good at keeping my attention . . ."

"It made me recognize relationships."

"You stay true to the character the whole time, so you can learn a lot about them and other characters you associate with."

"It also helped me see which characters were friends, family, and enemies."

Not only did students have a basic understanding of the play when they began reading the text, but they also had a newfound excitement for reading as they felt a connection to the characters and an interest in how the plot would play out. Once they began reading, students enjoyed comparing their experiences in the virtual world to that of the play.

During the role-play game the teacher is able to login and observe students during the activity. The teacher character is not locked out of certain places as are many of the student characters. Even though there is a teacher character, the teacher cannot be in all places monitoring conversation. So, there is also a script feature, which records all conversations that occur from each student-played character, and a transcript of their conversations is sent to both teachers and students, helping to keep students accountable and on task.

Getting Started

You are excited about taking one of your own classes into one of the Shakespeare virtual worlds now, but you don't know how to get started. First, know that there is help available. Creators love to see visitors and classes in their virtual worlds and will always be happy to help. You can contact Joseph at joseph.p.haughey@gmail.com and Jennifer at jennifer.m.barns@gmail.com. There are also other resources available to you and your students that can help you get started. At the literaryworlds.org web site, many worlds have associated web pages with information about the virtual space and how to use it. There you will find further descriptions of the worlds, character goal pages, tips and ideas for using the worlds in your classroom, pre- and post-activity writing prompts to use in classes that assess student learning, as well as other resources for making the lesson a success.

Joseph has also created a training world inside Literary Worlds, entitled the Shakespeare Learning Library. Unlike either *Midsummer Madness* or *The Virtual Tempest*, the Shakespeare Learning Library is a relatively small world with only a handful of rooms. There are no mazes or green worlds here. Instead, this is a world for beginners new to Literary Worlds, a relatively simple place where an individual or a small group can go in order to learn how to use the most basic commands and move from room to room. The game goal is relatively simple: a player enters the world and finds a librarian working at the "front desk" where they learn that in order to succeed they must find the key that unlocks a "glass cabinet" that holds a copy of Shakespeare's First Folio. We simply couldn't resist exposing players to a little bit of Shakespearean textual history too, but the main point of this particular world is to make sure that players have mastered all of the basic commands that they will need in order to play in either *Midsummer Madness* or *The Virtual Tempest*: commands such as "open" and "close," "get" and "drop," for example. This small world can help teachers explore the functions of Literary Worlds in a short time, and also serve as a homework assignment so that students come to class already knowing the basics of navigating a virtual space.

There are also a series of YouTube videos that walk you through the different worlds and give step-by-step directions for navigating the worlds and taking your class there. These YouTube videos can be found by searching "Literary Worlds" on the YouTube homepage or by visiting www.youtube.com/user/Literary Worlds. One YouTube clip walks players step-by-step through the Shakespeare Learning Library and is an especially good starting point.

Once you have decided that the activity is right for your classes, you'll need to contact either Joseph or Jennifer to set up a time for your class to visit the virtual world. Because the worlds exist in real time on a single server, it is not possible for two different classes to visit the same world at the same time. Don't worry, though, we are happy to hear from you and excited to have you visiting our worlds. When you contact us, you will also be assigned a teacher account that will allow you to monitor the space. During the role-play game, the teacher is able to log in and observe students during the activity. The omniscient teacher character has access to all of the rooms and special permissions. In addition, as described above, because a single teacher cannot be monitoring all of the vast interactions happening at once in the worlds, there is also a transcript feature, which records all conversations for each student-played character and emails a record of the conversations to both students and the teacher. Drawing on this recorded transcript capability, teachers can see how well students are performing their roles. Teachers might invite students to use Shakespearean vocabulary or draw on specific quotations from the play as they formulate their dialog. A teacher who wishes to use the virtual space in this way will need to prepare students accordingly. Looking closely at the language of the play, providing modeling and guided practice for using Shakespearean vocabulary or quotations will support students. Rubrics are available on the web site that teachers can use to measure student performance while playing in one of the virtual worlds.

Once you have reserved the space for your classes, it is time to assign the characters. On the Literary Worlds web site, you can find full descriptions of all of the characters. These character assignments can be given out randomly to students, assigned by the teacher, or chosen by students. It adds an entirely new dimension to the game play, though, if the character assignments are anonymous. This can add to the fun of the experience because identities of characters are secret until the activity is complete. Be aware there are certain specific characters that must be played because their success is contingent on others participating. The vital characters for *Midsummer Madness* are Oberon, Titania, Puck, Theseus,

Hippolyta, Lysander, Demetrius, Hermia, Helena, Bottom, Quince, Snug, Snout, Starveling, and Flute. The vital characters for *The Virtual Tempest* are Prospero, Miranda, Caliban, Ariel, Alonso, Gonzalo, Ferdinand, Antonio, Sebastian, Stephano, and Trinculo. These characters should be assigned first. If a student that has one of these characters is absent during the day of the activity, a student that does not have a vital character should switch. If there are more than twenty students in the class, students can work in pairs for the roles. Working in pairs can be helpful, especially for younger students.

We have found that time warnings are helpful during the activity to make sure students are moving efficiently through their goals and accomplishing what needs to be done. Because virtual world experiences vary from class to class, it is difficult to be precise about the time needed: the activities in these worlds require approximately an hour to complete. The game is a live event and, unlike some online games, it does not save your place when you log out. It is normal for some classes not to finish if only 30–45 minutes are allotted. Such an ending, however, still provides an opportunity for rich discussion the following day about why certain goals did not get accomplished.

While these worlds are designed as full participation role-play games, they can actually be used as teaching tools in a variety of ways. Both worlds can serve as a "virtual museum" space, one that could be visited before, during, or after reading the source text. In the room "Prospero's Library" in *The Virtual Tempest* there are essays that explore many themes from the play. The library contains "books" on the historical event that is thought to have inspired Shakespeare to write *The Tempest*, and there is information on the origins of names for several characters. The library also contains items such as "A note to Miranda," which includes excerpts of the play to highlight pivotal dialogue.

In many ways, this Shakespeare portion of the Literary Worlds Project is still beginning. In the same way that we both first worked as students to create these two spaces, it is our hope that other teachers and students will create their own virtual stages for other plays. There is no reason that middle school, high school, and college students interested in gaming and Shakespeare could not also continue to create and build. Imagine a virtual stage upon which the fierce ambition of Macbeth drives the action of a game play. Or an online stage dedicated to *Twelfth Night* or *The Taming of the Shrew*, or any other Shakespeare play for that matter. The possible variations are nearly limitless. In your spare time over the course of a few weeks, it is entirely possible to design and build an entire space and add it to our collection. We encourage both students and teachers interested in taking a larger role in helping to create these worlds to contact us to get started. There is plenty of room for this Shakespeare project to grow. Also, there are resources available to anybody interested in taking a larger role, and the basics of using the technology are not difficult even for younger students familiar with basic computing.

This type of foolish intervention with Shakespeare may at first seem sacrilegious, but as Henry Norman Hudson pointed out over a century ago, and as teachers for over the centuries have observed, to foolishly play at Shakespeare can bring a lot of good. Perhaps it's the best way to win a student's passion that may one day lead to more serious scholarly study. Join us. Bring your students. Build with us. Whether it be as a way to bring Shakespeare to life in your own class, or to dive into the aspects of building your own space, it will be an adventure that bridges Shakespeare into a new type of performance space.

4

FROM MIGRANT LABOR TO HIGH SOCIETY

Of Mice and Men and The Great Gatsby in Virtual Worlds

Gretchen Rumohr-Voskuil and Meghan Dykema

Of Mice, Men, and Migrant Labor

John Steinbeck's *Of Mice and Men* is a staple in secondary classrooms not only because the novella is short and easy to read, but also because its compelling plot brings with it a host of discussion questions about responsibility, friendship, and morality. Internet resources for this novel are abundant; my (Gretchen) recent web search for *Of Mice and Men* teaching resources yielded 43,000 results. Many of these results included traditional apparatus for teaching the novel, such as multiple-choice quiz generators and reproducible comprehension questions.

While some of these more rote approaches can help students make sense of plot events, I believe that they fail to foster authentic student interest or understanding of the work's most important themes. In this chapter I suggest an alternative—pairing *Of Mice and Men* with another text, a similarly accessible novella that addresses migratory labor, yet from a different cultural and historical perspective. The topic of migrant farm labor is not only central to *Of Mice and Men* but an important focus of Steinbeck's work, especially *In Dubious Battle* as well as *The Grapes of Wrath*. Somehow the topic of 1930s migrant labor is often missed in contemporary classroom analysis of *Of Mice and Men*. In the twenty-first century, migrant labor remains a compelling issue, though all too often invisible in our curriculum. I suggest teaching today should bring these topics together, and, moreover, students might consider the implications of unionization within the contexts of Steinbeck's *Of Mice and Men* and Rivera's . . . *And The Earth Did Not Devour Him*, a short novel divided into fourteen vignettes addressing Mexican–American migrant labor. Steinbeck worked as a migrant laborer in

California and later went on to win the Nobel Prize in Literature and the United States Medal of Freedom. Tomas Rivera grew up as a migrant worker in Texas and won the first Premio Quinto Sol for outstanding writing by a Mexican–American author. Rivera's work is accessible to high school readers, but for different reasons: each part of the book is a short piece of episodic fiction, lending itself to short readings for short attention spans; also, each piece can stand on its own so that teachers can pick and choose which pieces to actually teach. The text is bilingual, which may appeal to teachers with Spanish-speaking ELL students. (The Spanish title is . . . *y no se lo tragó la tierra*, also translated as *This Migrant Earth*.) Most notably, however, Rivera's blunt honesty about migrant labor conditions (the lack of water, nourishment, acceptable shelter, and safety) holds the attention and sympathy of young adult readers. Pairing a Mexican–American text with Steinbeck is especially appropriate given Steinbeck's great appreciation of Mexico (*The Pearl, Log From the Sea of Cortez*, and screenplay for *Viva Zapata*). Considering the benefits of this pairing, I have created the virtual world *Mice, Men, and Migrant Labor* so that students can consider the unionization process within the contexts described by both books.

Before the Virtual World Activity

I suggest students engage in a pre-reading activity such as an autobiographical journal prompt before reading the Steinbeck and Rivera texts. Because *Mice, Men, and Migrant Labor* asks students to consider issues of human rights, students could write about a time that they felt their own rights were violated, or about what they feel are the most basic of human rights. Sharing their responses in small groups, or as part of a large-class discussion, can help transition to similar discussions about human rights when reading Steinbeck and Rivera.

Character letters can also help students consider working conditions in the text. Students should act the part of a character, writing letters (regarding working conditions, or living conditions, or poor management, or yet another conflict) to other characters in the text. For example, Lenny could write a letter to Slim regarding the harassment he receives from Curley, or the unnamed child in the chapter titled "And the Earth Did Not Devour Him" could write a letter to a faraway uncle about his father's heat stroke. Students can trade letters, consider the recipient's point of view, and respond to these written concerns with the text in mind.

Once students have had a chance to consider their own opinions about human rights as well as the characters' perspectives, they can broaden their knowledge of unionization with some concise information about the labor movement. At this point, Web resources can prove valuable. PBS's "On the Border" (www.pbs.org/now/politics/migrants.html) details various aspects of migrant labor such as its early history, Cesar Chavez's involvement in the movement, the current state of migratory labor, and children of migrant workers.

Also, migrant.net has created a document titled "Migrant Farmworkers in the United States" (www.migrant.net/pdf/farmworkerfacts.pdf) that outlines statistics regarding migrant labor. Teachers seeking a more visual representation of migrant labor can have their students view photographer Dorothea Lange's collection titled "Migrant Farm Families" (www.historyplace.com/unitedstates/lange/index.html). Finally, moving to issues of advocacy and migrant work, teachers can have students view a simple slideshow of Cesar Chavez's life work at NPR's site titled "Memories of a Former Migrant Worker" (www.npr.org/blogs/pictureshow/2010/10/08/130425856/cesar-chavez), or have them read a brief biography of Chavez as well as an explanation of migratory working conditions at Gale's "Hispanic Heritage" site (www.gale.cengage.com/free_resources/chh/bio/chavez_c.htm).

Films may also provide students with insight into the unionization process and help them to anticipate their own actions as union supporters or dissenters in the virtual world. *The Fight in the Fields* (1997) tells the story of the life of Cesar Chavez as related to the United Farm Workers Union. *Norma Rae* (1979) is another possibility. This Oscar-winning film stars Sally Fields, whose mill-working character fights for better wages and working conditions in her small-town factory. Finally, *Salt of the Earth* (1954), a groundbreaking film about striking Mexican–American mine workers with a powerful feminist perspective, was banned and blacklisted during the McCarthy period (now in the public domain and available on YouTube and Google Video).

It is my hope that after their experiences with self-reflection, consideration of characters' points of view, and a heightened awareness of migratory labor conditions, unionization, and Chavez's work, students will be prepared to enter the *Mice, Men and Migratory Labor* virtual world.

Entering the Virtual World

Mice, Men, and Migrant Labor is a cross-textual role-play in which each character plays a key part in the unionization process. Students are asked to take on roles inspired by both the Steinbeck and Rivera texts. As described below, some characters are encouraged to convince others to unionize, while others are urged to halt unionization. Throughout the entire experience, characters should consider textual events from Rivera and Steinbeck as they move through the virtual world. After students have had a chance to freely explore the world, develop their roles, and dialogue with other characters, the class will have to determine whether unionization has actually been achieved—that is, that a certain percentage of workers have joined in supporting the union organizers.

Roles from the Rivera text include:

- *Cristobal, Marisol, Esperanza, and Juan,* who are advised to make enough money to send home to their families, and maybe realize the dream of owning a farm. They wouldn't mind a better place to sleep; they are passionate about their dreams, and are willing to take risks.

- *Rogelio and Helsie*, children of Domingo and Aron, who go to the migrant school and work in the fields every afternoon and weekend.
- *Esteban and Carlos*, who have a similar desire to stay out of trouble but lack dreams for a better future.
- *Domingo, Maria, and Aron*, who also want to stay out of trouble and care for children, and whose desire to work and make money far outweigh any other goals that they have.

Students performing in roles from the Steinbeck text are encouraged to consider the text when deciding how they will act/think/move. They include:

- *Lenny*, who is advised to stay out of trouble, to keep George happy, and to realize his dream of tending rabbits.
- *George, Crooks, and Candy*, who are encouraged to stay out of trouble and to realize the dream of owning their own farm. They are stubborn, not easily convinced by other people.
- *Curley*, who is told to make sure that all unionization efforts are halted and that any instigators are found and punished.
- *Curley's Wife*, who is encouraged to find her husband, determine what he needs, and help him carry out these wishes.
- *Carlson*, who is advised to make sure that a union is organized and that *everyone*—that is, all laborers—are on board.
- *Slim*, who is directed to make sure that a union is not organized and that everyone simply does his/her job.

Roles related to unionization include:

- *Union Organizers 1, 2, 3, and 4*, who are told to make sure that a union is organized and that *everyone*—that is, all laborers—support it.
- *Union Dissenters 1, 2, 3, and 4*, who are advised to break up any unionization efforts and ensure that all workers simply do their jobs.
- *Boss 1 and 2*, who are directed to make sure that a union is *not* organized and that everyone simply does his/her job.

Places and Objects

As students move about the virtual world, they find that their particular roles are permitted to visit only certain "rooms." However, they have one thing in common: all roles start in the Field. Described as "hot and dusty," and causing workers a terrible thirst, the Field is an ideal place to begin because it provides the conditions that fuel much of the conflict. Workers from the Steinbeck and Rivera texts may complain about these conditions; union organizers can quietly gather support by suggesting meetings elsewhere in the world. The more supervisory roles, such as Slim or the Boss, might add to this conflict by ignoring the complaints of workers, ordering workers around, or introducing further problems (threatening to reduce break times, or adding tasks or hours to the work day, for example).

From the Field, characters can visit various places where they can initiate, strengthen or discourage the unionization process. For example, worker characters from the Rivera text can visit the Migrant Shack, described as "housing [the] entire family—all seven of them," and having the remains of a meager breakfast on the table. The shack is an ideal place for discussions about unionization because the supervisory characters are not present. Family members can weigh their working and living conditions against the value of employment and engage in honest dialogue about whether they plan to organize. Children of workers can add to this discussion by sharing opinions as well as experiences in the School (during the week) and Field (on the weekends).

Rogelio and Helsie are permitted in the School room, where they are reminded that they have been doused with lice powder and called "Mex." This space, not frequented by their parents or their parents' supervisors, provides a venue for honest discussions about their parents' union-related intentions as well as any other frustrations related to their schooling.

True to the text, all roles from *Of Mice and Men* are permitted to visit the Bunkhouse, described with a passage from Steinbeck that includes whitewashed walls, burlap ticking, applebox shelves, the cast iron stove, and "a big square table littered with playing cards . . ." (Steinbeck, 19). Because all roles may visit this room, it does not provide a space for private unionization discussions between George, Lenny, Candy, and the like; roles from the Steinbeck text must rely on more public areas outside of the ranch (such as the Country Store or the Brothel) for such dialogue.

The Country Store is where workers meet at the end of a long day as well as on weekends. In this room, they can purchase whiskey, coca-cola, ice cream bars, and beer. And as a public place, the Country Store seems to be the most likely venue for discussions between union organizers and workers. It is there that they can approach all workers—whether from Steinbeck or Rivera's text—about further discussions about the union. It is also where union dissenters might spy on conversations and threaten workers that speak to union organizers. It provides an authentic representation of the complications one encounters when organizing, as all roles have to weigh their moves carefully, only speaking to the right people at the right times.

Finally, the Boss' House is only frequented by those in power, such as Boss 1, Boss 2, Slim, and union dissenters. Visitors to this room may find and keep a gun, which they can use to intimidate other characters. The Boss' House provides a space for the powerful to plan their next steps to halt the unionization process.

Regardless of which rooms students visit, which objects they gather, and which intentions they discuss, they are either encouraging or discouraging the formation of a worker's union. When this activity is complete, some post-world reflections can enrich their virtual world experiences—and textual responses—further.

Post-Virtual World

Once the success or failure of unionization has been determined, I recommend that students process their virtual world experience as a whole class or small group. They can consider questions such as:

- What did you expect to do with your role in this activity? Did your prediction come true? Why or why not?
- If you were a worker, what did you decide to do regarding unionization, and why?
- In this activity, what contributed to—or discouraged—the unionization process?
- As a character, what might you do differently next time, if given the opportunity?
- What might make this virtual world experience more valuable for you? Why?

Given ongoing local and national debates about unions and collective bargaining, discussions can be further enriched with contemporary news events, YouTube clips of contemporary public demonstrations, visiting speakers, and students can discuss parallels between the virtual world experience and contemporary union struggles.

Benefits of the Virtual World

The success of the *Mice, Men, and Migrant Labor* virtual world depends on several factors: investing sufficient class time preparing for the Steinbeck and Rivera texts, providing further information on unionization, setting aside ample time for the virtual world activity, and debriefing with students afterward. Executed with these key elements, *Mice, Men, and Migrant Labor* can bring about several benefits, including deeper engagement with the source texts. Students are likely to move beyond their knowledge of character attributes and plot to a deeper consideration of character motives, social and political contexts, and relevance to issues in the present day. In fact, after participating in *Mice, Men, and Migrant Labor*, a former student noted that the world helped her ". . . think about [her] character more deeply . . . and who to ask for help and what places to look in . . ."

Beyond engagement with the source texts, students will likely engage more deeply in the issues surrounding them. As one student noted, the activity "helped [him] to understand how difficult it is to form a union and what workers are up against." This engagement extends basic historical knowledge; playing the roles helps students to more powerfully comprehend the struggles of disempowered workers.

As with many classroom activities, we hope that students will develop their sense of empathy. I believe that the role-playing enabled by the virtual world, and the descriptions of living and working conditions therein, can move students in that direction. And with such empathy come questions of responsibility: What do we do with our new level of awareness? Moving beyond awareness to action, how can we change things, become involved, see ourselves as advocates for migrant workers? In asking these questions, and moving toward social action, *Mice, Men, and Migratory Labor* reaches its natural conclusion. Students can learn about the conditions of migrant workers in their area and across the country and world. They can gather food or clothing for the local migrant outreach program, write to local officials about migratory labor legislation, raise funds for migrant literacy programs, or educate others about the conditions of migrant labor. They can put their money where their mouth is and commit to buying products that are a result of unionized migratory labor. Putting their virtual world experience into practice, students can transform their virtual roles from the oppressive "Boss 1" or oppressed "Maria" to actual roles as "agents of change."

Gatsby's American Dream

I (Meghan) created *Gatsby's American Dream* as a role-playing environment for students reading F. Scott Fitzgerald's *The Great Gatsby*. Widely considered a literary benchmark exemplifying American life (or, more accurately, life for wealthy inhabitants of America's east coast) in the 1920s, *The Great Gatsby* is an immensely popular feature on secondary school reading lists, and therefore the virtual world was designed with primarily high school students in mind. Specifically, *Gatsby's American Dream* was created for the purpose of offering reluctant or indifferent readers a way to connect both visually and aurally to the characters and setting of the novel. My hope is that making the world of *The Great Gatsby* inviting and interactive will allow students to feel more comfortable investigating, interrogating, and manipulating the literary devices and the world of high society they encounter in the novel.

Students can enter the world as one of seven characters: Nick Carraway, Daisy Buchanan, Tom Buchanan, Jordan Baker, Myrtle Wilson, George Wilson, and, of course, Jay Gatsby. Teachers may give these character assignments to individual students, or, to allow more students access to the world at the same time, a small group of students may "share" a character and play from the same terminal. The relatively small number of characters in *The Great Gatsby* lends itself nicely to the role-playing environment—every student gets to feel as though his or her role is interesting and vital to the novel's action, and the game play does not become burdened by the presence of too many participants; play is fast-paced but does not leave anyone behind.

Ideally, students should be assigned their roles before they start reading the novel so they may study their character's actions, motives, and beliefs as they progress through the text and can begin to identify with their character early on. Thus, students can read the novel with their character in mind, keeping notes along the way about their character's personality, background, and relationships with other characters. This type of focused reading may afford students more opportunities to analyze the larger themes at work in the novel. For example, while reading, a student assigned the role of Myrtle, can keep notes reflecting on Myrtle's desire to join the ranks of Manhattan high society, while students playing Tom, Nick, or Gatsby can analyze the tensions between "new" and "old" money among the Long Island elite. Students can also benefit from keeping a journal written from their character's perspective in order to become more comfortable with the role-play and to prepare for the virtual environment. Maintaining this type of journal can also make for a more in-depth writing assignment once students have finished reading the novel and have participated in the virtual role-play.

When students log in to *Gatsby's American Dream*, they "wake up" in a welcome room containing a mural of a jazz club along with the following epigraph, which also appears on *The Great Gatsby's* first page:

> Then wear the gold hat, if that will move her;
> If you can bounce high, bounce for her too,
> Till she cry, "Lover, gold-hatted, high-bouncing lover,
> I must have you!"

This first room also features jazz music and the students' first encounter with a programmed bot designed to converse with the room's inhabitants. This particular bot is F. Scott Fitzgerald, who welcomes the students to *Gatsby's American Dream*, and, if provoked, asks students questions about the epigraph and its author as well as *The Great Gatsby's* title and the alternative titles Fitzgerald considered. Teachers can use this welcome room as a warm-up activity to let students familiarize themselves with the various features of the virtual environment, or they can have students write a brief journal entry in response to one of the Fitzgerald bot's questions. From here, the students can move to either the West Egg or East Egg villages and begin the role-playing session.

I selected the visual and audio elements that make up *Gatsby's American Dream* in hopes of immersing visitors in *The Great Gatsby's* setting and plot. Although most students are marginally familiar with the culture of the early 1920s, their knowledge may not extend beyond the somewhat ambiguous notion of the "roaring '20s." While this concept provides a fair foundation for understanding the context of *The Great Gatsby*, it does little to give students perspective on the social class issues at stake in the novel or to deepen their understanding of characters like George and Myrtle Wilson. Therefore, my goal in selecting images for the *Gatsby* virtual world was to offer more than just pictures of flapper girls and men in fedoras (though these images do make their way into the virtual environment occasionally as representations of the culture of excess that permeated post–World War I America). To offer as authentic a viewing and listening experience as possible for students new to the culture of Gatsby's Long Island, I chose 1920s New York City postcards to serve as the primary images for many of the world's rooms, including the "The Highway," which leads students from East Egg to New York City, and "158th Street," the site of Tom and Myrtle's Manhattan love nest. The West Egg room features an aerial photograph of Great Neck, Long Island, the peninsula on which Fitzgerald lived while beginning work on the novel; similarly, a map of Manhasset Neck, the peninsula that became the novel's West Egg, greets students in the Buchanan's posh, established neighborhood. The room dedicated to Gatsby's mansion also features music, and its visual is a photograph of Oheka Castle on Long Island's Gold Coast, one of Fitzgerald's inspirations for Gatsby's estate. The inclusion of these types of images combines the benefits of the role-playing environment with resources that could be found in a literary virtual museum. The maps, photos, and postcards provide background on Fitzgerald's life and some of the inspirations for *The Great Gatsby*, inviting students to make connections from the novel to the cultural identity of the era in which it was written. The maps became an important addition as well, allowing students to view the geographical landscape in which the novel takes place. I purposely selected Long Island maps as visuals in these first rooms because of the way many video games offer area maps to players early on to introduce the realm created for the game, thus giving the game's action a context. The images and music can also provide students with a starting point for potential research assignments about Fitzgerald, New York in the 1920s, prohibition and bootlegging, or the Jazz era. Photographs of New York and Long Island neighborhoods and businesses from the early 1900s are also featured frequently to provide an accurate and stimulating backdrop for the plot the students are recreating.

Game play within *Gatsby's American Dream* is fairly simple—students move through various rooms assigned to different locations within the novel's setting and follow, to a certain extent, the action of the novel's plot. In addition to the 1920s images and music featured in each of the rooms, the virtual environment's chat function, which utilizes one half of the screen, is a key component to the role-playing game. In the chat section of the screen, students talk to each other as their assigned characters, reacting to the novel's events the way they estimate their character would, and exploring the characters' relationships to one another in ways that may or may not get fully explored in the novel. The chat function also allows students to pick up, carry, and more closely inspect the objects they encounter, interact with the various bots in the game, and perform other actions as they choose. Teachers can facilitate this action by introducing major events that take place in the novel, thus ensuring all students are reacting to major plot points at the same time. Teachers can limit the amount of time students spend discussing or investigating each of the novel's events, or leave students as much time as they like to examine scenes the students deem significant. Another approach would be to have the characters be "shades" of their former selves who visit the world as a group (either during class or at a time set for the small group outside of class) and discuss the events of the novel in character as they move together from room to room. Transcripts of these discussions, or any discussions by the characters in the world, are sent to themselves and their teacher. Teachers also have the ability to control and restrict students' movements within the virtual world, encouraging them to remain in one area and discuss what's going on rather than allowing all students to move through rooms as quickly or slowly as they like.

That's not to say students don't have freedom to do what they please inside the virtual world—they can experience everything the novel has to offer, even if the character they're playing actually doesn't do so in the novel. Each character has access to all the rooms of the virtual world, so a student playing George Wilson could go to Gatsby's party and participate in a discussion of the events that occur there, even though George does not attend any of Gatsby's parties in the novel. If the teacher decides not to let students stray from the novel's plot in this way, he or she has the option of locking individual rooms or pathways. Otherwise, the virtual environment allows students to take several liberties with the text. Characters such as Myrtle Wilson, who do not live to the end of the novel, remain active participants until the role-play session is over, and all of the characters have the option of attending Gatsby's funeral if they decide doing so is appropriate. Whether they decide to follow the novel's plot exactly as it was written, or take advantage of some of the incongruities the virtual environment affords, students are actively interrogating the novel's plot rather than just taking it at face value. Within the virtual world, the text becomes malleable, and students are encouraged to explore the world Fitzgerald created, experimenting with elements such as plot and characterization as they make new discoveries about the literary devices they encounter.

Allowing students to experience *The Great Gatsby* through the virtual role-playing environment has several benefits, especially for those students who are not as vocal during traditional classroom discussions. When given a character and instructed simply to react to an event or accomplish a set of goals as that character, these typically silent students may feel less pressure to "give an answer" than they do in class; instead, they are using their knowledge of the text to engage in a conversation with their classmates that feels more natural than responding to a teacher's questions about the same text. The role-play has a distinctly collaborative atmosphere, encouraging students to pool their knowledge about their characters, and each student can feel empowered by contributing his or her knowledge set to the success of the game. In addition, students' ability to manipulate the text occurs fairly naturally in the online environment because students are ultimately in charge of the direction in which they lead their characters. As long as students are drawing on their knowledge of the text to support their decisions, game play should not be too heavily impeded by a student "changing the rules" and making a decision their character does not make in the novel. In fact, if a student does something during role-play that deviates from the actions taken by his or her character in the novel (for example, Tom telling George Wilson that it was Daisy, not Gatsby, who struck and killed Myrtle), the other students have an opportunity to question the decision and discuss whether or not it makes sense based on what they know about Tom's character. Thus, students are constantly assessing their own and each other's knowledge while they simultaneously play with familiar narrative conventions. When students play as they can when using the virtual environment, they become active participants rather than passive observers. I view this type of play as vital to students' understanding of and connection to literature, which makes the use of virtual environments such as *Gatsby's American Dream* a rewarding and enriching option for educators.

5

TEACHING *THINGS FALL APART* IN *THE VILLAGE OF UMUOFIA*

Cheryl Taliaferro

The virtual role-play made it easier for me to identify with the characters as well as the issues in the novel. By looking through the eyes of a character, I was able to better understand the culture, the background, and the world they lived in. The pictures and music also helped by adding to the atmosphere, which was firmly established by the other elements.

(Christine Roberts, 9th grade student)

Set in the imaginary late nineteenth-century Nigerian village of Umuofia during the years immediately preceding and following British colonization, Chinua Achebe's novel *Things Fall Apart* requires readers to orient themselves in a foreign land and understand characters far removed from their experience. Umuofia is inhabited by the Igbo, who believe the world was created by Chukwu, that the god Agbala speaks through their village oracle, and that egwugwu, their ancestors' spirits, take on physical form and walk among them. The villagers welcome friends into their homes by breaking a kola nut. They celebrate the yam harvest, tap palm wine, practice polygamy, leave newborn twins in the Evil Forest to die, and in many other ways, embrace customs and behaviors distant from those of my teenage students in Denton, Texas.

When I first began teaching this novel in a 9th grade World Literature and Composition course, I noticed that, comfortable in their familiar role as literature students, my students could analyze the novel, discuss characterization and theme, and identify relevant symbols, but they did not seem to have that kind of meaningful reading experience Louise Rosenblatt describes as "living through" the text (Rosenblatt, 33). My students did not, as Atticus Finch advises, "climb into [the characters'] skin and walk around in it" (Lee, p. 48). Their difficulty in reading *Things Fall Apart* may be unique in degree, but not kind; researchers point out difficulties students may have engaging meaningfully with multicultural works (Dressel; Louie; Poole). As I searched for new ways to help successive groups of students relate to this historically rich novel about a distant culture, I discovered the online virtual role-play *The Village of Umuofia* and decided to try it.

My initial reason for using *The Village of Umuofia* in my classroom, and the primary reason that I have continued to use it for several years, is that it does something for my students that I cannot do: it puts them in Africa. Adopting the persona of various characters in the novel, the students enter into the world of the Igbo on the characters' own terms. The virtual role-play requires students to think like the characters in the novel. It invites them to participate visually and aurally in the life of the village. As the students enter this new world, they are greeted with the sound of traditional music and photographic images taken by an anthropologist who worked with the Igbo during the early part of the twentieth century. Students immerse themselves in the authentic sounds and sights of Umuofia. Each year that I have used this activity, some students have expressed surprise upon discovering that some of the elements of the setting that they imagined were, in fact, quite inaccurate.

My desire to help students fully participate in their reading of the novel is not the only reason I continue to use this site. The role-play also provides an opportunity to address curricular standards that probably would not be covered by a reading of the novel alone, especially those standards that pertain to visual literacy. Currently, all states have some sort of standards that apply to media literacy (Baker); in addition, the National Council of Teachers of English and the International Reading Association (2010) include knowledge of non-print texts as one component of their English Language Arts standards, and the College Board's (2010) objectives for Advanced Placement English require that students be able to analyze images as text. This online virtual activity provides an opportunity to incorporate those standards in an authentic way into an existing unit of study.

Another benefit to using this site: it's fun. In general, students enjoy the experience of spending a couple of class periods in the computer lab "playing a game" rather than "working." The role-play is an intensely social, dynamic, and creative activity, ripe with opportunities for interacting and performing with classmates, injecting humor and wit into what may otherwise be experienced as yet another drab school day. For many students, the opportunity to be social, dramatic, and have fun in a non-threatening way is both motivating and encourages a deeper involvement with the object of study (Newkirk; Smith and Wilhelm).

The First Visit

Prior to playing the role-play game, students visiting the site are encouraged to complete a First Visit to orient themselves in the online world. When I first used this resource, I had students complete the First Visit during the class period prior to their playing the game. I quickly realized, however, that this activity produces many positive outcomes on its own that help it function as a worthwhile pre-reading activity. Now, my students' first encounter with *The Village of Umuofia* occurs before they even begin reading the novel.

Because my students' knowledge of Africa in general is fairly sparse, we spend about one week building background knowledge. This time affords me an opportunity to assess what preconceptions my students are bringing to their study of the book and to talk to them about why studying Africa is important. We primarily spend this time discussing Africa's connection to and impact on the modern world. We also explore customs and traditions typically followed by the Igbo people today. Placed in this context, studying the novel then becomes, in part, our attempt to analyze and evaluate the historical and social forces that contributed to contemporary Igbo society. After building this type of knowledge, I send my students to the computer lab to work on the First Visit. While this activity can be assigned for homework, I've found it's helpful to have students begin it under my supervision. This ensures that they all know exactly how to log in, which buttons to click, where to go, and what to do once they've entered the world.

For most of my students, the First Visit takes 30–45 minutes to complete. Students log in to the world as a guest and are instructed to spend time simply looking around. In this way, they become familiar with the enCore interface, learning how to navigate and to use the basic commands that the game requires. From a practical standpoint, the First Visit makes the role-play they will engage in later much easier. Since students already know how to use the virtual world, they can focus more of their thoughts on the role-play activity rather than on the technology. As the students become comfortable using the site during the First Visit, they select three photographs and write about them as a journal activity. The next day in class, we discuss their journal entries.

Students' responses to the photographs may vary considerably, and debating their reactions affords a good opportunity to discuss specific elements of visual literacy as well the Igbo culture itself. The discussions of these photographs also reveal the ways in which students use their own lives and their own know-ledge to connect to elements of this foreign culture, and, when that knowledge fails them, raises questions that they carry with them into their reading of the novel.

For example, one of the pictures that the students encounter is titled "Musicians and Boys" (see Figure 5.1). Students in one class who chose to write about this picture made the following comments in their journals:

- I think they could represent something like the fine arts program at [our school]. They might be learning how to play a song for a tribal dance.
- There is a huge xylophone. They look like they are having fun. There are boys watching them from behind. Maybe they want to learn how to play.

FIGURE 5.1 Musicians and Boys

- They probably play music to entertain ... They could also play music to release their emotions. They look like they are enjoying themselves so they probably do this for fun. They are also playing together so it is strengthening their unity.

Clearly, the students' journal writing illustrates how they draw on their prior understanding of groups of people playing music together as they interpret this picture. When we discussed their comments in class, my students debated whether the picture depicts music lessons or people just having fun. Several questions were raised in this discussion that the students could not definitively answer. How are children in this village educated? In what subjects are they educated, either formally or informally? What purposes does music serve within this society? What other instruments are common?

Additionally, the discussion that occurred about this picture led to inquiries about gender roles. One student noted that two females are positioned in the top right of the photograph. Most of the students had not initially picked up on the female presence in the photos, but upon it being pointed out, they agreed that these must be females because they are dressed differently from the others.

Students wondered why the females are on the periphery of the group. One is actually not even completely in the picture. Is it because they are less important than the boys? Were they just bystanders in this event, or did they have their own role to play? Are women allowed to play musical instruments?

A second picture that captured students' interest is titled "Masked Man." The caption underneath this photograph reads "This man is protesting the Christian mission" (see Figure 5.2).

Two students wrote the following in their journals:

- This gives off a different tone [than the picture titled "Disguised Man"], even though this one has a mask in it too. The text says he is protesting the Christian mission. One might guess he is very firm in his beliefs by wearing such a mask. For all we know, he could become a martyr in the future.
- Primarily, I wonder what the mask means. Could it be a traditional mask worn in this situation to stand up for customary beliefs? I am also curious as to what actions this protester may be taking . . . Would he be punished? . . . How many of the Igbo did not agree with the Christian reformers? If this protester was alone, he was very brave.

During the class discussion of this photograph, students wondered about the creation of the mask. One art student noted its intricate details and speculated about how it might have been made. This line of thought led to questions once more about education. How is this carving skill learned, who practices it, and in

FIGURE 5.2 Masked Man

what contexts? In addition, we analyzed the placement of the mask within the photograph. The mask takes up such a large portion of the photograph, causing the viewer to focus on the mask itself rather than on the actions of the protester. The protester's body cannot be seen at all. Was the photographer implying that the mask held some special power for the wearer? Did it represent something by itself that would cause the wearing of it to be considered an act of protest? The photograph also led to questions about colonialism. What role did religion play in colonization? How many native people resisted colonialism and/or Christian conversion, and in what ways? What happened to those who resisted? How does the colonization of Africa compare to the colonization of North America?

Clearly, the discussions centered on the pictures encountered during the First Visit raised more questions for the students than they answered. This is one of the benefits to using the First Visit as a pre-reading activity. The students carried their authentic questions with them as they began reading the novel. In many cases, the students found close parallels between their own questions and the themes and ideas that Achebe raises in the novel. Also, the raising of so many questions, and the offering of various interpretations of the specific photographs, sets the tone for the larger questions *Things Fall Apart* brings up about the nature and impact of colonization—rich questions that do not have one right answer for students to dutifully seek out and repeat.

Writing Preparation

The Village of Umuofia virtual role-play requires students to assume the identities of characters from the book, a task that does not come easily to all students. Each year, a small percentage of the students in my class are unsure how to proceed with this type of activity. Therefore, I've found it helpful to have the students practice assuming the perspective of characters throughout the course of our time reading the book by journal writing from the point of view of various characters. How often we do this depends on how comfortable the students in that class are with adopting another persona and speaking through a new voice. Perhaps if this type of activity is one that students are already accustomed to, it may not be necessary to practice it as much as we do in my class. Nonetheless, I do recommend that once students are assigned a role to play, they complete at least one first-person journal entry from their character's perspective.

The first year I did this, I learned that the students needed time to write this entry in class rather than as a homework assignment. The students who struggle with adopting the persona of the character need time to talk to their classmates and me about events in the book that may be important to their character, and they often need my support and feedback as their writing progresses. As an added incentive to do well, I offer to let the students use these entries when they participate in the role-play to help them remember key points about their characters. While most students do not directly draw on them during the fast-paced activity, it can be reassuring for some to have their journals nearby as a type of "cheat sheet."

Some years the students ask me for suggestions to guide their journal entries. When they want a more specific framework to guide their writing, I write the following questions on the board for them to address in their entries:

- Who are the members of your family? How do you feel about each of these family members?
- What is important to you? Why?
- Who is important to you? Why?
- What are your opinions about Okonkwo? What is the basis for these opinions?
- What is your opinion about the way the Igbo live? Is there anything that you think needs to be changed? Why or why not?
- How do you feel about the Christian missionaries' attempts to convert the Igbo? Why?
- How do you feel about the British colonial government officials and their actions? Why?

Of course, not all of these questions can be clearly answered based on the information in the novel. I encourage students to draw on their understanding of the book, and the time period in which it is set, to develop ideas and perspectives unique to each character that seem logical, based on their close reading of that character and other characters in the novel.

The Virtual-World Role-Play

In order for students to log in and participate, the teacher needs to obtain user-names and passwords from the site's creator, Allen Webb. When he emails these, he includes a detailed set of instructions for how to set up the activity. I've found these instructions to be helpful, and I typically follow the role-play as Allen designed it. As teacher I play the role of the Village Crier, making announcements about events from the novel that the characters can then discuss. The instructions come with suggested announcements to make, but it's quite easy to add your own prompts to these, based on ideas that were emphasized during the novel study. The discussion of each announcement generally lasts about 5 minutes, which seems to be about the right amount of time for students to discuss before running out of things to say. The entire game usually takes my students one full 90-minute class period to complete. For 50-minute classes the role-play could be split into two smaller sessions or simply shortened.

The teacher also has the capability of locking different characters in rooms so that they can discuss announced events with like-minded people, or with people whose views differ from their own. For example, the Christian missionaries and converts can be locked into a room together in order to plot their next movements, or they may be locked in a location with some of the Igbo so that they have to debate and defend their beliefs and actions. For some parts of the game the doors may be unlocked so that the students may wander around and talk to whomever they choose; however, I've found that conversations tend to be more focused when the students are locked into particular areas so that they do not have the option of running away from conversations, avoiding conversations altogether by simply moving from place to place rather quickly, or congregating with all of their friends in one particular area. When the latter happens, the conversation of my fourteen-year-old students can quickly turn to plans for the weekend or something that happened at the last party they attended.

Besides playing an active role in the game, the teacher also needs to be able to monitor the students as they are playing. After I make each announcement as the Village Crier, I generally walk around the computer lab, reading what the students are doing and making suggestions as needed. Sometimes students need to be redirected when their conversations veer off topic, but I have not found these off-topic conversations to be any more frequent than those that normally occur during a regular class period. If anything, they occur less frequently because all members of the class have a vested interest in everyone doing what they are supposed to be doing so that the game can continue smoothly.

One of the things that impressed me when I first tried this activity was that the students held each other accountable for the work they were all doing. In fact, I often find the spoken conversations in the computer lab that the students have among themselves as they play just as interesting as the online virtual conversations they create within the game. Generally, a few students will quickly emerge as leaders of sorts, offering others suggestions for things to say and keeping their classmates on topic. These students are not always the ones who emerge as leaders during typical class discussions. Sometimes they are the quieter students who have experience with and enjoy role-play games. These students know that such activities require a "willing suspension of disbelief" and they want this one to work. They are, in effect, teaching the others how to imaginatively engage in virtual learning.

A certain level of playfulness occurs as students experiment with anachronisms, using modern slang in their conversations and invariably threatening another character with some sort of advanced weapon that could wipe out the entire village. This is part of the playfulness that keeps the activity fun and engaging for the students, but I think it also demonstrates a way in which the students are making sense of the novel by using their own experiences, understandings, and vocabulary to help them relate to the characters. Okonkwo is a tough guy, and since the students don't know any tough-guy nineteenth-century words, they have him speak using the roughest modern American slang words they can. I suspect that these anachronisms also indicate that the students recognize that their own world is, in some ways, re-enacting the past as modern man continues to struggle with many of the same issues that the novel raises. It's easy for us to imagine a man saying "Screw you" to someone who is oppressing him or to hear a leader threaten to use a nuclear warhead, because we've seen that happen. However, the students generally have a sense of when this playfulness begins to go too far, and someone among the group will say, "This is getting ridiculous. We need to get back to the book" or perhaps, "Hey! Stop it. I don't want to have to stop playing." In most cases, these admonishments from a peer are all that is needed to refocus a discussion.

Students devote a much greater amount of their spoken conversation, though, to reviewing the book. They question and correct each other when online comments are made that are factually inaccurate or don't represent a character appropriately. They also ask for help when needed, seeking clarification about events or other characters. I have found that students become acutely aware, at this time, of misunderstandings they may have had about this book and work to correct those misunderstandings so that they don't embarrass themselves in front of their peers, or become excluded from an online conversation. At moments like this one, when a student realizes that he or she doesn't know something that is necessary in order to continue participating in the discussion, a shy student may quietly ask a friend for clarification before proceeding, while a less-inhibited student may loudly ask, "What are you talking about?!" The students do work as a community to help ensure that they all possess the knowledge that they need in order to continue engaging in the virtual-world role-play.

Each year, the direction that the activity takes varies according to the particular group of students playing it. One of the slight oddities about it, which again is one of its interesting strengths as an instructional tool, is that characters in the game interact with one another in ways that do not occur in the book. For example, the character Ikemefuna is killed fairly early in the book. However, the student playing the part of Ikemefuna continues to play the game after his death. Students have to discuss verbally how they should handle such anomalies, and they generally come to some sort of group consensus about how to proceed. Most groups decide that Ikemefuna's spirit is what survives, and they take advantage of the opportunity they see in the game for Ikemefuna's ghost to confront Okonkwo about his role in the murder. However, sometimes students decide that Ikemefuna actually survived the murder itself; this solution is a trickier one, but it generally does not seem to interfere with Achebe's intentions, since the Igbos' decision to kill Ikemefuna, and Okonkwo's participation in the murder, is the primary focus of the event.

In a similar way, the character of Okonkwo usually continues playing a part in the game even after he commits suicide. Sometimes students have his spirit return to exact revenge or to prophesy the complete destruction of the Igbo, reminiscent of the ways in which the ghosts of Caesar and King Hamlet function in Shakespeare's works. Other students have had Okonkwo's spirit return to bring back a message that he learned about the way he should have lived his life in a way that is more like the story of Scrooge in Dickens' *A Christmas Carol*.

Also, characters such as Mr. Brown, Mr. Smith, and Ikemefuna all appear together in the virtual world even though they are not in the same scene in the book at any time. I've watched students deal with these situations in a variety of ways. Sometimes Ikemefuna, like Nwoye, converts to Christianity. Other times, he takes the opposite stance, standing in solidarity with the traditionalists. Once, he even managed to convince Mr. Brown that he should forsake the Christian mission and his European heritage to become a full member of the Igbo instead. These liberties that the students take with the plot, far from being weaknesses in the way the activity is set up, give the students sufficient control over their characters to explore alternatives to Achebe's story. In doing so, students demonstrate their understanding of how literature works. The choices that they make also reveal their recognition that the choices that the characters make in this book are not the only ones that exist. Other paths could have been followed, and the students have the opportunity to explore what the outcome might have been had characters made different decisions.

Listening to the conversations students have as they participate in the virtual role-play, and afterwards reading the transcripts of the online discussions that are automatically emailed to the teacher, provides excellent opportunities to informally assess what the students are learning and how they are processing information from the novel. Following are two small excerpts from online conversations and what I learned about my students from them. The first excerpt contains part of a conversation between Ezinma and her mother that occurs after they have learned that Okonkwo beat his wife during Peace Week:

> *Ezinma*: Did you hear what my father did?
> *Ekwefi*: Yes, I did hear.
> *Ezinma*: I hope that he does not beat you anytime soon.
> *Ekwefi*: I hope that he doesn't too. But you know how your father can be.
> *Ezinma*: Yes . . . maybe if he drank more palm wine and just mellowed out once in a while . . .
> *Ekwefi*: Yeah, he really needs to unwind a bit.
> *Village Crier*: The Oracle of the Hills and Caves has just ordered the death of Ikemefuna.
> *Ezinma*: What!
> *Ekwefi*: Oh no! . . . What should we do?
> *Ezinma*: There is nothing we can do to stop it if the oracle has decreed it.
> *Ekwefi*: Very true. I feel sorry for Ikemefuna.
> *Ezinma*: Nwoye will be upset.
> *Ekwefi*: You're right . . . and I think my father will be sorry as well.
> *Ezinma*: Yes, he would never admit it but I think he became very close to Ikemefuna.

These two students enacted a private conversation that might have occurred between these two characters. The students demonstrate their understanding of the close mother–daughter relationship that these two characters have by having them share their worries and concerns about family members. They worry about Okonkwo's bad temper and its effects on the family, yet they also sympathize with both Okonkwo and Nwoye over the emotional distress they will feel when learning that Ikemefuna must die. The love that they feel for their family members is evident, but it does not blind them to reality. The students' understanding of various cultural elements is also revealed in the way they easily include elements such as palm wine and the role of the oracle in their discussion.

The second excerpt comes from a conversation that Mr. Brown has with Osu and Nwoye at the Christian mission:

> *Mr. Brown*: Greetings primitive people of Umuofia . . . I have come to you in peace.
>
> *Nwoye*: For what purpose?
>
> *Mr. Brown*: I will build you a hospital.
>
> *Osu*: I believe you.
>
> *Nwoye*: As do I.
>
> *Mr. Brown*: Well then my children we should get to work.
>
> *Osu*: If the gods do not punish you that means you're not an evil spirit.
>
> *Nwoye*: Get to work? I am no slave.
>
> *Mr. Brown*: Right-o mate, we will work together.
>
> *Nwoye*: I fear my father will be angry that I am talking to you.
>
> *Mr. Brown*: First I must take a tea break. So, while I eat my crumpets, you should begin laying the framework for the hospital.
>
> *Osu*: What's tea?
>
> *Mr. Brown*: A drink made from soaked herbs.
>
> *Osu*: Our medicine man makes that.
>
> *Mr. Brown*: How right you are my friend but my methods are better . . . I have brought cures from the end of the earth and technology.

In this excerpt, the students playing the roles of both Nwoye and Osu show that they understand some of the forces motivating these characters. Nwoye worries about provoking his father's anger, but not enough to stop him from talking to the missionary. Osu reveals that he trusts the missionary at first, but not completely; he is willing to trust the man totally once he receives confirmation that the gods are not going to punish Mr. Brown for his actions.

The student playing the role of Mr. Brown captures both the positive and the negative sides of his character. Mr. Brown brings some good to the Igbo, such as a hospital, new forms of food, cures, and technology. However, even the kind Mr. Brown carries with him an air of superiority. Although he offers to "work together" with Osu and Nwoye, he then proceeds to tell them to work while he takes a break and refers to both of them as "primitive" and "my children," neither of which completely reconcile with the other term he uses, "my friend." He also assures them that his own "methods are better." The student playing Nwoye also seemed sensitive to the inequality inherent in their relationship when he protests, "I am no slave." The students in this group display their understandings of the characters as well as some of the inherent complexities within the colonial system. The fun that they were having during this conversation was evident. The student playing Mr. Brown joked aloud that Mr. Brown didn't have enough personality in the book, and he decided to use the humorous phrase "Right-o mate" and to add in the detail of the tea and crumpets in a sort of fun homage to the British.

Addressing Potential Problems

As with any activity, there are some difficulties that teachers may encounter when they use this game. Being aware of these potential problems upfront, however, can help minimize their effects. Although Literary Worlds does not require special software, be sure that the computers students will be using are not blocked from the site by a school filter or firewall (may need to be opened), that Java is installed, which browser works best, and that it is set to "accept popup windows."

Second, it is important for the teacher to spend time on the site prior to having students use it so that the teacher knows how everything works. After getting the instructions for the game, the teacher can practice with the various commands needed to use as the Village Crier, and learn how to activate them. That said, technology is never perfect. My last piece of advice is to be flexible and expect some minor problems. One year, I had a student accidentally unplug an entire bank of computers in the middle of the game. It took some time to restart the computers and get those students back online playing, but the game continued. Another year I somehow managed to lock one student in a room alone. While waiting on me to unlock the doors, she performed a soliloquy.

Another problem teachers may observe is that some students, especially those with reading difficulties, may have a hard time with the game initially. Conversations tend to move pretty quickly, and when multiple students are participating, they move even faster. Several students may be responding to a comment all at the same time, or a couple of students within the group may branch off on a different topic while the rest continue the conversation that they were having. I have seen a small number of students become frustrated at trying to follow what is being said. Allowing these students to pause in their participation can be quite helpful, as it allows them time to acclimatize to the format and to learn how best to read and process the information. These students usually want to be part of the activity and will figure out how to do so if they are given the time. It can also be helpful to get these students alone in a room on the site with just one other player so that they can have an uninterrupted conversation for a while.

Teachers need to rely on their knowledge of their students as they negotiate how they group students into different rooms. Online conversations can become challenging to follow if too many people are participating at one time, and sometimes one or two students may encounter or create more difficulties than others. I have found that, in general, most students benefit from participating in conversations that are limited to four or fewer players whenever possible.

The final problem that I've encountered is that sometimes students simply aren't prepared. Perhaps they didn't read all of the book, or perhaps they didn't understand what they read, but they do not have enough knowledge about the book to carry out their role in the game. Sometimes their knowledge gap is slight enough that help from their classmates can help them progress through the game. In the process, they will fill in some of the gaps in their knowledge base. However, if the knowledge gap is great, classmates may become exasperated and simply refuse to interact with the unprepared student. I have found that explaining the activity well at the beginning of the unit, and informing the students of the possibility that they could embarrass themselves or not be able to play if they don't do all the reading, is usually enough to ensure that students do the reading and make an effort to understand the book. I have only once had a student who found herself completely unable to participate.

Benefits

There are significant benefits from using this virtual world to study literature. The First Visit activity acclimatizes the students visually and aurally to life in an Igbo village as it was lived almost a century ago. The game itself allows students to review the entire book while assuming the identities of characters whose lives differ greatly from their own. It also provides them with valuable opportunities for self-correction and for socially constructing new knowledge. It also helps me informally assess my students' understandings, and I can then adjust their next assignments according. Lastly, it helps bring humor and fun into the classroom, which all students appreciate.

6

CONTENT LEARNING IN LITERARY VIRTUAL WORLDS

The Village of Umuofia

Allen Webb

Narrating the impact on a fictional Igbo village in Eastern Nigeria of the incursion of British missionaries and colonial administration, Chinua Achebe's *Things Fall Apart* (1958) is an important study of cultural interaction, the best-known literary work from Africa, and one of the most frequently taught novels in the world. Using usernames and passwords, students enter into the virtual world I created based on *Things Fall Apart*, which I call *The Village of Umuofia*, and "wake up" as a wide range of Igbo villagers, British missionaries, and colonial administrators in a visual space based on an extensive archive of authentic black and white photography taken by an anthropologist at the turn of the century in the region of Nigeria where the novel is set. The village is filled with images, characters from the novel, and recordings of traditional West African music. Students visiting *The Village of Umuofia* have commented:

> I have never seen anything like it before. The most important thing for me was seeing the pictures of huts, walking sticks, and tools. I was amazed at the quality of craftsmanship and the amount of time these people must put into carving them. Also the website did a good job reinforcing how characters communicated with each other and how they came to their decisions.

> This activity helped me to place myself in a villager's shoes and try to think like they did. I got to kind of experience first hand what they went through.

> I enjoyed my online experience in *The Village of Umuofia*. It really made you feel as if you were in the book and living as your character.

Like many of the virtual worlds we have created, *The Village of Umuofia* is accompanied by a web site that provides information and resources for students and teachers (www.literaryworlds.org/umuofia/).

The *Village of Umuofia* is a flexible, experimental virtual environment where teachers follow specific pedagogies that I have developed for its use, and/or invent new approaches. As of February 2011, 239 teachers have requested the usernames and passwords for *The Village of Umuofia*. Though some of these teachers did not actually use the resource, others have used it multiple times. A handful of these teachers are at university level, but the majority teach in high schools across the United States and the world. From alternative schools in inner city New York to public schools in North Dakota teachers have taken their students to *The Village*. I have had many requests for passwords from England and Canada, from Anglophone Africa, including from Nigeria, South Africa, and Zimbabwe, as well as English-language schools in Mexico, Senegal, India, and Thailand. I maintain an email list of these teachers and occasionally share with them information about new developments in *The Village*, teaching ideas, relevant conference presentations, and publications.

The previous chapter ("Teaching *Things Fall Apart* in *The Village of Umuofia*" by Cheryl Taliaferro) illuminates the experience of a class of 9th grade students using this virtual world in Denton, Texas. Drawing on the experience of college students in Kalamazoo, Michigan, this chapter will examine how a literary virtual world organizes, informs, and develops the response and interpretation of literary texts. Understanding a virtual world as a critical and creative reading process is central to helping us understand the pedagogical value and possibilities of virtual worlds for teaching literature.

Configuring Virtual Space: The Literary Map

A literary virtual world must in some sense reproduce the setting of a literary work. At the most primary level that reproduction takes the form of a map of connected virtual spaces. Depending on the geography of the source text many different maps are possible, and any virtual mapping emerges from a textual analysis and constitutes an interpretation or reading. Which physical spaces in the setting of the work should be represented in the virtual world? How do the spaces connect to each other and how should virtual characters travel between them? How closely should the map follow the source text? Is the map highly complex and difficult to navigate (as in the Shakespeare virtual worlds described in Chapter 4, which contain over one hundred rooms)? Or is the space small, contained, and easily understood? In *Graphs, Maps, and Trees* (2005) Franco Moretti develops literary maps for stories and novels from eighteenth- and nineteenth-century England, France, and Germany. He describes the way a literary map interprets texts by reducing and emphasizing specific aspects of textual geography:

> What do literary maps do [?] . . . First, they are a good way to prepare a text for analysis. You choose a unit—walks, lawsuits, luxury goods, whatever—find its occurrences, place them in space . . . or in other words: you *reduce* the text to a few elements, and *abstract* them from them the narrative flow, and construct a new *artificial* object [. . .] it offers a model of the narrative universe which rearranges its components in a non-trivial way, and may bring some hidden patterns to the surface.
>
> *(ellipsis and emphasis in the original, 53–54)*

The Village of Umuofia is a relatively small, thirteen-room virtual space based on my artificial mapping of key locations in the village and surrounding locations described in Achebe's novel. The layout or map of the virtual world becomes, as Moretti describes, an "artificial object" that is also a textual interpretation— an interpretation that students or scholars of the novel traverse and can also analyze. In considering a virtual world as an interpretation of a source text there are several key questions to ask: Why this map? How does the layout of the map emphasize particular settings, characters, perspectives, or themes? What other maps are possible and how might they interpret the novel differently?

I mapped *The Village of Umuofia* to facilitate specific character groupings, afford spaces for a range of role-playing activities, and foreground specific themes and tensions in the source novel (see Figure 6.1).

The map centers on the village square, and radiating from it there is access to an Elder's Compound (where the family of the main character lives) and, in one direction, the Christian Mission and British District Commissioner Headquarters, and in the other direction the village meeting hall, cave of the oracle, and the remote village of Mbanta. There is nothing in the novel that indicates that these settings are in this linear arrangement. Instead of representing a geographical "reality" from the novel, the artificial virtual world map of *The Village of Umuofia* locates the village in tension between the British missionaries and district commissioner on one side and the traditional African values of the oracle and cave on the other. At one extreme, the colonial prison created by the British; at the other extreme, the remote traditional village (Mbanta).

Each of the characters in the role-play is assigned a "home" where they first "wake up," and these "homes" group together more or less like-minded characters: the missionaries and their converts at the mission, the district commissioner and his enlisted Africans in the Commissioner HQ, Okonkwo and leading village men in the Meeting Room, women at the Elder Compound, and so on. The activity often begins by having students as players "talk" with people in their "home" before entering other areas. (It would be possible to set certain rooms as closed to specific characters, but that is not something I have done in *The Village.*) The Meeting Hall represents a space where Africans can discuss public issues farther from European influence; the Village Crier, played by the teacher, can move all traditional Africans there and lock the door. The Crier can also

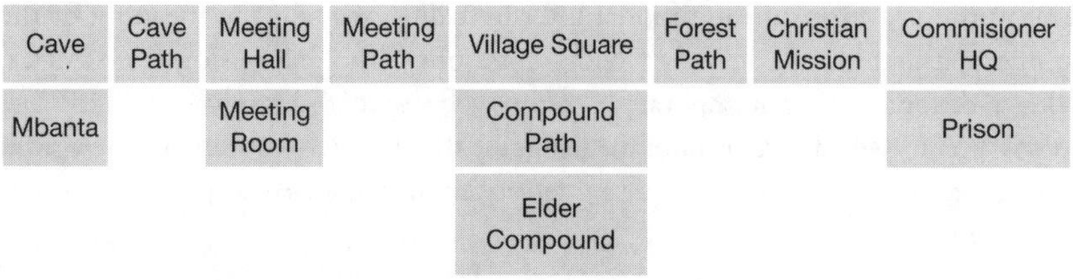

Cave	Cave Path	Meeting Hall	Meeting Path	Village Square	Forest Path	Christian Mission	Commisioner HQ
Mbanta		Meeting Room		Compound Path			Prison
				Elder Compound			

FIGURE 6.1 *The Village of Umuofia* Map

move British characters and African sympathizers to the Christian Mission and lock that door. As characters leave their homes and the groups of like-minded fellow citizens they are first surrounded by, they move through the village from one end of the continuum of conflicting cultures to the other, with the Village Square caught between the cultural conflict, and Elder Compound, in a small measure, a retreat from it.

Aural Dimension: Immersion and Interpretation

The music that plays in the virtual world also develops an interpretation of the source text. An attentive reading of *Things Fall Apart* will show a close integration of music, story telling, dance, and ritual celebration in the lives of the Igbo, and visitors to real West African villages soon recognize the social importance of music even in the present day. Entering many rooms and examining certain objects in *The Village of Umuofia* initiates the playing of a variety of traditional West African compositions by Yaya Diallo, a Malian drummer, author, and recording artist who specializes in the djembe, an hour-glass shaped hand drum common throughout West Africa. The presence of music, and of many images of African villagers playing music, adds to the verisimilitude and interest of the virtual world. In *The Village of Umuofia* music functions also as background to enhance the immersive effect. Background music in immersive virtual worlds has been shown to create statistically significant increases in remembering factual aspects of those environments (Richards et al., 243).

Properties of music that are congruent with accompanying media act to highlight certain features of that media over others and hence can greatly influence how those media are remembered (ibid., 242–243).

Although I have not systematically researched the impact of the music in *The Village of Umuofia*, I believe it has two specific effects in this context. Because the music is new to students it enhances the sense of the experience as exotic and different; the virtual world sounds "African." At the same time that the music is exotic, it is also attractive and even apparently joyful, thus enhancing the appeal of the African characters and village. The music selected for the virtual world is then also an interpretation of the novel, and its representation of African culture.

The music is a form of multimodal intertextuality, shaping the meaning of the source text and linking it with a wide range of cultural expression from Africa, both traditional and contemporary. On the web site that accompanies *The Village* (www.literaryworlds.org/umuofia), I suggest that teachers can use West African music as another starting point for student examination of African culture and its worldwide impacts.

Visual Dimension: The Virtual Gallery

Black and white photographs decorate the interface of each room in *The Village of Umuofia* and exist in different rooms as "objects" that can be opened and viewed. Given the unfamiliarity and the cultural, historical, and geographic remoteness of the setting of *Things Fall Apart*, this gallery of images constitutes a compelling and persuasive envisioning of the novel. The images were taken in the 1930s by the anthropologist Gwilliam Jones in south-eastern Nigeria where the novel *Things Fall Apart* is set and include many pictures of ritualistic artifacts and practices, village life, and even indigenous Africans dressed in apparent satire as British colonials and native messengers (see Figures 6.2 and 6.3). They are included in *The Village* (and in this publication) with the express permission of the G. I. Jones Photographic Archive of Southeastern Nigerian Art and Culture administered by the Museum of Archaeology and Anthropology at Cambridge University. Like the music, the photographic images add significant interest and an aura of authenticity to the virtual world.

Taken thirty years before the writing of the novel and perhaps twenty to twenty-five years after the events they describe, the photographs were certainly not composed for the purposes of illustrating the text, nor were they shot in the precise setting of the story, a setting which is, after all, a fictive composite created by Achebe and likely based on the Onitsha people, who lived near Ogidi where Achebe was born (Wren, 534). Yet, the inclusion of the photographs in *The Village of Umuofia* virtual world create another multimodal intertextuality with the novel that can be highly influential for interpretations of the work. The writing that the students do in their First Visit helps them to compare what they have imagined from reading *Things Fall Apart* with the photographs taken from the same region of Nigeria. Analyzing this visual imagery connects students' reading of the novel with students' prior knowledge of Africa. Here are two representative comments from students examining images in *The Village of Umuofia*:

> There appears to be some type of ceremony in progress. The villagers are dressed in what I assume to be ritual garb. Their faces are covered in elaborate masks. This scene reminds me of the chapter in *Things Fall Apart* where the entire village gathers to hear a trial presided over by the egwugwu. I find it so fascinating that although I'm aware that this book takes place in Africa I'm so westernized in my view of the world that I'm

FIGURE 6.2 Village Celebration

FIGURE 6.3 African Dressed as British Colonizer

FIGURE 6.4 Villagers in Ceremonial Garb

FIGURE 6.5 African Building

almost surprised to see people standing bare foot on dry earth wearing masks and feathers. The pictures are beautiful however and I just wish that I could see them in color to get the full effect.

(Student 1)

The most interesting image I came across was simple but very powerful and moving to me. The image involved a young man sitting on the step of a hut. The image interested me so much I think because it is so peaceful. The man is sitting there with his hands crossed in his lap, sitting in a straight up position, just gazing at the camera. The hut has quite the designs along the walls. All identical but very detailed. This image shows me the humanity of these people. All too often people can view images of a different culture and see these masks and other artifacts and view them as a lesser people. But here is a peaceful person, sitting in front of a hut. The same thing one might do on a summer night. Simply sit on the porch and reflect. Also the detail of the hut shows the creativity of the people. It once again shows their humanity. I really enjoyed this image and think it is one to keep.

(Student 2)

Both students view the people depicted in the images not so much as individuals but as representatives of a cultural other. In *The Conquest of America: The Question of the Other* Tzvetan Todorov analyzes the "typology of relations to the other":

We must distinguish among at least three axes, on which we can locate the problematics of alterity. First of all, there is a value judgment (an axiological level): the other is good or bad, I love or do not love him, or, as was more likely said at the time, he my equal or my inferior . . . Secondly, there is the action of *rapprochement* or distancing in relation to the other (a praxeological level): I embrace the other's values, I identify myself with him . . . I impose my own image upon him . . . Thirdly, I know or am ignorant of the other's identity (this would be the epistemic level).

(Todorov, 185)

Student 1 draws a connection between the image and a scene described in Achebe's novel, suggesting some knowledge of the other from prior reading (epistemic). The picture of a person depicted as barefoot or wearing masks and feathers serves to make the student aware of the large cultural difference between her and the Igbo people; it demonstrates to her her own ignorance of their lives (praxeological). This difference seems to be the site of aesthetic pleasure: "the pictures are beautiful," which is also a value statement (axiological). Student 2, on the other hand, finds commonality between himself and the subject of the photograph, and consciously refuses to judge the depicted person as "lesser" (praxeological). The description of the image as "peaceful" and the hut designs as "detailed" constituted a positive value judgment (axiological). Student 2 strongly identifies with the other, who is seen to be performing a similar action "sitting on the porch" (epistemic).

We can begin to see from this brief analysis of the response of only two students to two images the richness of interpretation the gallery dimension of the virtual world can foster. Class conversations after students have undertaken the First Visit have led to many observations, questions, and new understandings about the novel. Notice that in their analysis of these images, students are highly self-conscious about themselves, their perspective, and distance from the Africans portrayed. As Todorov suggests, students are engaged in axiological, praxeological, and epistemic analysis of alterity—an important way to think about the activity of interpretation of texts or images of cultural difference. We will now consider how the process of interpretation is influenced when *The Village of Umuofia* virtual world moves from gallery to a stage for live action role-play and devised work.

Verbal Interaction: The Writerly Text

During the role-play students, as characters, write in text boxes to form a dialogue stream that allows group communication. Prompted by "events" in the village announced by the teacher, students can move, communicate, and interact in an enormous variety of ways. The dialog stream of student verbal interaction in *The Village of Umuofia* constitutes a form of writing that extends and interprets the novel *Things Fall Apart*. While drawing on Achebe's characters, the dialog that develops might be either familiar or unrecognizable to readers of the source novel. In *S/Z* Roland Barthes distinguishes between the "readerly" text, "what can be read, but not written," what he considers "classic text," and the "writerly" text, "the goal of literary work (of literature as work) is to make the reader no longer a consumer, but a producer of the text." Barthes believes that:

> our literature is characterized by the pitiless divorce which the literary institution maintains between the producer of the text and its user, between its owner and its customer, between its author and its reader. [With the readerly text] this reader is plunged into a kind of idleness . . . instead of functioning himself, instead of gaining access to the magic of the signifier, to the pleasure of the writing, he is left with no more than the poor freedom either to accept or reject the text.
>
> *(Barthes, 4)*

The Village of Umuofia converts *Things Fall Apart* into a "writerly text" where students engage in a form of interactive, collaborative, and creative writing deeply informed by their reading and understanding of the source text.

Below is a portion of a transcript taken from one of forty-nine transcripts sent to me from *The Village of Umuofia* on February 13, 2007, a day when I worked with an African Religion class taught by Dr. Mustafa Mirzeler at Western Michigan University. This was the fifth time that I had personally directed the use of *The Village of Umuofia* and, working together with Dr. Mirzeler, we carefully wove the activity into his lesson plans, including having the students know their identity before the role-play, having them engage in the First Visit (samples above are from this class), and having them write and discuss the experience and complete a survey afterward. The transcripts are generated as recordings of the conversations that take place in each room the student visits during the role-play. Since there are thirteen rooms in the virtual village of Umuofia, at any one time there could be thirteen different conversations going on. Students who are in a room together at a given time will have the same transcript for that portion of their transcript. As they move through the virtual world continuing to talk with other virtual characters their transcript develops. Thus, no two students will have the same transcript unless they enter and exit each room at the same time. At the end of the role-play unique transcripts are sent to each student and their teacher. Printed below is approximately one-fifth of one student's transcript, a transcript that was created during the 22 minutes that she participated in the activity. This is obviously a tiny part of the mass of transcripts generated, and was selected randomly.

During normal play, students role-playing characters can come and go from the rooms. The teacher usually role-plays a unique character, the Village Crier, who has several special powers. This teacher-character can speak so as to be heard in every room at the same time, can "lock doors" so that students cannot move between rooms, and can magically transport groups of characters to different rooms, such as placing all the British and British-sympathizing characters in the same room, all the African traditional characters in the same room, all the characters in the same room, all the characters spread in small groups throughout the village, and so on. There are thirty-nine possible characters in the village, and during this role-play all were used; some characters were played by two students working together at the same computer. The activity lasted for 1 hour and 40 minutes, and during that time some students logged in and out (thus creating more transcripts than the total number of characters). Although the event took place during the regular time of the class meeting, students were at computers either at home or in dispersed locations.

This transcript is from the room called "Village Center," and while characters come and go, and there are at the most nineteen characters present at any one time. These characters include traditional Igbos, including the novel's main character, Okonkwo, members of his family including his father, three wives, a son and daughter, respected tribal leaders, Africans from other villages, and one of the British missionaries. The discussion begins when the teacher announces an event that actually happens in the novel. As you read the transcript watch for the relations between characters, how they interact based on their roles, and how the conversation develops. Consider what the students might be learning from the activity, how the activity and student writing compare with other language arts activities, and how this kind of writing involves both interpreting and extending the source text. (The transcript has been edited for spelling and punctuation.)

Village Crier [the teacher] announces "Attention villagers of Umuofia: It is Peace Week and Okonkwo, while angry at his youngest wife, has beaten her mercilessly. Please discuss this event."

Okagbue [medicine man] says, "Okonkwo has committed a grievous error."

Chielo [priestess of oracle] says, "How could Okonkwo do such a thing!"

Ekwefi [Okonkwo's second wife] says, "Okonkwo is sadly prone to anger."

Ukegbu [senior member of the clan's sacred society], says, "I am very mad and upset with his action."

Ozoemena [female survivor of a massacre of another village] says, "Okonkwo should be punished."

Okagbue says, "This kind of thing has not happened for many generations and must be punished."

Nwoye [Okonkwo's son] says, "Our yams will not grow now."

Mr. Kiaga [Christian convert from a different village] says, "There is no excuse for his behavior."

Obierika [Okonkwo's friend] says, "Okonkwo should not have struck his wife in the week of peace."

Unoka [father of Okonkwo] says, "Okonkwo is the best fighter in the village."

Chielo says, "Yes, he should be punished."

Ojiugo [Okonkwo's youngest wife] says, "He is just a physical man."

Ukegbu says, "It is to be a week of peace not violence."

Uchendu [Okonkwo's uncle] says, "He must make up for his actions. Then all will be right."

Chielo says, "He needs to make the proper sacrifices to make up for this incident."

Ozoemena says, "The Gods will be angry."

Ekwefi says, "I will comfort his wife."

Ojiugo says, "I am used to his beatings."

First Wife [Okonkwo's eldest wife] says, "But this is Peace Week; it is not acceptable."

Akueke [daughter of Obierika, Okonkwo's friend] says, "There is no way I would let my husband beat me, especially during Peace Week."

Obierika says, "If a man was to rob another man, the one robbed must wait until Peace Week has ended before taking action."

Unoka says, "His wife is probably in much pain. I will play music for her."

Nwoye says, "He must sacrifice to the gods so that our yams will still grow."

Mr. Smith [Christian missionary] says, "Beating one's wife is a sin any time of the year."

Ojiugo says, "But I was shocked that he would beat me during the week of peace."

Ibe [fiancé of Akueke] says, "I can't believe such a good man would do such harmful things to his wife."

Okagbue says, "No one must be above the law. To allow this shame to go unpunished would be to invite chaos into our presence."

Obiageli [daughter of Okonkwo] says, "The elders say they can only remember two or three times when the Peace Week has been disgraced."

Ekwefi says, "Ojiugo, I will take care of your duties today. You should rest."

Ibe says, "May peace be with us."

Okonkwo says, "I was hungry and she didn't cook. She needed a good beating!"

Mr. Kiaga says, "It is not our place to punish him; God himself will punish Okonkwo."

First Wife says, "We three wives must stick together."

Mr. Kiaga says, "Not our Gods, the White Man's God."

Uchendu says, "Okonkwo are you mad? It is Peace Week. No man should beat his wife during this time."

Ibe says, "You have two other wives Okonkwo, not one will cook for you?"

Obierika says, "A wife is less likely to cook after being beaten; even a fool knows that."

Okagbue says, "Perhaps, Okonkwo, but NOT during peace week."

Chielo says, "Okonkwo . . . you knew what week it was . . . there is no excuse!"

Kotma [African who works for the British commissioner] says, "Your god is too savage."

Akueke says, "Why would he do that to his wife? Dinner isn't cooked *once* and he lashed out . . ."

Unoka says, "Okonkwo will see his faults."

Okagbue says, "You show a lack of respect for our traditions by acting so foolishly."

Unoka says, "When his wife is not able to care for him."

Ojiugo says, "I try my best to care for him. A wife's work is much harder than most men think."

Mr. Kiaga says, "It is not right to beat another person, for any reason."

Mr. Smith says, "Okonkwo needs to repent from his sins and give up his pride. He is a very proud man."

Okagbue says, "Perhaps you are correct, Mr. Kiaga, but our ways are not your ways."

Kotma says, "Okonkwo you have to pay 200 cowries for your crime."

Mr. Kiaga says, "Your ways were once my ways."

Unoka says, "You have brought your family shame."

Okagbue says, "And you left us, Mr. Kiaga. You have become a servant of the white man and his ways."

Mr. Kiaga says, "No, I am simply showing you the way."

Ekwefi says, "Mr. Kiaga, what will happen to your ancestors? Who will care for them if not you?"

Okagbue says, "Your ideas are divisive, Mr. Kiaga. Go back to your white men and leave us be."

Mr. Smith says, "The bible says that polygamy is a sin. Maybe if Okonkwo had one wife he would not feel so stressed . . . He is breaking God's law!"

Ekwefi says, "Perhaps Peace Week would be less prone to violence if the men could wrestle away their anger."

Mr. Kiaga says, "Yes, Mr. Smith."

Ekwefi says, "It would provide a good time for everyone."

Unoka says, "The bible?"

Uchendu says, "Your God's law is not our law."

Ukegbu says, "We don't believe in the bible, Mr. Smith."

Nwoye says, "But that would violate the peace."

Mr. Kiaga says, "One wife is God's way."

Okagbue says, "And did you not also teach, Mr. Smith, that your Abraham had more than one wife?"

Unoka says, "That God does not respect our ways."

Ibe says, "Amen to that Mr. Smith."

Chielo says, "He is breaking no laws of ours with his many wives, Mr. Smith."

This transcript illustrates how the student communication in the virtual world can be fast paced and highly interactive. Students rarely write more than a sentence or two before entering it into the conversation, and sometimes it is difficult to know exactly to whom responses are directed. The pace is amplified by having so many characters present; at the same time in the village there may be rooms where there are only three or four characters and the conversations are typically slower and involve longer entries. Some who use this platform believe that five or six is the ideal number; in the previous chapter Cheryl Taliaferro recommends four. I have found during a typical role-play event I like to have different numbers of students in rooms: at the beginning smaller numbers to allow more slow-paced conversations, and then, when dramatic events are announced, bringing larger numbers of actors together in the same space generates energy and excitement.

The interactive dialog in this sample is deeply engaged with the novel *Things Fall Apart* and shows a high degree of character identification. As students "speak" as their character they explore character motivation, both as individuals and as participants in different groups in the village and different cultural groups: Igbo and British. In this sense the writing expresses substantial social knowledge from the text. For example, the apparently simple comment by the student playing Ekwefi (Okonkwo's second wife), "Okonkwo is sadly prone to anger." shows not only knowledge of Okonkwo's behavior, but the word "sadly" illustrates awareness of affection between Ekwefi and Okonkwo, knowledge that such behavior is wrong in the context of the novel, especially during Peace Week: the tone, factual not outraged, suggests that such behavior is common, if not entirely acceptable in the Igbo world of Achebe's novel. Another example of demonstrating content knowledge takes place when the student playing Ekwefi says, "Ojiugo, I will take care of your duties today. You should rest." In the novel Okonkwo's wives, despite jealousies, perform understated actions to help each other. Often student demonstration of careful reading of the text is subtle. When the student playing Uchendu (Okonkwo's uncle) says, "He must make up for his actions. Then all will be right," referring to Okonkwo beating his wife, there is a close fit with events later in the novel when Okonkwo must be punished for inadvertently killing a tribal member by a banishment that will balance the action—indeed, it is the character Uchendu who takes Okonkwo into his village in the novel. The student here playing Uchendu draws on knowledge of the character from events later in the novel and projects that knowledge backward to the earlier event of the wife beating to devise a statement for the thinking of the character.

The transcript also shows students performing not only personally different viewpoints, but cultural conflicts in complex, multiple, and interacting social worlds. The comment by Mr. Smith, the Christian missionary, that, "Beating one's wife is a sin any time of the year" demonstrates the student's awareness of the social and religious beliefs of the British and how they contrast with the Igbo (epistemic). When Mr. Smith says, "The bible says that polygamy is a sin. Maybe if Okonkwo had one wife he would not feel so stressed . . . He is breaking God's law!" the student goes a step further, not only making a cultural comparison and judgment (axiological), but devising an analysis of behavior based on a differing belief system (praxeological). One of the most interesting interactions is the discussion involving the virtual Mr. Kiaga, an African from the coast who speaks a different dialect of Igbo and who has been "educated" by the British to become a Christian minister. Here we have a complex cross-cultural situation. When Mr. Kiaga says, "Your ways were once my ways," the student performing this character demonstrates/performs assimilation as a value, which allows him to both relate to the other African characters and offer himself as a model for a change in their behavior and values. Unoka says, "You have brought your family shame," (appropriate remark given his role as a father figure in the novel) and when Ekwefi says, "Mr. Kiaga, what will happen to your ancestors? Who will care for them if not you?" they are both American students projecting themselves into the hypothetical position of an Igbo villager and responding to an Igbo from a different village who has been assimilated in western culture. Although the student role-playing Okagbue has most likely not read Frantz Fanon's analysis of the psychology of the colonized, when he says, "And you left us, Mr. Kiaga. You have become a servant of the white man and his ways," and, "Your ideas are divisive, Mr. Kiaga. Go back to your white men and leave us be," he is insisting on a Manichean understanding of the colonial context that Fanon described as necessary for the colonized to adopt to free themselves of European domination. In both cases the Manichean argument arises as a response to the valorization of assimilation to western culture and values.

The transcript illustrates not only knowledge of the text but also the interpreting and extending of the text. Again, there are many interesting examples in the cited passage. When the student playing Okonkwo's close friend Obierika says, "A wife is less likely to cook after being beaten; even a fool knows that," he makes a statement of information that is actually not known from the novel, but one which might be inferred based upon behaviors described in the novel, or projected, based upon knowledge of human nature that the student brings to the text and ensemble production of the virtual role-play. (I note that the sentence uttered here by the student performing Obierika does seem especially appropriate to Obierika's character in the novel; it is thoughtful and shows a flexibility of mind not merely controlled by accustomed behavior. It demonstrates a willingness to judge his friend Okonkwo, though not showing disloyalty to him.) When Okagbue says, "And did you not also teach, Mr. Smith, that your Abraham had more than one wife?" he adds an argument that was not in the novel but which makes perfect sense given the extensive conversations some of the Igbo characters have had with missionaries.

While this transcript does not demonstrate it, in the virtual world students sometimes transgress strict adherence to remaining "in character," writing in a way that self-consciously violates the time period and cultural situation. This writing is often humorous or playful, and the humor depends upon the juxtaposition of culturally inappropriate language or ideas. In some circumstances this can be seen by teachers to pose a challenge to the "intended" activity. After the activity one student wrote,

> People started goofing around and just chatting for the heck of it. Once that happened, there was almost no way to restore order, and, consequently, the assigned missions went unaccomplished. Personally I found the conversations fun and humorous; but I'm pretty sure that it was not supposed to be that way by means of joking and mockery.

This student's comments suggest that the virtual role-play activity generates both its own expected norms and counter-norms. While this "mockery" may very well have intellectual interest, as a developer of the world the tendency has been to create protocols that diminish this behavior. In the role-play the teacher cannot be in every room at the same time, yet the transcripts allow teachers to assess, evaluate, and hold students accountable for their participation after the event, and the role for the teacher as Village Crier enables them to enter conversational topics, move students, and lock doors. In this way teachers can reduce activity that they view as "off task."

Student Assessment of *The Village of Umuofia*

Students were overwhelmingly positive about their experience in *The Village of Umuofia* on February 13, 2007. Thirty-four students completed a survey about their experience, twenty-six female and eight male. (Approved HSIRB protocols required that the professor be out of the room while the survey was administered and students be informed he would not see survey results until after grades were submitted.)

	YES	NO
1. Was this your first time in a virtual world?	33	1
2. Did the activity help you better understand characters and motivation?★	29	4
3. Did the activity help you understand historical context and themes?★	26	7
4. Was it enjoyable?★	28	5
5. Was it intellectually stimulating?★	27	6

★ Not all students answered these questions.

Although the numbers are too small to make firm conclusions, males were more positive than females. (For questions 2–5 there was only one male that responded "no.") Typical written comments included:

> It made the character come alive and allowed me to imagine myself in that time and environment.

> The music and the images really helped to make me feel more a part of the village and my character.

> It was interactive, fun, and much better than a traditional lecture.

> It helped me to get a better understanding of the book.

> It made the material easier to relate to for me.

> It reminded me of class discussion, but this took those discussions to a whole new level.

> A lot was going on and so many people were talking at times it was hard to follow.

> The world was extremely stimulative, almost to a fault.

Continuous Development of Virtual-World Pedagogy

Repeated experimentation with virtual worlds is essential to developing effective strategies for enhancing their use as a tool to develop a richer interpretation of literary works. Early tests with *The Village* indicated the importance of students developing thinking from the point of view of their character before entering into the virtual experience. Thus we evolved, as mentioned, pedagogies to prepare students for virtual-world participation. During early experiments designing *The Village* I held what I later considered to be unrealistic expectations for what kind of actions could be taken during the role-play. I thought, for example, that characters might make collective decisions to take specific actions, such as groups of traditional Africans deciding to burn down the missionary church (as happens in the novel), or the British district commissioner deciding to take some of the African leaders prisoner (another event from the novel). While several of the Literary Worlds have been designed to allow for quite complex character actions and collaborations, I did not develop the skills as a builder of the world I needed to make this kind of collaborative activity possible in *The Village of Umuofia*. Rather than this lack of knowledge becoming a handicap, however, eventually it allowed me to recognize that *The Village* functions well as a conversational role-play space. Clarifying this expectation allowed me to help other teachers using the resource.

A literary virtual world becomes a richer experience when students write and discuss what they are learning soon after the activity. It is valuable for students to analyze at least a portion of the transcript of their experience. Questions they can consider include: How was our experience similar to and how different from the novel? Why did certain characters act the way they did during our experience in *The Village of Umuofia*? How has *The Village of Umuofia* virtual reality changed or enhanced my interpretation of the novel and the historical events on which it is based?

7

BUILDING A SECONDARY
BRAVE NEW WORLD

Robert Rozema

It is the winter of 2002—my last semester teaching high school. I am in the middle of teaching my senior literature class the science fiction satire *Brave New World* by Aldous Huxley. Originally published in 1932, the novel is a dystopian portrait of the future, in which a powerful global government controls every aspect of its citizens' lives, not through brutal oppression, but through biological, psychological, and socioeconomic conditioning. To maintain social stability, the global government—the World State—engineers its citizens in laboratories, alters their intelligence and abilities to fit a stratified class hierarchy, and keeps them in blissful ignorance by encouraging sexual promiscuity and by pushing a recreational drug called soma. Part satire of modern existence, part caveat about the future, *Brave New World* has been popular in secondary literature curricula since its publication—though it has often been challenged for its sexual content and drug references.

On this particular day, my seniors return to the computer lab to continue their construction of the *Brave New World* virtual world, the text-based virtual environment we designed to simulate the setting of the novel. Working together in small groups, students have logged into the world, navigated their way to specialized conference rooms, and are now discussing what sort of buildings they might add to the *Brave New World* landscape. A group of three students, who have chosen the in-world aliases Wilbur, Stalin, and Iven, begin planning a research center for Alphas, considering how to incorporate important ideas from the novel into their virtual building. Wilbur suggests designing caste-restricted rooms and a soma-vending machine for building residents; Iven thinks there should be laboratories, offices, and a main lobby. Each will eventually contribute textual details to their final creation, the Alpha Center for Research and Development of the Turbine Engine.

Today, Wilbur, Stalin, and Iven are acting out of character, but on earlier visits to the environment, they role-played as World State Citizens. For this purpose, the *Brave New World* environment was designed to replicate, as closely as possible, the setting of the novel. Wilbur, Stalin, and Iven, for example, are Alphas, the top caste in the futuristic World State. As such, they have privileged access to all of the rooms within the *Brave New World* virtual world, while other lower castes, particularly the Deltas and Epsilons, are refused entrance to particular locations. All castes, however, are subject to hypnopaedia—the subliminal indoctrination of the World State—as messages about consumerism and social position flash across the screen. Players may also take soma, though students were quick to discover that overindulgence results in temporary paralysis.

On other days, students drop out of character completely and use the virtual world to discuss the novel from a more detached perspective. My students used the *Brave New World* "world" to talk about the major ideas of the novel, including its critiques of consumerism, technology, and the culture of recreation. On such days, students log in, navigate to discussion rooms, and hold conversations on pre-assigned topics for 30–40 minutes. That the computer lab is all but silent on these days, except for the clicking of keys, is not an indicator of student apathy. On the contrary, the log reveals these conversations to be fairly profound, as students grapple with the implications of a challenging text.

Traditionalists may find the picture painted here unsettling: a roomful of students gazing intently into monitor screens, nearly silent as they immerse themselves in a secondary digital world. English language arts teachers may even find the student's fixed stares eerily reminiscent of the World State citizens that Huxley satirizes in the novel. Indeed, *Brave New World* is often invoked by a range of cultural critics who decry the increased presence of technology in classrooms and society at large. Neil Postman, for example, contends that modern society has largely realized Huxley's fear—that "people will come to love their oppression, to adore the technologies that undo their capacities to think" (Postman, 64). C. A. Bowers argues that educational software "reproduces the same cultural patterns experienced as normal in our modern, technological, and consumer-driven society," a sort of state-sanctioned brainwashing that might be likened to the hypnopaedia of the novel (Bowers, 127). Clifford Stoll complains of "edutainment" technology that "shout[s] the magical mantra: 'Here's the no-effort, fun way to learn!'" (Stoll, 147). Such a mantra does resonate with the recreation-driven ideology of Huxley's World State.

Critics like Postman, Bowers, and Stoll are part of a larger cultural countermovement that views computer-mediated education with no small degree of skepticism. Most of these critics share some common objections, namely that computers limit the imagination; equate learning with information gathering; promote superficial understanding; remove the teacher from the classroom; waste time; foster poor reading and writing behaviors; break down frequently; widen the digital divide between the technology haves and have-nots; and even cause physical injury. To this litany, we might add a newer complaint: that laptops, tablets, and smart phones are preventing learning, as distracted students text and Facebook their way through class after class. No doubt, many of these claims have validity, particularly in contexts where computers are misused or misunderstood.

In the scene I have described above, however, technology is being used to support and expand meaningful literature instruction. I believe that as my students worked to build part of an immersive literary environment, they were also enriching their understanding of *Brave New World*. In fact, creating a *secondary world* that goes beyond the details provided by the text is a critical part of the reading process. As we shall see, reader-response theory has long held that readers *must* create this world if they are to understand the text at all.

Foundational Theory: Experiential Reader-Response

I taught *Brave New World* for five years, to high school seniors in a required British Literature class. While many of my students enjoyed the novel, no small percentage griped that *Brave New World* was difficult to get into. Or, they just plain misunderstood its satirical thrust, leading to challenges about its controversial content. To me, these complaints illustrated that at least some of my students were reading the book at arm's length, not entering the literary world or reflecting critically on that world. I sensed that students were not *experiencing* the text as fully as they might. Year after year, low test scores and uninspired essays confirmed this intuition. My question was this: How can I get these students to experience *Brave New World*?

In asking this question, I invoked the language—*experience*—of reader-response theory. As Richard Beach observes, however, reader-response theory is large and contains multitudes of approaches: "Writers who have been called 'reader-response critics,'" he writes in *A Teacher's Introduction to Reader-Response Theories* (1993), "embrace an extremely wide range of attitudes toward and assumptions about, the roles of the reader, the text, and the social/cultural context shaping the transaction between the reader and text" (ibid., 2). Beach categorizes reader-response theories into five broad categories: textual, psychological, social, cultural, and experiential. My question moved me toward the experiential model of reader-response theory, which is broadly concerned with how students engage or experience literary texts. Experiential reader-response theory seeks to identify and describe the strategies readers employ—for example, how they identify with a character, visualize the setting, elaborate on the textual world, draw connections to their own lives, and detach themselves from the story in making a critique. I wanted to make these meaning-making strategies more explicit to my students, in hopes that doing so would create more engaged and effective readers.

One particular explanation of the reading act stuck with me as I thought about *Brave New World*—the three-part model of reader-response proposed by Jeff

Wilhelm in *You Gotta Be the Book* (1997). Wilhelm suggests that proficient readers engage literary texts on three different levels, or dimensions. The first of these Wilhelm labels the "evocative dimension." On this dimension, readers enter the story world, show interest in the plot, relate to characters, and visualize the story world. On the second level, the "connective dimension" in Wilhelm's terminology, readers engage in more analytical activities, including elaborating on the story world and connecting literature to life. Finally, the third level, the "reflective dimension," engaged readers to consider significance, recognize genre conventions, understand reading as a transaction, and evaluate both the author and themselves as readers.

Sophisticated readers operate on all three levels simultaneously, moving between evocative, connective, and reflective stances. "The dimensions point out that there are various purposes and ways of reading," Wilhelm writes. "When reading in different ways, readers operate on different levels—privileging the ones useful to them and responding less, if at all, on other dimensions" (ibid., 48). This three-part model, broadly representative of an experiential approach to reader-response theory, eventually became a conceptual framework for my inquiry, as I asked how my students might experience *Brave New World* more fully.

The first level of response in Wilhelm's experiential model is the evocative dimension. While each of the dimensions includes particular reading strategies, measuring and describing these strategies can be somewhat speculative, since doing so involves, as Michael Benton observes, "the unavoidable difficulty of monitoring and analyzing an invisible and instantaneous process in the absence of empirical evidence" (Benton, 29). This difficulty notwithstanding, Wilhelm derives his experiential model from over 1,000 of his own secondary students, relying on a range of data-gathering protocols, including student conferences, interviews, literary letters, and symbolic story representations. Based on their input, Wilhelm proposes that the evocative dimension of literary reading consists of entering the story world, showing interest in the plot, identifying with characters, and seeing the story world.

The process of entering the story world begins when the reader first encounters the text, drawn by its cover, its title, or perhaps the recommendation of a friend. In this opening move, the reader makes superficial inquiries about the text, forming images or making predictions based on their brief encounters. If this quick evaluation looks promising, the reader continues; if not, she moves on to another book, unless of course the text is required reading. Should she decide to carry on, she begins to develop her initial impressions of the text, entering further into the story world by "getting into the story's sense of play and action" (Wilhelm, 51–55).

Other theorists have similar understandings of this first, important step of engaged reading. Judith Langer labels this initial act "being out and stepping into an envisionment," in which the reader makes a brief incursion into the text world, searching for clues about its characters, plot, setting, and situation (Langer, 16).

Like Wilhelm, Langer suggests that the reader first tries to gain a sense of what the text will be about, by gathering surface details. The reader relies on this information—and her previous experiences with other texts—to begin building an envisionment, or a temporary understanding, that changes as the reader enters further into the text (ibid.). And as Michael Benton observes, the concept of entering a world is germane to the idea of fiction itself: "The notion of a *world* [his emphasis] in discussions of fictional experience," he writes, "is the single most common idea. It appears in a variety of guises, not least in recent developments in the broad church represented under the title 'reader-response criticism'" (Benton, 29). In keeping with this idea, Benton uses Tolkien's term, "secondary world" to describe the story world of the literary reader. For Benton, a secondary world is the product of two unique imaginations: that of the writer, who creates a virtual world between his inner self and the external world; and the reader, who creates a virtual world between his inner self and the external world (ibid., 26).

The next dimension of Wilhelm's experiential response model is the connective dimension. According to Wilhelm, readers on this dimension make two distinct moves: they make explicit connections between their own lives and those of characters, to "consider how the reading experience might inform choices and actions the reader might take in his or her own life," and they elaborate on the text to "extend the story world beyond what was explicitly described in the text" (Wilhelm, 65). Wilhelm further classifies the second of these moves—elaborating on the story world—to include making intertexual connections, and imagining extra-textual events, and filling the gaps left by the text.

This idea of filling gaps is central to Wolfgang Iser's model of reading. Like Louise Rosenblatt, Iser sees reading as a dynamic transaction between the reader and text. And like Rosenblatt, he posits that the reader and text co-create a virtual text that exists halfway between the two. In his 1978 work *The Act of Reading: A Theory of Aesthetic Response*, Iser proposes a phenomenology of reading, the chief assumption of which is that "the linguistic signs and structures of the text exhaust their function in triggering developing acts of comprehension" (Iser, 107–108). The text, for Iser, is the catalyst for the reader's production of meaning.

It is the structure of the text that allows it to function as a catalyst. More specifically, the text contains semantic gaps that the reader fills in during the reading process. Because an entire text can never be perceived at one time, the reader takes what Iser calls a "wandering viewpoint," or a temporal perspective that experiences the text as a manifestation of separate segments, rather than all at once. In essence, each textual segment contains reading instructions, information that helps the reader construct the secondary world. At the same time, however, the text leaves room for that which is not said: "The incompleteness of each manifestation," writes Iser, "necessitates syntheses, which in turn bring about the transfer of the text to the reader's consciousness" (ibid., 109). In a complex process, the reader synthesizes what is known with what remains unknown.

As Wilhelm notes, Iser's understanding of the reading process privileges the act of elaboration, in which the reader makes intra-textual connections to other works or authors, fills in missing information in the story, and imagines extra-textual events (Wilhelm, 67–69). Langer also emphasizes the importance of elaboration. In the second reader stance of her model, "being in and moving through an envisionment," the reader uses the knowledge he already possesses—personal knowledge, knowledge about the text, knowledge about context—to go beyond what is explicitly stated about the setting, plot, or characters (Langer, 17). We will return to this act of textual elaboration in a moment, since the idea of textual elaboration is key to building secondary worlds.

The final tier in Wilhelm's reading model is the reflective dimension. As Wilhelm notes, readers operating on this level separate themselves from the story and examine it from an objective perspective. This detached perspective may be applied to the text itself. Readers on this level become detectives, asking "How does the text work?" and posing answers through a careful examination of its details. Coming under close scrutiny during this stage are all the elements that constitute a text: its genre conventions, characters, plot, themes, symbols, and other literary features. At the same time, readers on this level focus on their own reading experience, working to revise their interpretations while recognizing themselves as key players in the literary transaction. Finally, readers also critically evaluate the author, as they seek to identify his or her purpose in writing the text (Wilhelm, 74–84).

In Judith Langer's model, taking a detached perspective involves "stepping out and objectifying the experience." For Langer, this fourth and final reading stance occurs when the reader "distances [himself] from the envisionment [he has] developed and reflects back on it." Much like Wilhelm, Langer suggests that the reader objectifies the text, her interpretations, and her reading experience. "In this stance," she writes, "we become critics, aware of tensions between the author's and our own sense of the world, aware of insinuations of conflict and power, and aware of critical and intellectual traditions and the place of this work within them." In this stance, readers see the text at a distance, from a more objective perspective (Langer, 18–19).

Building as Understanding: Extra-Textual Elaboration within the Virtual World

If reader-response theory establishes the importance of extra-textual elaboration—the ability to generalize an entire secondary world from the specific textual details—then a virtual-world environment allows this world building to occur in a literal way. In the case of *Brave New World*, I encouraged my students to elaborate on the setting of the novel by contributing their own buildings to the *Brave New World* simulation.

I began by modeling the process, reproducing key locations from the novel inside of the virtual space. To do so, I sampled passages from the novel. There was no shortage of description to choose from: Huxley spends the first three chapters of *Brave New World* detailing the strange world of his satiric imagination, even delaying the introduction of main characters until his setting is well established. The richness of the setting made it easy to reproduce inside the virtual world with just a few commands. To begin, I built a key location from the novel: the London Center of Hatchery and Conditioning. From this hub, I created and connected over twenty rooms, in many cases using Huxley's own words. Developing these rooms and programming their special features was time-consuming, but became easier as I went along (for more technical help on building, see Chapter 13). I also created a gateway room, somewhat like the old wardrobe in the *Narnia* series. When players first logged into the *Brave New World* virtual world, they found themselves in the Coffee Shop:

—Coffee Shop—

You are in a coffee shop. There are several comfy chairs here, a few tattered couches, and a scattering of tables. On one of the tables, a few books rest. Among them is a copy of *Brave New World* by Aldous Huxley. You may enter this book by typing "in." Otherwise, you may stay here to talk. Conversation topics to consider: Are you enjoying the virtual world experience? What is rewarding or frustrating about it? Is it enriching the experience of reading *Brave New World*? Why or why not? You see a coffee bar here.

In creating the Coffee Shop, a sort of drawing room to the secondary literary world, I hoped to emphasize the idea of entering, making the process described by Langer as "being out and stepping into an envisionment" explicit and concrete. Like Wilhelm, who uses drama and art to help remedial readers understand their positions in relation to the story world, I used the Coffee Shop to help my students recognize that literary reading can involve an active and deliberate entrance into a secondary world. A player enters *Brave New World* by typing "in." When she does so, she enters the Main Lobby of the London Center of Hatchery and Conditioning, the opening location of the novel itself:

—Main Lobby—

Welcome to the Brave New World MOO. You are in the main lobby of the London Center for Hatchery and Conditioning. The room is large and industrial looking, with polished green marble floors and stark white walls. Sitting at a large metallic desk in the center of the room is a Beta-minus receptionist. There is also a large bulletin board on the east wall. Exits include an elevator to the west and a hallway to the east. To the south, you see an indoor bumble-puppy court. You see a receptionist and a bulletin board here.

—Hallway—

The hallway is long and narrow, but exceedingly well lit. It leads east to a door labeled Fertilizing Room: Authorized Technicians Only and west to the Main Lobby.

—The Lift—

This elevator is operated by an Epsilon semi-moron, clad in Epsilon black and looking rather sullen. "What floor?" he croaks as you enter. You have access to the Basement (b), the Main Lobby (m), the Psychological Conditioning Center (5), the offices suites (28), and the roof (35).

—Neo-Pavlovian Conditioning Room—

A large, bright room, lit by sunshine from a huge window on the southern wall. Half a dozen nurses, dressed in sterile white uniforms, are setting bowls of roses and brightly colored books on the floor. You see khaki-clad babies and a lever here.

I tried to create room descriptions that were evocative enough to help students see the story world but spare enough to allow students to fill in the gaps with their own details. My goal was to have students move through the *Brave New World* virtual world, construct mental images based on the text and their own imaginations, and become immersed in the story world. Then, to help my students identify with the characters of the novel, I required them to create and role-play as characters who might have existed in the futuristic World State. As shown in Assignment One: Creating Your Character, this involved choosing an appropriate name for the character and writing a fitting *Brave New World* description.

Huxley, of course, names his characters after prominent political thinkers and industrial capitalists alike, satirizing his contemporaries Marx, Hoover, Ford, and Lenin by naming his vacuous characters after them. I wanted my students to capture the same spirit in naming their own characters, so I encouraged them to research politicians, psychologists, industrialists, and scientists from Huxley's own time— individuals whom Huxley might also choose to satirize in the novel. After finding appropriate names, students described their characters by detailing their physical description, caste, occupation, and hobbies.

By creating their own characters, students identified with characters in the novel and found a perspective from which to view the *Brave New World* MOO

Assignment 1: Creating Your Character

You have been given a virtual character with a rather generic description (e.g. Gamma4) and a password that is difficult to remember. Your first assignment is to rename your character, change your password, and describe your character—in other words, to add a little personality to your character. To do so, complete the following tasks.

1. First, you need to rename your character. After connecting, you'll need to type the following command to change your name: @rename Gamma4 to Vladimir.

   Your character is now named Vladimir. Pretty simple.

2. More importantly, your character must have a name that fits within the setting of the novel. So, renaming your character "MikeTyson" might be amusing, but not really in keeping with the spirit of the novel. For possible names, peruse the book, but avoid naming yourself after a major character like Bernard or Helmholtz.

3. Now for the fun part. Currently, your character has no description. Type "look me" and you will see what I mean. You need to add a description of your character. But remember, your character is a part of *Brave New World*, and should fit within the context of the novel.

   You may also note that you have been assigned a caste (such as Beta). Your description should be defined by your caste. If you are a Delta, do not write that you are 6'5", when the novel suggests that Deltas are quite short. Get it? To add a description of yourself, type the following command: @describe me as <your description>.

   While you're at it, you might want to set your gender. Do so by typing: @gender <gender> where gender is male or female.

4. When all of this is done, you should: (a) roam the world, role-playing as your character, interacting with others, and figuring out how this whole thing works; (b) evaluate your virtual world experiences with others in the Coffee Shop.

---

and the novel itself. The literary virtual world, in other words, made another implicit reading process more tangible and deliberate, as students created fixed reference points for reading and experiencing the novel. Moreover, their character descriptions below are informed by textual details, as students created their personas by reading the novel for important information. The results were virtual characters created by my students who could have occupied the pages of the novel alongside Bernard Marx and Lenina Crowne:

- Iven Skinner (an Alpha): Iven is a tall, handsome man who is head of the World State Island Management Program. He towers over you with his powerful presence and chiseled stature. As you gaze into his mysterious eyes, you see the incredible depth of his knowledge and wisdom.
- Wilbur (an Alpha): An Alpha-plus who looks like he knows everything about everything. (He does, actually). Wilbur currently works as an aircraft engineer and test pilot for his privately owned aircraft manufacturing corporation. He is fairly tall for an Alpha and obviously very, very strong. Wow!
- Tito Hoover (a Delta): A short man, but strong in stature. Born cousin of Benito Hoover, and proud owner of his DDC card (Distinct Deltas Club). Tito prides himself in his khaki color clothes and his vast collection of soma bottles from all over the World State. Tito works hard at being the best Delta helicopter pusher and it shows. He's received seven awards for Best Helicopter Pusher in his union, the Delta Devils.
- Bambino (a Delta): A boy whose job in this Brave New World is to box thousands of packages of soma. The soma is then shipped to various parts of the World State and distributed to those who need it. He makes sure his job is done well and enjoys it completely. He is very pleased with his role in this Brave New World.

Within the virtual world, students role-played as these characters. I designed the space to allow students to experience what it was like to live in this world, albeit in a limited way. Huxley foresaw a society rigidly divided into five castes, ranging from the elite, super-intelligent Alphas to the mentally impaired Epsilons. The World State, the global government of the future, predetermines who belongs in each caste through biological and psychological conditioning. I assigned each of my students a particular caste, which raised few objections until they discovered that certain rooms were restricted to certain castes. In addition, participants were fed messages that appeared on the screen periodically, a sort of textual indoctrination meant to simulate the sleep-teaching (hypnopaedia in Huxley's language) practiced by the World State. Hypnopaedic phrases such as "Ending is better than mending," "Everyone belongs to everyone else," and "A gram is better than a damn," were soon being parroted by all of my students, demonstrating the power of suggestion, and prompting a few to think critically about television advertisements.

Since the socialization of its citizens was of crucial importance to the survival of the World State, the *Brave New World* virtual world also emphasized togetherness. Just as Bernard Marx, the protagonist of the novel, is ostracized because he enjoys solitude, participants who spent more than 2 minutes alone in a room were first reprimanded and then whisked off to join their nearest companion. Virtual characters could also take virtual soma, the wonder drug of the World State, whenever they felt distressed or unhappy. Taking soma gave players a "pleasantly narcotic holiday from reality," but paralyzed them when they overindulged. The point of this, of course, was not to make light of or encourage drug abuse, but to give students further insight into the recreational culture that Huxley critiques.

Outside of the virtual world, I used these characters as reference points in class discussions. As we progressed through the novel, I encouraged students to imagine where their character was at that point. At the end of the fourth chapter, for example, the protagonist Bernard Marx suspects that he and another character, Helmholtz Watson, are being overheard as they discuss a potentially subversive subject—the meaninglessness of hypnopaedia—in Helmholtz' office. I asked students to insert their character into the story at this point, asking the Alphas, for instance, to speculate on what they might do if they knew Bernard and Helmholtz were acting in an unorthodox way. In so doing, I hoped that the students would enter and live in the story world of the novel itself, ultimately seeing themselves as part of the tale.

To encourage my students to shape the very landscape of the story, I asked them to complete a second assignment within the world. As shown below, this second assignment asked students to work collaboratively to construct their own buildings in the *Brave New World* virtual world. A more sophisticated task than creating a character, this assignment required students to master the virtual world commands necessary to build and connect their buildings, to write imaginatively, and to think critically about the way Huxley uses setting as the central vehicle of his satire. While students were allowed to recreate buildings that were mentioned but not described at length in the text, nearly all chose to design original buildings that *could* exist in the World State. Working in small groups, students created the London Hospital for the Dying, the Nightclub, the Alpha Center for the Research and Development of the Turbine Engine, and lastly, a country club called Club Aqua. Once these buildings were constructed, students visited and interacted in them. A player visiting Club Aqua, for example, would encounter the following rooms:

~ Main Lobby ~

You are in a spacious, atmospherically lit room with several pneumatic chairs and couches grouped about in it. The air has a pleasant aroma that is coming from the sweet-smelling plants in the corners. There is a bulletin board on the wall and a bookshelf in the corner. There are exits to the north to an elevator, south to a chapel, east to a Social Gathering Room, and west to the changing rooms. You see a bulletin board here.

~ *Chapel to Our Ford* ~

You are in a fairly small, dimly lit, hexagon-shaped room. There is a circular table in the center with twelve chairs around it. At the head of the table is a small podium, with glowing buttons on it, and a metal T on the front. It is a console for playing synthetic music. In one corner of the room is a small, metallic refrigerator filled with bowls of soma-laced strawberry ice cream. In the center of the table is a large book of Fordism hymns. There is an exit to the lobby to the north.

~ *Social Gathering Room* ~

You are in a room where *Brave New World* citizens socialize. There is a soft glow of red light and a faint perfume of soma gas wafts around you. The purple carpet is plush and deep purple, your feet are soothed as you walk about. There are pneumatic couches scattered about and a dance floor serviced by a synthetic music plant. Around the north and east sides a balcony runs around the room. At the south end is a well-stocked bar. You may exit north to the balcony and west to the lobby.

What is immediately apparent about the student-created rooms described above (distinguished from the rooms I designed by the tilde [~] symbol) is that they illustrate some of the novel's key ideas: class distinction, consumerism, biological and psychological conditioning, and state-sponsored religion. In the Social Gathering Room, for example, students took the idea of promiscuous socialization—a major virtue in the World State—and rendered an environment where such socialization would be encouraged. There is a sensuality in the description of the room: its plush carpeting, soft glowing lights, comfortable couches, and whiff of soma all hint that the room hosts the casual sexual encounters that Huxley satires.

The details in the Social Gathering Room were supplied both by the text—my students said the assignment required "scanning the text for ideas and details"—but also by the imagination of my students. In the Social Gathering Room, for example, students programmed hypnopaedic phrases to reflect its recreational purpose. A player who lingers here is told that "You feel a pleasantly narcotic holiday due to the soma gas," and that "The red light beckons you to the dance floor." He also hears lines from a popular song emanating from the synthetic music plant: "Hug me till you drug me honey," "Bottle of mine, it's you I've always wanted!" "Bottle of mine, why was I ever decanted?" The name of the room is also a student invention, though its bureaucratic-sounding title is pitch-perfect in its imitation of Huxley.

Other student inventions were equally creative: one group developed a minor location in the novel—the Hospital for the Dying—into a more three-dimensional

Assignment 2: Building the Brave New World

By now, you should be familiar with the *Brave New World* virtual world. You should have created a character, described that character, and wandered through the rooms in the London Center for Hatchery and Conditioning.

Your next step is to demonstrate that you understand the world that Huxley creates in *Brave New World*. That is, you need to show me how Huxley uses the setting of the novel to communicate his ideas about modern society. To complete this task, your group must do the following:

1. Discuss and design a building for the *Brave New World* virtual world.
   * The building must have at least four rooms.
   * Each room must have at least one object with its own description, but no more than three. For example, the microscope in the Fertilizing Room is an object.
   * The building must be consistent with Huxley's vision of the future. In other words, you must stay within the world Huxley creates. This is one critical way to show you understand what the novel is all about.
   * You may take your idea for a building from the novel itself (you might want to design a "feely palace," for example), but you may not directly lift descriptions from the novel. Of course, you are free to improvise your own idea, as long as your building could feasibly exist in *Brave New World*.
   * Your building must illustrate some of the novel's key ideas: class distinction, consumerism, genetic and psychological conditioning, state-sponsored art and religion, etc.
   * You may construct individual rooms for your own characters within your larger building (e.g. an office for an Alpha-plus doctor).

2. Write a description of your building using Microsoft Word.
   * The description of each room must be at least 100 words long, but no more than 250.
   * For every object you include, please include a description. See me about how to build special objects like notes and containers.
   * Each room must have at least one exit, and one room in the building must exit to the roof. All rooms should be interconnected.
   * You should include a physical map of your building. A hand-drawn map will be fine, but if you can use Word, more power to you.

3. When you have finished the above steps, each group member should write an individual paper (2 pages, double-spaced, typed) that answers the following questions:
   * How does your building reflect the setting of the novel?
   * What aspect of society does your building criticize?

space by adding a lobby and a garage for hearses. Another group reasoned that the World State relied on Alphas to develop its technology, and invented a research center for the turbine engine. These elaborations illustrate that students did more than enter the novel; they re-imagined and extended the story. In Wilhelm's words, they went "beyond what was stated or even suggested by the book," until "the story world [became] what could be called a 'reader's world'" (Wilhelm, 66).

At the same time, the building assignment asked students to make personal connections by reflecting and writing about their virtual world creations. After finishing their virtual buildings, students were required to write short essays in which they explained how the buildings reflected the setting of the novel, and what aspect of modern society their buildings critiqued. Looking critically at the world around them, students applied lessons from *Brave New World* to their own lives. In describing the swimming pool locker room in Club Aqua, for example, one student wrote:

> The products that are available to use in the locker rooms are a total downplay on our world today. We have so many beauty and health care products out on the market, that it is disgusting. Even though we don't have testosterone hand lotion or wrinkle-ridding towels, we do have products that claim to take days, years off our aging. Looking beautiful and young is a part of who we are as a culture today. If you look, models just keep getting younger and younger each day, plastic surgery is considered the norm when you reach your mid-life crisis, and we have so many drugs that claim the impossible it's amazing we aren't a World State.

Designing a locker room (as part of Club Aqua) compelled the student to reflect critically on the beauty myth of contemporary American culture, a phenomenon that as a student in an affluent and brand-conscious high school, he had no doubt experienced first-hand. Making a similar personal connection, another student describes the rationale behind the Chapel to Our Ford:

> The religion of the World State, Fordism, and the practices of it were Huxley's criticism of organized religion and the commercialization of it. I personally don't have a problem with organized religion, being a Christian and a regular-attending church member. I do feel as though the over-commercialization of the Christian faith, and the turning of a church service into a multimedia, rock-and-roll extravaganza is a bit unsettling and I don't think it's a good thing necessarily.

Another student saw his group's building—the Alpha Center for Research and Development of the Turbine Engine—as an implicit critique of the modern reliance on technology. While his comments are slightly less personal, they nevertheless indicate that he has applied the lessons of the novel:

The idea that we need an enormous building with thousands of employees to research engines is absurd. Yet that very thing is currently present, only on a smaller scale. General Motors, for example . . . What would Americans do without their personal vehicles, not to mention buses and airplanes? The idea of increasing consumerism through transportation is no foreign idea to the modern world either. Every successful American is expected to have his own personal vehicle, or is considered too poor to afford one . . . It is so engrained in our minds that we must have our own car that one could almost call it conditioning.

As evidenced by their essays, these students considered *Brave New World* in a very personal and critical way, seeing the world around them through the lens that Huxley provides. By building the virtual secondary world—first constructing characters, then collaborating to create rooms—my students used their own imaginations to fill in gaps left in the story world, thinking critically about the novel in the process.

Despite the frustration some students experienced as they worked to create within the MOO, the platform was designed to allow users to add their own contributions to the world. This is fairly rare in massively multi-user environments, and all but non-existent in multiplayer games. Today, the only notable environments to give users building ability are graphical, three-dimensional platforms such as *Second Life*. In such environments, users typically design their own avatars, or representations of themselves, and create objects such as clothing, vehicles, and buildings with a set of in-world tools. These tools can be challenging to master, and graphic platforms such as *Second Life* usually charge for the privilege of owning virtual land. So while creating *Brave New World* within *Second Life* is feasible, building within Literary Worlds is free and, more importantly, is language-based. Several literary simulations within Literary Worlds allow participants to co-construct the world, including *Lord of the Flies* (see Chapter 2), Pied Piper (Chapter 8), *Moll's World*, a recreation of Daniel Defoe's England (Chapter 10), *and Island Barrio*, a world based on *An Island Like You* by Judith Ortiz Cofer. Indeed, this last feature—the ability to create with language—may be enough to recommend a text-based environment such as Literary Worlds for literature study: in such spaces, students must write to render worlds.

8

RIFFING ON THE PIED PIPER

Combining Research and Creativity

Linda Dick[1]

Few college students know details of the Pied Piper story. Most remember vaguely that it is a story about someone who led rats away from a town, but then wasn't paid and ended up leading children away. Scholars believe the story has a basis in truth, but the question becomes, what is that truth? About one hundred years after the supposed disappearance, the event was recorded on the walls of a church in Hamelin, Germany:

> In the year of 1284, on Johns and Pauls day
> Was the 26th of June
> By a piper, dressed in all kinds of colours,
> 130 children born in Hamelin were seduced
> And lost at the calvarie near the koppen

A stained glass window commemorating the event was installed in the same church in the fourteenth century. The mysterious disappearance of the children has long created fascination. A number of ideas have been suggested. A young man, Nicholas, came through the area of Hamelin at about the time of the children's disappearance and may have taken them on a children's crusade. Perhaps families migrated because of civil wars to the south and east of Hamelin—there are family names synonymous with Hamelin families on street signs in other areas such as Hesse, Saxony, Transylvania, Moravia, Pomerania, Uckermark, Prignitz, and lands even further east. Finally, the church wall inscription suggests that the children were taken to "calvarie." Perhaps the children died, so the story could be an allegory about the Crucifixion. The Black Death plague was not an issue during this time period in Germany, but there could have been any sort of small epidemic.

These mysterious and diverse interpretations suited this story to the open-ended, exploratory and experimental virtual world my students created. My teaching approach drew on theories of reading and pedagogy that foster active student involvement in literary interpretation. In reader-response theory the meaning of a text is created in the transaction between the words on the page and the individual reader who brings his/her own historical context and repertoire to the reading. Folk and oral traditions, as well as children's literature, are especially ripe for unique and interesting engagements with readers. In deconstruction, texts in themselves are considered to have multiple, irreconcilable, and contradictory meanings that make single interpretation impossible—certainly true for the Pied Piper story. Both reader-response and deconstructionist theories led the students to engagement with the story itself on a more concrete level—"textual intervention"—a strategy advocated by Rob Pope in which students intervene in, reorganize, and rewrite literary works in order to further understand their meaning and their own position as readers. (Pope).

In the Pied Piper project, I encouraged textual intervention on a large scale. Class after class of students were encouraged to invent the lives of the Hamelin townspeople and create and recreate everything about the location as well as the story line. Fostering research skills and critical thinking, and locating stories, people, and objects in historical context were important objectives in all of my classes. In this case, the end product of our work was the creation of a medieval town full of people and activity—a virtual version of Hamelin, Germany.

In jazz, a "riff" is the repeated improvisation of a specific melody or progression. The term has come to include the verbal exploration of a particular subject, even the act of improvisation itself. My students in the Pied Piper world engaged in a "textual riff," a term that points both to a pedagogical approach for literary and cultural study and a style of participatory virtual-world building that could be brought to a great variety of texts and settings.

First, we visited the literary world together in a computer classroom. Students signed in as guests and browsed the rooms, avenues, and spaces I had created to get us started. We explored the three possible scenarios presented by scholarship on the reality and truth of the Pied Piper story. We discussed the idea of historical context and how it shapes our interpretation of the past.

Next, I asked students to try to figure out what it was like to live in the Middle Ages around 1284. I asked them to work within a decade of the date in the church inscription. They were to validate and cross-check sources and produce at least five pages of information and ideas about geography, people, customs, economics, politics, trade routes, food, or another aspect of medieval life that interested them. The assignment was wide open. I felt as though I was pushing my students over a cliff, and I stepped right off the cliff with them. The results were so interesting that I was to repeat the assignment a number of times over the next two years.

Throughout the research, students discovered cultural values/artifacts that could help explain the townspeople, the type of government they operated under, the economy, and various combinations of factors that shaped Hamelin as a unified group of people. Students learned that climate may have played a role in the story. A "Little Ice Age" was in effect from 1150 to 1460. The fluctuation in climate caused lost crops and widespread famine across Europe for generations. Students also found that the middle European states had a flourishing textile industry: co-ops were formed and alliances made. Thus, the political and economic arenas were open for students' investigation. John (all student names are pseudonyms) found that "during this time period ladies wore metal hair nets, veils and draped throat covers called wimples. Men wore hoods that had long tails called liripipes." He also found that "most . . . homes were cold, damp and very dark." Details like these helped the class to understand the medieval era.

I asked students to find biographies of people who lived during the late 1200s in order to shed light on cultural values as well as politics and economics. Students also investigated art contemporary to the time frame. David explains, "Another thing the Gothic artists did for the culture of Europe during its height was to solidify Christianity as the major religion. Along with this surge of art came the building of huge, decadent Gothic cathedrals marked by pointed archways, instead of rounded ones." Cathy writes, "The thirteenth century was a huge turning point for the Pope as well as the Catholic religion itself . . . Religion became incorporated in the governments of European countries, which eventually resulted in the Crusades throughout Europe and Asia." Cathy also found that "the economy in the thirteenth century was much different from that of today . . . England . . . exported raw materials such as metals and even coal to other countries due to the expanding population."

Next, I had students move from historical research to something more creative. I wanted them to use their creativity to apply what they had learned in their research to help us build and develop the universe of the Pied Piper. They asked me, "What does that mean?" So I told them:

> Use your critical thinking. Draw on what you are learning about the time period—all aspects of life are important to address. Be the baker, write me a story about the baker. What's the best price for rye today, June 26, 1284? Tell me what the weather was like last Sunday in Hamelin Town on April 16, 1284. What are the politicians arguing about?

My goal was to have the students build up the virtual world so that it was richly and diversely imagined, a place they could step into and experience, in some measure, Hamelin during the year of 1284.

Taking the researched materials and interpreting the results of that research, students began writing. They wrote stories. They wrote biographies. They wrote grocery lists and gave recipes. They recorded meeting minutes. They wrote letters. They wrote diaries. They wrote conversations between people in the town. From their research and creative pieces they built a new historical context, certainly much of it conjecture, but plausible conjecture tied to their research on the period. As the undergraduates wove a tapestry of what was, and what could have been, they brought together knowledge of the past with modern-day language and ideas. Yet, the creative work could not have come without an understanding derived from their scholarly research.

After the initial push to find information to develop familiarity with the lifestyle of the townspeople of Hamelin, the students and I focused on building the Pied Piper's virtual world from scratch. The task was to flesh out the characters, the place, and the time frame. Each creative piece produced by a student had to be supported by research. The learning objectives for any class that covered this part of the assignment addressed learning research techniques and critical thinking skills. In order for Janice to produce recipes for German bread dumplings and red wine cake, she had to first research what food was like in the 1200 time frame. The same goes for Allison when she looked up the history of the children's crusade led by Nicholas. All aspects of the story were up for investigation and expansion.

In order for students to gain an understanding of the historical context of the original story, I asked them to give meaning to the story in their own words, interpreting and re-creating their research. Some of their creative efforts included family interactions that reflect contemporary social trends more than medieval realities. Sometimes violating conventions of the time and bringing modern views back into the past helped students see the constraints people were under within the cultural setting of the story. Their textual intervention riffed on the traditional storylines from the Grimm Brothers and Robert Browning.

For instance, in a creative piece, a mother and father argued over whether to let young Johann go off to the children's crusade led by Nicholas when, in the culture of the Middle Ages, mothers might not have had much say over the children because children were under the father's sphere of influence. Another creative example was when the students had the Councilmen argue about whether or not to pay the Piper. In another creative exploration, a student had young girls pen love notes in their diaries. During the Middle Ages, young girls were not generally taught to write, nor did they have the funds to purchase and keep writing material, so this type of creativity shuttles between current culture and the past. For every question that can be asked about the story, the location, the events and the people, students found ways of creating a written dialogue between their own understanding and between the fictional characters of the story. The imaginative *what if* factor was in full force. If girls had been taught to write, what would they write about? If writing paper had been available, who would have access to it? What if children had gone on a children's crusade and ended up instead being sold as slaves in northern Africa by an unscrupulous sea captain? What if the Pope were to offer up a prayer for the missing children? Did the Pope even know that children were on their way to visit him?

I found asking questions crucial to student engagement in this history-based virtual environment. Allowing students the freedom to step way outside the box and bring a discussion of feminism to a Middle Ages cottage in Hamelin Town may seem far-fetched, but there were advantages. How better to understand a modern concept by setting it down within an ancient setting? And feminism is just one possibility. What were medieval trade practices? How was money used? What political influences guide a town and influence how it operates? Were people of the time period "ethnocentric?" How do these factors affect the way contemporary readers understand an ancient story?

When students were asked to research the past, questions about life in the present inevitably came forward. As they married past and present through fiction, they created new understandings and another textual riff. Writing for the virtual world energized student work, and giving students open-ended assignments created a freedom and motivation all too rare in school. Because they were invited to participate in building the virtual world, my students developed a vested interest in the story and its historical context.

In the third stage of the experiment students had to justify their creative pieces in a reflective essay that explored how they came to understand the historical context as revealed through research. That reflection allowed me to assess their thinking and evaluate how well the virtual platform served to facilitate their learning. Over the course of the three weeks of the project, we shared research results and creative works at least once a week in an open forum. At the end of the project, we went back into the computer lab and revisited the Pied Piper's world. This time the students went in as characters and did some role-playing with their classmates in the world that they had newly enlarged. While these computer sessions were not scripted for anything in particular, except to share the wide variety of critical thinking results with all the students, I felt that the variety itself was a great benefit. The message that thirty students are going to produce thirty different results while working on the same project came across loud and clear. The diversity of projects helped illustrate the fact that cultural artifacts are not stagnant objects made in a vacuum of time or space.

The first students to try this project were working with a barren landscape: they had a paper map of the virtual world reducing the problem of getting lost or bumping into a dead-end alley. The second and subsequent groups of students had an easier experience as they built on what the first group did. Each successive generation of students who worked on the Pied Piper world added a new layer of materials while interacting with the ones already in place. This project remains ongoing and I invite interested teachers and students to participate.

In the Pied Piper's story students found a surprisingly rich literary tapestry already in place, but at the same time they also discovered wide-open spaces just waiting for interpretation and expansion. These spaces allowed for students' individuality as they extended the social and geographic landscapes where the story unfolded. Regardless of time and place, people are influenced by social morality, economics, and politics. Helping my students understand the interconnectedness through cultural artifacts, such as works of art, was a main objective. Understanding social and historical interconnections in the modern world was a secondary objective. For example, students discovered that the social and economic position for the baker's wife, a character developed by several students, spans across time from the past to now. The question of women's rights, then, surfaces not in isolation, but within a contextual reading of the literature and the culture. Learning how the social, political, and historical contexts of a story work together to provide meaning in the past fostered holistic thinking about the present as well.

The students who participated in the project expanded their creative writing skills as well as their research skills. Some students wanted to take a short cut and write a straightforward essay, as they were uncomfortable when venturing into the creative writing world for an academic project. They thought they could not write fiction. They were often uncomfortable writing fictionalized accounts of what went on in Hamelin Town. To do so was making them work outside of their comfort zone. I asked these students to be one of the children and write a letter home. Or these students could be a mother or a father, and they could write out a conversation that those two parents might have over the kitchen table. Or students could find a portrait of the great uncle of the Pied Piper to hang in the Great Hall. Or they could find a map that shows the route from Hamelin Town to the Pope in Rome. All of these investigative efforts stretched the students' abilities to seek out and interpret materials not normally associated with an academic paper written for a college course.

For different courses our Pied Piper experiments had differing foci. For the course focused on writing research papers, the main thrust was research and analysis; for the art history course, the focus was more on the factors influencing art-making in the Renaissance. All my students from multiple disciplines were contributing to the same project, and this resulted in a rich tapestry of intertwined historical contexts and creative textual riffs.

Regardless of the course they were taking, I asked students to view the project in a holistic way—to incorporate ideas into their creative endeavors. All students developed research and critical thinking skills, learned how to utilize a wide variety of sources, marry non-fiction materials to fictionalized accounts, and extend analysis in self-reflective writing. Learning how to cite unusual sources and create accurate bibliographies was another skill set practiced with the assignment.

Looking closely at some sample student writing can further illustrate the activity. Here is a snippet from a piece titled "Garth's Dream" by Val:

> "Garth! Get out of your bed. Get in here and eat your bread before these rats carry it away!"
>
> I mumble something back to my mother, but my focus at this moment is directed to catching the very large roach that was scurrying to hide in the straw. John, Lizzie, Mary, Gunner and little baby Sarah had already left the bed to eat their morning bread. This is one of my favorite times of day when they all leave me alone and I can lie back and pretend I am a rich noble lord or knight on a great crusade.

I get out of bed and my bare feet hit a cold, hard-packed dirt floor in a two-room basement flat in the village – though I dream of my feet softly treading on fancy rugs in front of a blazing hearth. My breakfast then would consist of the fine white breads my father bakes for the titled instead of the dark, barley-laden stuff we have to gnaw through. My imaginary breakfast even consists of eating an orange! Not just on the Yule morning, but EVERY morning.

The story doesn't stop there, but continues with references to attending school at a monastery, and Val shares a few games that boys might play such as "prisoner's base" or "hood man's blind." The food choices such as rye bread and pottage are typical for the time period Val is describing. This textual riff comes from this simple expansion of one boy's life in a German village in the 1200s. None of the above materials is indicated in the story itself. Instead, Val has taken the basic story and developed one character in the virtual world, the baker's son. Val's contemporary voice is evident in her diction. In this sense she is clearly interpreting her research, not only conveying information but also adding layers to the boy's life, such as living under the bakery, gaining lessons at the monastery, fabricating dreams, and defining goals the boy might have had. Most importantly, Val adds her original ideas to shape the boy's life. Val's character does not want to take over his father's bakery as would be expected of the oldest son in the family. Val decided that this boy wanted to leave Hamelin and make his own mark on the world. This, then, is a contemporary viewpoint shared within the story and brings the story forward to the present. As an added dimension, Val inserted a picture of the sculpture of the Pied Piper located in Hamelin from a visit she had to Germany. Who would have thought that a tourist's photograph would end up in an academic paper? This is one example of how students expanded their ideas beyond the basic assignment's requirements. They learned that it is appropriate to use unusual, non-academic sources in an academic paper as long as their presence is relevant. Once the floodgates were opened, students felt free to contribute a fascinating range of materials to the literary world of the Pied Piper.

Alex gives the story an entirely new imaginative dimension by portraying for the reader a meeting among the rats. Using the rats' point of view, he reviews the situation Hamelin Town finds itself in—besieged by rats. Here's an interesting passage that speaks to acceptance, diversity, and alienation from events not fully understood:

One day the rats all gathered at the high point of the town for a meeting. The discussion was called to inform all of the rats that they needed to become fellow citizens of the town and no longer seen as a danger or just flat out filthy and disturbing creatures.

Rats took turns discussing how the townspeople spend their time and ways that rats could possibly fit into these daily activities that took place.

The meeting lasted the whole night because the rats were debating what they would do to finally be recognized and brought into the town that had rejected them for so long.

When the meeting was adjourned, the rats decided to join the human community at the next bonfire and explain who they were in the grand scheme of things. Their voices would be heard, they would be accepted, and they would be taken seriously.

[The next day,] the rats inched closer and closer to the fire, the orange color burning and radiating on top of their backs. One rat took charge and approached the crowd. He let out a soft squeak, a lump in his throat. He tried again, but this time he got more of his throat into the squeak, and a loud hissing sound erupted from him. A man in the crowd turned around and saw the large crowd of rats that stood behind him, their orange and yellow eyes burning against the fire. Their lips curled over their teeth, trying to smile but coming off as more of a scowl. The man tapped a woman next to him, and she immediately turned around to gaze upon the group. Her mouth shook violently as she took step after step away from the rats. The rats sensed something terrible about to happen. The woman finally let out a large shriek that made even the fire cringe. Instantly, the rest of the townspeople turned around and took on the same gaze that the other two had plastered on their faces.

The rats squeaked more and more loudly, and the townspeople screamed. Men ran towards the group, swatting the rats with their arms and kicking their feet at the rats. The rats hurried back up the hill with some of the men chasing right behind them until they reached the plateau where the rats normally hung out.

"Normally hung out" is a phrase directly from today's vernacular, and this quotation demonstrates Alex's textual riff by clearly incorporating yesteryear and today in language use and expression.

Michelle takes "The Pied Piper of Hamelin" and marries it to "Hansel and Gretel" in her piece "The Seduction of Music" by simply placing Hansel and Gretel inside the Pied Piper story. In Michelle's version, Gretel hears the piper's music and loves it, but Hansel can't hear the music at all. Gretel wants to follow the music, yet Hansel only hears the birds singing their morning song. Here is the last sentence of Michelle's creative piece: "With that the Piper winked, and the children were gone." Clearly, Michelle has generated another textual riff by adding a bit of magic to the disappearance of at least these two children. She does not use any of the original "Hansel and Gretel" plot; Michelle simply borrows them as characters. Furthermore, in the original story there is no mention that some children hear the music while some do not. So Michelle has added a layer to the Pied Piper literary world.

Sometimes students experimented with the gender of characters in their creative pieces. Doug turned the tailor (always a male character during this time frame) into a woman. He named her "Inderb," a name plucked from the Middle Ages as a common girl's name. He gave her the status of being a widow and made her have a strong personality that motivated her to defy other people. Doug substantiated his choices by researching Hamelin in the 1200s and found that it was a Saxon settlement and also part of the Hanseatic League, a mercantile league set up to protect and promote trade among the Saxons, London, and Prussia.

An art student provided a surprising twist. Instead of writing or researching or making up stories, Krystal did five pen and ink character sketches. She was not afraid to draw one of the characters with an arm amputated below the elbow. In this graphic rendition, she reminds the reader that living in the Middle Ages was dangerous and difficult.

One of my favorite pieces in the virtual world is entitled "The Confessions of a Mayor," in which Sam describes the anguish that the mayor suffers after the children are gone. A true textual riff occurs here because in the Grimm Brothers' version the mayor never expresses sorrow over the mistake.

What exactly did the students gain from the Pied Piper project, and how can other instructors repeat this success story? At the end of the project, I wanted students to reflect on the process of creating their literary world. Passages from several student reflection papers illustrate their reaction to working on the project:

> The true story of the Pied Piper is interesting in that there are an infinite number of possibilities of what happened to the children. Through this assignment, I was able to explore different ways that researchers and histor- ians have viewed this story. There is much more documentation of the real and the fictional Pied Piper than I had ever anticipated. I think this is a great project to incorporate into classrooms and to explore an old story in a new way. I think this project will be especially useful in middle school or high school because students can incorporate prior knowledge with the newly acquired knowledge.

> Children need something that is high tech but still teaches the basics . . . 5th and 6th graders will benefit from this web site. It will allow teachers to try more innovative ways to get children interacting. Not only will students be able to interact with each other but also with children around the world. This will teach children diversity without having to be "preached" at.

> At first, I felt some resistance to this project. I couldn't figure out what I might be interested in, and I'd never given a lot of thought to the Pied Piper story. But it was surprisingly interesting. I enjoyed visiting some of the Pied Piper web sites and learning more about the background of the story. And once I hit on the pipe/flute as a point of research, I was further

interested. My favorite part of the project was discovering the information about Pan. Things kind of clicked into place in my mind. I'm sure that anyone with a good background in Greek and Roman mythology would find my "discovery" simplistic, but since I did not have that background knowledge and I didn't see anything similar to the Christian motif of the devil being a pipe-playing shepherd on any of the Pied Piper web sites, I felt that I was making my own little discovery. I enjoyed it.

I think that the Pied Piper Literary World is a great idea for children and teachers in the classroom. It not only tells a story as they are playing this game, but they are also learning history while they are doing it. For example, with my story, they would learn what a monk was because normally children would not know what one was. They also can learn what cities or towns, people, and places looked like in other time periods because all they know is now.

It is not difficult to shape any historic event as a "textual riff" project, with or without a virtual space. For example, even 3rd grade students could benefit by riffing on the characters in *Dear Mr. Henshaw* and engaging in behind-the-scenes activities relevant to this story. The story itself reveals the results of the character's thoughts and actions in the letters to his teacher. But the riff could expand upon those activities in terms of what the children do in a math or science class on any given day. Students in the 5th grade could riff on *The Giver*, a novel about a utopian society gone wrong. The ambiguous ending of the story is ripe for interpretation by students of that age. There are many aspects of this story that lend itself to research, creativity, and interventions—studies of government styles, of cultures, of education settings, of geography. The writing and research could center on any number of learning objectives from multiple disciplinary areas. The advantage of undertaking this project in the virtual world is that any group of students can now come into the Pied Piper Literary World, look around, and add their own creative materials.

The students did achieve the more finite purpose of this exercise: to explore the historical context of a cultural artifact through research, analysis, and creative writing. Students re-created the Pied Piper's world in a variety of creative fiction and creative non-fiction pieces which I then added to the Pied Piper Literary World experience. There is no reason, however, why the students could not have entered the world as builders and entered their own works inside the platform. Because I didn't want to take the time to teach the students how to be builders, I decided not to invite them to participate in that part of the work and I posted their writing and illustrations myself. In retrospect it would have been, however, a rich and rewarding experience for them to feel more like artists of the Pied Piper virtual world had I let them step behind the scenes and build their little nooks and crannies inside the world itself.

My project is unusual among the others outlined in this book owing to extensive student involvement in the ongoing creation of the virtual world. I wanted my students to be actively engaged in the literary world of the Pied Piper, and undertake concrete research where they would see immediate results. My students were builders of the project from an outside perspective in that they did not enter materials directly into the Pied Piper Literary World; I did that for them. But they did have the freedom to explore any aspect of the medieval world and apply what they learned to their individual contributions. While taking in the past, students combined ideas in the documents they created in response to the assignment. They weren't afraid to bridge the generations of time that had passed or mix time frames with abandon as they created their kitchen table conversations, letters and diaries.

Before I started this project, I didn't know what a literary virtual world was, or whether it would work for my students and achieve the learning objectives set for my diverse courses. I did not immediately envision how I was going to create a learning environment that explored historical context not only for paintings, sculpture, and architecture but for literature as well. Yet gaining perspective on historical context allowed surprising things to happen: change, innovation, new directions, and originality.

With the ever-changing landscape of the World Wide Web, students will continue to be challenged to conduct plausible and concrete research for academic work as they move through their academic careers. Indeed, it becomes increasingly difficult for teachers to control the student's research efforts as the web continues to increase in scope and depth. Just as in the Pied Piper story, we may have to wonder, where are those young people going and what will they find when they arrive?

Note

1. This chapter reports on five semesters over a two-year period and more than 350 undergraduate students in ten different classes I taught at Western Michigan University and Kalamazoo Community College in five academic departments. The courses included Children's Literature, Art History, Mythology, Western World Literature, First-Year Seminar, Composition Studies, Creative Writing, Art in the Community, College Readiness, and Modern Culture and the Arts.

9
VIRTUAL *FLANERIE*

Strolling through *Mrs. Dalloway's London*

Todd Kuchta

I first read Virginia Woolf's 1925 novel *Mrs. Dalloway* a few months after my first visit to London. This coincidence would be crucial to my understanding and appreciation of Woolf's complex and breathtaking text, one I've since taught many times to both undergraduate and graduate students. Set on a single June day in the early 1920s, *Mrs. Dalloway* follows a small group of characters as they walk the streets of London's West End. Famous locales such as Big Ben, the Houses of Parliament, Bond Street, and Regent's Park feature prominently, and much of my fascination with the novel stemmed from my ability to visualize and mentally "map" the movements of Woolf's characters as the plot unfolds. This ability can be crucial, given the difficulty of Woolf's style. Along with James Joyce, T. S. Eliot, Ezra Pound, Gertrude Stein, and William Faulkner, Woolf is considered one of the foremost modernists, that diverse group of early twentieth-century writers who sought to revolutionize literature and, in Pound's words, "make it new." In *Mrs. Dalloway*, Woolf developed an experimental, stream-of-consciousness technique she called "tunnelling," in which her narrator not only burrows in and out of the minds of different characters, but also shifts quickly between their past memories and current perceptions."[1] "So fluid are the boundaries between past and present" in *Mrs. Dalloway*, one critic points out, that the challenge for readers is to know whether they are "encountering an image from the character's past or something part of the character's immediate experience" (Wolfreys, 173).

Not surprisingly, Woolf's style presents a challenge for first-time readers, particularly those unfamiliar with London's geography and history. Yet familiarity with London can also provide the solid ground that first-time readers need to offset the flux and fluidity of Woolf's experimental style. While one critic suggests that knowledge of London can accentuate our enjoyment of *Mrs. Dalloway*, giving it "an added savour" and making "its spatial relations ... clearer" (Johnstone, quoted in Beker, 376), others argue that such knowledge is absolutely crucial when reading the novel. Jeremy Hawthorn claims that "part of the central experience of *Mrs. Dalloway* is that at any given point in the novel the reader is nearly always able to pinpoint the exact location of what is happening with complete accuracy" (Hawthorn, 66). David Daiches and John Flower concur, adding that the geographical movement of the characters "is both precisely indicated and important to the novel's structure and meaning . . . If one does not follow the topography of the novel one loses a great deal" (Daiches and Flower, 82–83, 89). In addition to helping readers understand the novel's organization, a knowledge of London is central to Woolf's characterization. Susan M. Squier claims that the characters "are defined by the streets through which they pass. The buildings, people, and events of their common urban surroundings establish their characters and social circumstances for themselves, for each other, and for the reader" (Squier, 95). Daiches and Flower identify a mutually constructive relationship between London and Woolf's characters: "Woolf's sense of London helps her to define the characters and her sense of the characters helps her to define London" (Daiches and Flower, 89).

A number of maps are available to help readers chart the topography of *Mrs. Dalloway*, and scholars have commented extensively on the symbolic and ideological significance of the characters' movements throughout London.[2] While many of these maps and commentaries are valuable for readers already familiar with either *Mrs. Dalloway* or London, they prove less useful for those struggling to read the novel without this knowledge. I designed the virtual world *Mrs. Dalloway's London* to immerse first-time readers in Woolf's London in a way that cannot be easily replicated by studying maps or textual commentaries. This virtual world is based on the premise that an understanding of London's geography— its streets, buildings, parks, and monuments—can contribute immensely to reducing student confusion and increasing student appreciation of Woolf's novel. *Mrs. Dalloway's London* uses photographs and maps of London from the early twentieth century to help students visualize and learn about the areas central to the novel, and to follow the journeys of two main characters both in the text and on a map. Rather than simply providing background information, however, *Mrs. Dalloway's London* also encourages students to use this information to engage with the novel, asking them to think about why Woolf might use the particular places she does, what we learn about different characters based on the places they visit, and how the setting of various scenes relates to the thoughts of the characters while there. *Mrs. Dalloway's London* thus has two complementary purposes. While the virtual world seeks to make Woolf's complex novel more accessible— both for first-time readers and for those unfamiliar with London—it is also meant to raise questions about the novel from the perspective of its setting. Ideally, *Mrs. Dalloway's London* should help students not only to see Woolf's setting more clearly but also to ask new questions about this complex and engaging literary work. In the case of *Mrs. Dalloway's London*, the virtual world that emerges from the literary work draws deeply from the source text and its unique construction of space. At the same time, this virtual world recreates the novel's depictions of space in order to understand the source text in a new way.

Woolf's London in Context: History and Theory

Before examining *Mrs. Dalloway's London* in more detail, I'd like to expand on the historical and theoretical significance of Woolf's depiction of London. First let's consider how some of her most famous predecessors portrayed the city. Woolf was a child in 1887 when Arthur Conan Doyle wrote his first Sherlock Holmes tale, which opens with a haunting image of London as a "great cesspool" drawing in all the flotsam and jetsam of Britain's global empire (Doyle, 15). Likewise, at the turn of the twentieth century, Joseph Conrad called London a "monstrous town" (*Heart of Darkness*, 7) and compared its foggy streets to "a slimy aquarium from which the water had been run off" (*Secret Agent*, 122). For E. M. Forster, London's constant movement made the city like a platter of dirty gelatin, "a tract of quivering grey, intelligent without purpose, and excitable without love" (*Howard's End*, 79–80). For H. G. Wells, London was an unruly disease, "something disproportionately large, something morbidly expanded," "the unorganised, abundant substance of some tumorous growth-process" (*Tono-Bungay*, 108–109). By the 1920s, T. S. Eliot invoked Dante to describe London not only as the center of a vast waste land, but as a modern purgatory peopled by the living dead: "Unreal City, / Under the brown fog of a winter dawn, / A crowd flowed over London Bridge, so many, / I had not thought death had undone so many" (Eliot, 62).

Compare these depictions of a diseased and damned urban landscape to the London of *Mrs. Dalloway*. Woolf's novel begins with the title character stepping through her front door as if taking an exhilarating "plunge" that recalls her youthful visits to the beach. "How fresh, how calm . . . the air was in the early morning; like the flap of a wave; the kiss of a wave" (3). As Clarissa Dalloway proceeds on her way to purchase flowers for a party she'll host that evening, she takes pleasure in London's vibrant rhythms everywhere she turns:

> In people's eyes, in the swing, tramp, and trudge; in the bellow and uproar; the carriages, motor cars, omnibuses, vans, sandwich men shuffling and swinging; brass bands; barrel organs; in the triumph and the jingle and the strange high singing of some aeroplane overhead was what she loved; life; London; this moment of June.
>
> *(ibid., 3–4)*

With its accumulation of sensory details straining the limits of conventional sentence structure, this passage reflects the exhilaration and freedom Woolf felt upon moving back to London after ten years in suburban Richmond, which she had grown to despise. Upon returning to the city, she wrote in her diary that "London is enchanting. I step out upon a tawny coloured magic carpet, it seems, & get carried away into beauty without raising a finger . . . One of these days I will write about London, & how it takes up the private life & carries it on, without any effort" (*Diary* 2, 301). *Mrs. Dalloway* is the culmination of that desire. It not only reflects her personal view of London as a source of energy that is life-giving and life-sustaining. It also challenges the dystopian, if not apocalyptic, view of London as depicted by Woolf's famous male predecessors.

Indeed, Woolf's novel is a distinctly feminist response to the male-dominated character of cities in general in the early twentieth century. An ideology of "separate spheres" became the norm in modern industrial societies during the nineteenth century, as women were relegated to the home and family (the private sphere), while men engaged in work, professional life, and politics (the public sphere). As the site of so many public experiences and encounters, the city was a predominantly masculine domain. One of the central literary characters epitomizing modern urban life was the male stroller known as the *flâneur*. A figure whose central traits were his mobility and his roving eye, the *flâneur* perpetually meandered the metropolis in the hopes of stumbling upon remnants of individuality and beauty in an increasingly industrial and bureaucratic society. The *flâneur* luxuriated in the voyeuristic pleasures of the modern city—aimless wandering, chance encounters, window shopping, people watching. The *flâneur* eventually exploded into a variety of literary and real-life characters—detective, journalist, photographer, spy—but the experience of *flanerie* continued to dominate modern literary epics such as Eliot's *The Waste Land* and Joyce's *Ulysses*. Woolf was very much aware of this phenomenon. By organizing *Mrs. Dalloway* around a woman's simple journey to buy flowers for a party, Woolf attempts not only to highlight the female experience of modern urban life but to appreciate the city from a female perspective. She also engages in an effort to reclaim the city for women—in life and in literature. The sociologist Janet Wolff argues that because of the dominance of the separate spheres, there was no such thing as a *flâneuse*, a female counterpart to the *flâneur* (Wolff, 210). Yet Clarissa Dalloway is arguably one of the first examples of a *flâneuse* in literature.

Thus we should not conclude too hastily that Woolf's love of London is superficial or naïve, nor that Clarissa Dalloway's engagement with London serves merely as a distraction from her domestic boredom. Indeed, in a diary entry recorded once she had begun *Mrs. Dalloway*, Woolf wrote: "I want to criticise the social system, & to show it at work, at its most intense" (*Diary* 2, 248). London serves as the primary lens for this criticism, and Woolf depicts the city as if it gives shape to all the male-dominated social forces—patriarchy, class conflict, commodity culture, militarism, and imperialism—that she wanted to question. London thus provides Woolf with a model of both negative and positive social interactions. Peter Kalliney claims that "by commingling the most exhilarating and most depressing aspects of metropolitan life, the novel consists of equal parts celebration and critique" (Kalliney, 77). Woolf's London thus functions as a spatial analogy for interpersonal relations and communal dynamics at their best and worst. Moreover, London in *Mrs. Dalloway* does not simply serve as a "setting" in the conventional sense—an inert backdrop for the actions of the characters. Rather, London is a character in its own right—and perhaps the novel's central character. As one critic suggests, some of Woolf's descriptions "seem to emanate from the city itself . . . It is as if Woolf gives voice to the city" (Thacker, 158).

Recent developments in literary theory and criticism can help us appreciate Woolf's view of London as a living, breathing entity that affects the beliefs and interactions of its inhabitants. Three thinkers in particular have been instrumental in the recent "spatial turn" in the humanities, encouraging scholars to examine how particular places and spaces shape—and are in turn shaped by—our lived experiences. These thinkers have also been influential to me in developing the virtual world of *Mrs. Dalloway's London*. The first is French philosopher Henri Lefebvre. His book *The Production of Space* considers how the construction of social spaces serves to produce and reproduce different kinds of social relationships. One of his central claims is that space is not an empty container that we fill with the contents of our lives (a view that has dominated western consciousness since Descartes). Nor is space for Lefebvre a predetermined structure set in stone and impervious to our presence. Social space, according to Lefebvre, is made "neither by a collection of things . . . nor by a void packed like a parcel with various contents." Likewise, social space cannot be reduced to "a 'form' imposed . . . upon things" (Lefebvre, 27). Rather, for Lefebvre, space is a *process* and as such is constantly in motion. This is because space is always produced, always constructed in certain ways for certain ends, and in turn because space is always productive, always shaping social relations in particular ways.[3] Lefebvre's insight is very much in keeping with Woolf's desire to use the experience of *flanerie* in London "to criticise the social system, & to show it at work, at its most intense."

Another influential "spatial" thinker is the Russian literary theorist Mikhail Bakhtin. Although best known for his concept of dialogism, which refers to the way that novels put competing social voices in dialogue with one another, Bakhtin also analyzed literary works using what he called the chronotope. Combining the Greek words for time (chronos) and place (topos), the chronotope refers to the way works of literature make palpable the interactions between temporal and spatial elements that are abstract or otherwise invisible to the naked eye. "In the literary artistic chronotope," Bakhtin claims, "time . . . *thickens*, takes on flesh, becomes artistically visible; likewise, space becomes charged and responsive to the movements of time, plot, and history" (Bakhtin, 84). From this perspective, the places represented in any literary work—Bakhtin examines the public square, the road, the castle, and the provincial town—are not merely static settings. They become active players in shaping how characters relate to one another and the kind of social vision that the literary work provides. Given Virginia Woolf's intense concern with the relationship between the spaces of London and her characters's past memories and present experiences (her novel was originally to be called *The Hours*), Bakhtin's interest in the literary melding of time and space in literature also proves useful in appreciating *Mrs. Dalloway*.

A more recent literary scholar whose work blends the insights of Lefebvre and Bakhtin is Franco Moretti. The central concept behind Moretti's fascinating *Atlas of the European Novel 1800–1900* implicitly echoes Lefebvre and Bakhtin. Moretti writes that

> geography is not an inert container, is not a box where cultural history "happens," but an active force that pervades the literary field and shapes its depth. Making the connection between geography and literature explicit, then—mapping it: because a map is precisely that, a connection made visible—will allow us to see some significant relationships that have so far escaped us.
>
> *(Moretti, 1998, 3)*

As Moretti suggests, the purpose of his own atlas is "bringing to light relations that would otherwise remain hidden," thereby helping us to "see a book, or a genre, in a fresh and interesting way" (ibid., 3, 4). What is it that such an atlas can help us see differently? Echoing Bakhtin's notion of the chronotope, Moretti claims that the first is "the place-bound nature of literary forms: each of them with its peculiar geometry, its boundaries, its spatial taboos and favorite routes." Second is "the internal logic of narrative," the way in which a story and its language organize themselves into larger spatial patterns of meaning (ibid., 5). Lefebvre, Bakhtin, and Moretti emphasize the importance of understanding the construction of space and its link to storytelling, and in doing so they point toward the intellectual value of pedagogical experiments in the construction of literary virtual worlds and interactive maps like *Mrs. Dalloway's London*.

Using *Mrs. Dalloway's London*

The historical and theoretical context I've outlined above has informed my own production of space in designing *Mrs. Dalloway's London*. This virtual world does not replicate the geography of Woolf's entire novel, nor does it follow the movements of each character who moves about London. It focuses instead on the two central figures, Clarissa Dalloway and Peter Walsh, whose journeys together occupy a substantial portion of roughly the first quarter of the novel. These journeys are more or less symmetrical and complementary, allowing readers to see the parallel movements of male and female characters taking differ-ent routes northward through London (see Figure 9.1). Both characters begin from the Dalloway home at Dean's Yard, near Big Ben and the Houses of Parliament (Clarissa's husband is a member of Parliament). Both journeys can be

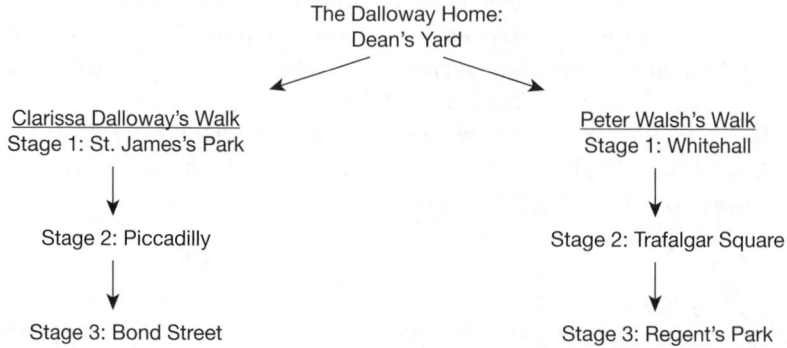

The Dalloway Home:
Dean's Yard

Clarissa Dalloway's Walk
Stage 1: St. James's Park

Stage 2: Piccadilly

Stage 3: Bond Street

Peter Walsh's Walk
Stage 1: Whitehall

Stage 2: Trafalgar Square

Stage 3: Regent's Park

FIGURE 9.1 Overview of *Mrs. Dalloway's London*

divided relatively equally into three main stages, each representing a major area or thoroughfare in London's West End. From her home, Clarissa Dalloway first walks through St. James's Park, then along bustling Piccadilly, arriving finally in Bond Street, where she enters a flower shop (we do not follow her as she returns home, an issue over which John Sutherland speculates). Peter Walsh, a longtime rival for Clarissa's affections who has been stationed in India for a number of years, arrives at her home later that morning, and we follow him as he departs after their rather awkward reunion. Although Peter moves in a direction similar to Clarissa's morning trip, his route takes him through a very different terrain. Peter first marches up the governmental district of Whitehall, then through the crowds of Trafalgar Square, arriving finally in Regent's Park, where he stops to rest.

At each of the seven primary locations, visitors to *Mrs. Dalloway's London* are given an opportunity to engage in a number of different learning activities, including:

- Reading the corresponding text of *Mrs. Dalloway.*
- Reading brief descriptions of each area, with information relevant to the historical and symbolic significance of the related passages in the novel;[4] viewing photographs of the area, many taken by the renowned German-born British photographer E. O. Hoppé during the 1920s and 1930s.[5]
- Viewing an early twentieth-century color map of the area from the 1900 edition of J. G. Bartholomew's long-running *Pocket Atlas and Guide to London.*

For example, when visitors to *Mrs. Dalloway's London* arrive at Piccadilly, the second stage of Clarissa Dalloway's journey, they find an image of the street's pedestrian traffic from the early 1920s, a brief description of the area, and the corresponding text from the novel (see Figure 9.2).

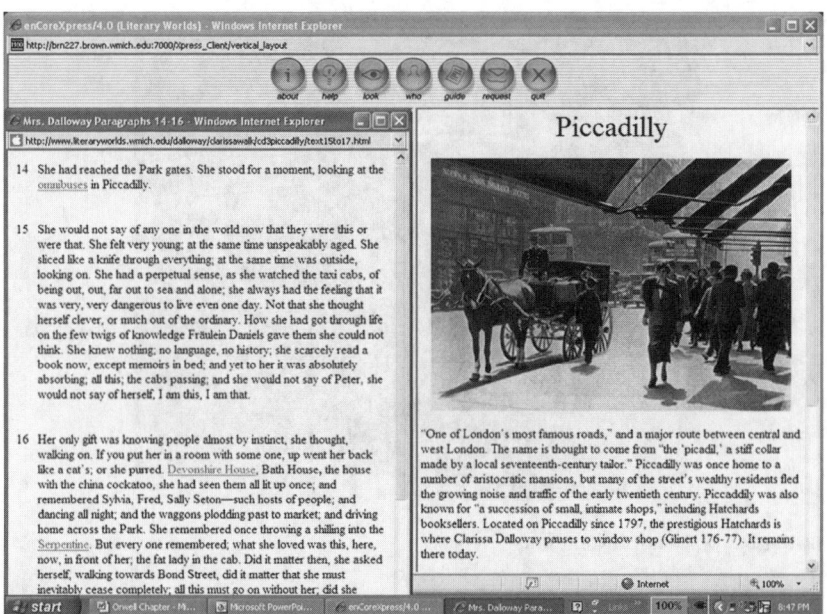

FIGURE 9.2 Description of Piccadilly and Corresponding Text of *Mrs. Dalloway*

As this passage and photograph suggest, my descriptions provide glosses for some of the locations identified or alluded to in the novel, while also offering details relevant to theme and character development. More advanced readers might discern elements of Clarissa's identity that are related to both the photographs and area descriptions. Reflecting the ways in which "Woolf's sense of London helps her to define the characters and her sense of the characters helps her to define London" (Daiches and Flower, 89), Clarissa becomes, in this part of the novel, an embodiment of Piccadilly's own history, hovering between an almost aristocratic prestige and a desire to be at one with the masses of people around her. The photograph of Piccadilly, with the central female pedestrian emerging between a regal horse cart and a group of (largely male) pedestrians, echoes the tension in Clarissa's own identity—which moves fluidly between past and present, individual and crowd, eccentricity and convention.

The virtual world also provides verbal and visual links for particular words, phrases, locations, and objects referred to in the text of *Mrs. Dalloway*. When Woolf writes that Clarissa "stood for a moment, looking at the omnibuses in Piccadilly," a link on the word "omnibuses" opens a window with a representative photograph from the 1920s (see Figure 9.3).

Likewise, when Clarissa has a momentary flashback in which she recalls throwing a coin into the Serpentine, a lake in the middle of Hyde Park, viewers can click on "Serpentine," see a photograph (see Figure 9.4), and read a brief

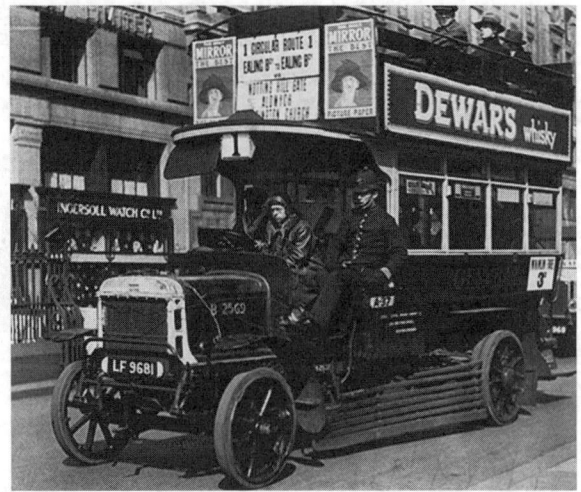

FIGURE 9.3 A London Omnibus

FIGURE 9.4 The Serpentine

description noting that this was the site where the wife of poet Percy Bysshe Shelley drowned herself in 1816. This detail has thematic relevance for Clarissa's own thoughts of death and foreshadows the suicide of another character later in the novel. In addition to clarifying the historical and cultural context of Woolf's own "production of space" in *Mrs. Dalloway*, these descriptions and period-specific images attempt to help viewers visualize the scene as Woolf might have imagined Clarissa herself doing.

Finally, I have developed a series of reading and discussion questions that ask students to consider how Clarissa's location or movements at any given time reflect her thought processes. For example, students can attempt to apply their knowledge and understanding of the relationship between Woolf's text and each area Clarissa visits by considering questions such as the following (for a full list of questions, see appendix):

- As a setting, how does Piccadilly mark a shift from Dean's Yard and St. James's Park? How do Mrs. Dalloway's thoughts about people and herself change here?
- Mrs. Dalloway seems to be heading up Piccadilly, but after looking at books in the window at Hatchards, she reverses her direction and walks towards Bond Street. Why does she change her direction? How is this change reflected in her thinking?

These questions are meant to be open-ended enough for students to develop their own interpretations and yet specific enough to guide those who might otherwise have difficulty drawing connections between Woolf's novel and the locations and images represented in the virtual world. In my own class, I have used these questions as prompts for both discussion and writing.

No virtual world or online environment could fully replicate the experience of *flanerie*—of strolling freely through a city with little more than your sensations and your curiosity to guide you. Nor could such a world allow visitors to fully experience the production and reproduction of social spaces, or the melding of temporal and spatial chronotopes, in Woolf's novel. Nevertheless, *Mrs. Dalloway's London* does accommodate a variety of pedagogical uses and approaches. Because visitors enter the world in the same areas of London where the novel itself begins, *Mrs. Dalloway's London* can serve as a socio-cultural introduction or preview of the novel before students begin reading it. Because visitors can also read from the first quarter or so of the novel, the world provides a valuable inter-text for understanding the early part of the work. The supplementary glosses, location descriptions, maps, photographs, and reading questions also allow visitors to use the site as a research source and an interpretive aid. These activities in turn can be used as a launching point for both discussion and writing.

Student comments on *Mrs. Dalloway's London* suggest that the virtual world allowed them a certain level of mobility to determine the purpose, pace, and intensity of their experience. Comments from students who used the virtual world in my Spring 2007 section of a 300-level British Literature II survey course include the following:

- Provides relatively uncommon information.
- It helped to visualize the novel.
- I could pull up information as I pleased, could digest it at my speed.
- The site allowed for a more personal exploration of the text, yet offers a good amount of guidance to aid interpretation.

The quantitative responses to the HSIRB-approved student evaluation of the virtual world reflected these comments. Fourteen students used *Mrs. Dalloway's London* (eight seniors, one junior, three Sophomores, and two dual-enrolled high school students). Twelve of them responded that the activity helped them understand the historical context and themes of *Mrs. Dalloway* more deeply. Eleven of them responded that they enjoyed their use of the virtual world.

The relative freedom of movement students described was also reflected in the extra-credit writing assignment they could submit in conjunction with our reading of *Mrs. Dalloway* and our use of the virtual world. I gave students the following prompt:

- Write a 2–3 page essay that in some way uses *Mrs. Dalloway's London* to analyze some aspect of the novel. For example:
  - Analyze a specific paragraph or passage from Clarissa's or Peter's walk in relation to its particular setting.
  - Connect the history, images, or other information about London to other sections of the novel.
  - Compare/contrast Clarissa's and Peter's walks. How are they similar? How are they different?

In response to my second reading question on Clarissa's journey along Piccadilly (Why does she reverse her direction and head for Bond Street?), one student drew on the descriptions of both Piccadilly and Bond Street to consider how these locales comment on her shifting perception of her own character:

> Clarissa's abrupt decision to revert her path on Piccadilly and head back to Bond St. [. . .] occurs just as she changes her mind about how others view her. She scolds herself for acting in regard to other people and wishes to think and act only for herself.
>
> When she reaches Bond Street, she is faced with conflicting ideas of what thinking for herself means. [. . .] Old Bond Street represents Clarissa's yearning to be well-respected and noble, where New Bond Street denotes Clarissa's true inner self, which might seem less like the façade of the upper class.

Another student discussed Peter Walsh's journey through the environs of Trafalgar Square, in this case drawing out compelling contrasts between the locale and Peter's identity:

> Peter finds a welcome escape [. . .] in the anonymity that the city offers, which is ironic, given that Trafalgar Square is a public plaza brimming with people. Peter finds isolation even in the most crowded of spaces, which he finds liberating. [. . .] But this same solitude is menacing, because it makes Peter insignificant, and it is significance that creates worth in this society, as the spire of Nelson's Column reminds him.

Like the previous student response, this one makes use of the geographical and historical information to develop an in-depth character study. However, its focus on the tensions between escape and isolation, anonymity and individuality, represents an even more sophisticated account of the *social* contradictions Peter experiences. This student uses Peter's movements and experiences to show how particular kinds of social spaces—in this case, Trafalgar Square—can shape the social relations that occur within them. Peter's simultaneous feelings of isolation and escape within a large public space like Trafalgar Square demonstrate how such a space can provide both a refuge from powerlessness at the same time as it encourages and monumentalizes acts of individual power. As such, this kind of insight could provide a useful way to discuss the qualities of modern urban life in a course that emphasized the historical or cultural contexts of particular literary works.

A third student pursues a similar kind of analysis of Peter, again drawing on the historical descriptions, to consider the end of Peter's journey—his arrival in Regent's Park after pursuing a beautiful young lady:

> Regent's Park was once a hunting ground. This pushes the connection that Peter is seen as a hunter looking for girls to seduce. Peter is now in a place that was once used for the thrill of the hunt. [But] with the London zoo and its caged animals nearby, Regent's Park also connects to Peter's inner turmoil. He is caged in by his desires to be with women that he cannot have.

Like the previous student response, this one uses historical and geographical knowledge to show how Woolf attempts "to criticise the social system, & to show it at work, at its most intense" (*Diary* 2, 248). More specifically, and like much of the criticism on Woolf's depictions of London in *Mrs. Dalloway*, this student emphasizes the distinctly gendered aspects of Woolf's social critique. What emerges from such an approach is the recognition that Peter's pursuit of the young woman not only serves as a compensation for his failure to woo Clarissa years earlier, but that this "hunting" is itself a game in which Peter ends up feeling trapped. Though such an insight does not excuse Peter's behavior towards the young woman he follows, it shows how that behavior may actually undermine the feelings of power it seems to reflect.

Insights of the kinds that these students provided in their written work, as well as in the class discussions based on use of *Mrs. Dalloway's London*, reflect a complex engagement with Woolf's novel—one that uses a consideration of place and space as its point of departure. But such engagement is also meant to foster students' ability and desire to re-enter the novel again and again as more informed readers—aesthetically, historically, and socially. While I have not discussed the theoretical perspectives of Lefebvre, Bakhtin, or Moretti when teaching with *Mrs. Dalloway's London*, the student writing above also suggests an implicit recognition of these thinkers' key insights. As I mentioned earlier, no virtual world could fully replicate the experience of *flanerie* as represented in a novel like Woolf's. However, an environment like *Mrs. Dalloway's London* can facilitate student engagement and understanding of this complex novel in a way that will bring them back to it again and again, hopefully to experience it as Woolf would have hoped—as a form of socially conscious *flanerie*.

APPENDIX

Reading and Discussion Questions for *Mrs. Dalloway's London*

General Questions

1. Why might Woolf use the *particular* places she does to plot Mrs. Dalloway's walk?

2. What do the places Mrs. Dalloway travels through tell us about her character?

3. How does the setting of particular scenes relate to her thoughts while there?

Dean's Yard Questions (see *Mrs. Dalloway, 3–5*)

1. What do the history, images, or location of Dean's Yard (note its proximity to Parliament and Westminster Abbey) suggest about the Dalloways and their social status? How does this status relate to Mrs. Dalloway's seemingly trivial decision to buy flowers in the novel's opening line?

2. In the novel's second and third paragraphs, Mrs. Dalloway steps out of her home and is flooded by memories of a beach vacation in her youth. How does Dean's Yard relate to these memories? How does Dean's Yard compare or contrast with the beach as a setting?

St. James's Park Questions (see **Mrs. Dalloway, 5–8**)

1. Mrs. Dalloway runs into an old friend, Hugh Whitbread, just as she enters St. James's Park (paragraphs 6–7 in *Mrs. Dalloway*). How does the tone of her thinking begin to change here? What kind of thoughts and memories does Hugh elicit for Mrs. Dalloway?

2. How do the history or images of St. James's Park relate to Mrs. Dalloway's thoughts during her exchange with Hugh? In other words, why might Woolf have chosen to set their exchange here?

Piccadilly Questions (see **Mrs. Dalloway, 8–11**)

1. As a setting, how does Piccadilly mark a shift from Dean's Yard and St. James' Park? How do Mrs. Dalloway's thoughts about people and herself change here?

2. Mrs. Dalloway seems to be heading up Piccadilly, but after looking at books in the window at Hatchards, she reverses her direction and walks towards Bond Street (see paragraph 19 in *Mrs. Dalloway*). Why does she change her direction? How is this change reflected in her thinking?

Bond Street Questions (see **Mrs. Dalloway, 11–14**)

1. Mrs. Dalloway's walk ends at a flower shop in Bond Street, a setting that Woolf links specifically to Mrs. Dalloway herself (Woolf's novel began as a short story titled "Mrs. Dalloway in Bond Street"). What do the history or images of Bond Street say about Mrs. Dalloway and her sense of identity? (She could probably have gotten flowers somewhere else, but chooses to buy them here? Why?)

2. Much of Mrs. Dalloway's journey up Bond Street is spent thinking about her daughter Elizabeth's tutor, Miss Kilman. What does Mrs. Dalloway think of Miss Kilman, and how might the setting of Bond Street reinforce these feelings?

3. How does entering the flower shop alter Mrs. Dalloway's thoughts? To what extent is the flower shop meant to compare or contrast with the earlier images of nature (the beach at Bourton, St. James' Park) during Mrs. Dalloway's walk?

Notes

1. In her diary entries on *Mrs. Dalloway* Woolf writes: "I dig out beautiful caves behind my characters . . . The idea is that the caves shall connect, & each comes to daylight at

the present moment" (*Diary* 1, 263). "It took me a year's groping to discover what I call my tunnelling process, by which I tell the past by installments, as I have need of it" (*Diary* 2, 272).

2. For maps see Beja; Daiches and Flower, 85; Dowling, 53–55; and Sutherland, 462–63. For discussions of the various journeys and their significance see Beker; Brewster; Daiches and Flower; Kalliney; Squier; Sutherland; Thacker; and Wood. See Wilson for a biographical account of Woolf's life in London.

3. For helpful overviews of Lefebvre and *The Production of Space* see Soja, 26–82 and Thacker, 16–22.

4. I have drawn this information from sources including Glinert; Moore; and Weinreb and Hibbert.

5. These images are available from Corbis at www.pro.corbis.com.

10

VIRTUAL MUSEUMS

British Literary Works in Historical and Cultural Context

Christopher Nagle, Ilse Schweitzer VanDonkelaar, and Cynthia Klekar

As this chapter will illustrate with three examples drawn from British literature (medieval, early eighteenth century, and early nineteenth century), the online literary virtual museums created in the Literary Worlds Project provide an archive of textual, visual, and audio resources that support and enhance in a variety of ways the experience of reading and studying a literary work. Visitors can go to a literary virtual museum as individuals, or in pairs or small groups at prearranged times. A distinct advantage when more than one person visits is that they can engage in conversation about the exhibits and their relation to the literary text, sharing and deepening understanding. Indeed, groups or entire classes of students can visit the museum simultaneously, accessing it from home or school computers. If the teacher or scholar visits at the same time he or she can act as a virtual docent explaining, responding to questions, and leading discussion. These museums can be projected during a face-to-face class meeting and used as a support for discussion or lecture. The branching pathways through the museum galleries make it a more flexible presentation tool than slides or PowerPoints. Visits to a literary virtual museum can occasion a variety of student writing assignments. Indeed, a number of the museums offer specific research or other "hands-on" activities in an exploratorium format. These virtual museums created by literary scholars comprise carefully constructed resources providing intellectually and academically engaging experiences for student learners with varied skills and levels of experience.

Linking Anglo-Saxon Material and Literary Culture: The *Middangeard* Virtual Museum

As a student of medieval culture in general and Anglo-Saxon literature in particular, when I (Ilse) thought about creating a virtual world I began with the best-known and perhaps most widely taught Old English text—the epic *Beowulf* — intending to recreate the poem as a second world or role-play environment. In this initial effort, the visitor would enter Heorot to find the legendary hall deserted and "blood-bedewed" by the ravages of Grendel, and must speak to various programmed bots (a "bot" is a robot, a talking character who responds in programmed ways to specific words or phrases from a visitor; the bots I worked on acted as characters ranging from a nameless *scop*—the Anglo-Saxon singer/ poet—to King Hrothgar) to piece together what has happened and to chase down the monstrous outcast. Somewhere along the way I concluded that, in my painstaking process of programming the bots to recite selections from the epic poem, I wasn't really adding anything to the text, and I also wasn't creating a teaching tool that was much different from, or more useful than, other modern responses to the poem, be they updated retellings in modern English or film versions of *Beowulf*.

I went back to the drawing board, so to speak, and thought about what might actually be useful to *me* as a teacher of early English literature. In a typical survey class, an instructor might only have time to teach *Beowulf* as the "standard" or most famous of the Anglo-Saxon poems, or perhaps only modern English selections from *Beowulf* as are typically included in secondary textbooks. While *Beowulf* is a memorable masterpiece, this text, populated by monsters and heroes and set in a kingdom predating Anglo-Saxon England, is not necessarily indicative of the entire corpus of Old English poetry or culture, a body of work that includes elegiac, gnomic, scriptural, hagiographical, historical, and enigmatic texts, among others. Students at the secondary and post-secondary levels might rightly ask, "But how did people actually *survive* in Anglo-Saxon England? Were there really halls like the grand Heorot? What does the remaining literature tell us about this long-gone culture?" Instructors at both levels might have need for tools to introduce the cultural context of Anglo-Saxon society—the society which produced *Beowulf*—to their classes.

To create an interdisciplinary teaching resource, I found myself constantly looking to the disciplines of history and studies of material culture to flesh out and illuminate the literary remnants of a long-gone society. Archaeological finds, such as the seventh-century Sutton Hoo ship burial, and manuscript evidence, including the poetry of the tenth-century Exeter Book and richly illuminated Anglo-Saxon gospel books, provided a wealth of images and texts that I incorporated into this virtual landscape. Anglo-Saxon texts are provided in translation in this museum, as they would be taught in secondary and under-graduate classes. However, where possible, I have provided external links to the original Old English texts in order to allow students to see the ancestor of modern English on the page, as well as external links to audio files of selected poems to enable students to experience the alliterative and rhythmic power of Anglo-Saxon in performance. Thus, for *Middangeard*, the Anglo-Saxon literary virtual museum I created, I chose to focus on the poetry that often does *not* make it into the standard survey course curriculum as well as the objects recovered from that society that might pique a student's interest in medieval culture.

Middangeard (or "middle earth") is constructed as a virtual museum where students can navigate individually or in groups through an imagined Anglo-Saxon landscape. This virtual experience begins in a mead-hall, the central symbol of civilization in medieval Germanic culture, where students are encouraged to explore the layout of the timbered structure, its inhabitants, and objects that reflect the material culture of an Anglo-Saxon agricultural settlement. Among the objects are tapestries, horns, a lyre, and a carved whale-bone box, several of which are modeled on actual finds recovered from Anglo-Saxon England (the Sutton Hoo lyre and the eighth-century Franks Casket, to be specific), and for which I provided links to external web sites so that students may investigate images of these finds. (Despite the fictional nature of this landscape, wherever possible, I incorporated links to external web sites featuring actual medieval objects and archaeological sites, providing resources for further research, should students and teachers have need for them.) A virtual "window" within the hall provides a view to the virtual settlement outside, via a link to an external web site with a 360-degree view of the reconstructed Anglo-Saxon settlement of West Stow. One of the "inhabitants" of the hall, a bot programmed to behave like an Anglo-Saxon *scop*, responds to greetings with selections from the Exeter Book poems "Widsith" and "Deor," texts concerned with the oral tradition of poetry in Anglo-Saxon culture and reflecting the experience of the travelling poet in Germanic society.

Moving outside the hall, students can wander freely through several landscapes, many of which are inspired by descriptions of the natural environment in Anglo-Saxon poetry. In the agricultural settlement surrounding the hall, students can read descriptions of the plants and animals that supported life in the hall. Beyond the typical livestock that one might expect, students will find a virtual swarm of bees, along with texts meant to elucidate the value of these insects: an Anglo-Saxon metrical charm for controlling the swarm, as well as an Exeter Book riddle describing the production of mead from honey, both indicative of the somewhat surprising economic value of bees in medieval culture.

In various other areas of the landscape, students can look in and around a funeral barrow, complete with links to images and information about the actual seventh-century Sutton Hoo funeral hoard and a comparative description of the hoard from Scyld Scyfing's sea-burial in the opening lines of *Beowulf*. A foray into the woods leads students to encounter not only the wildlife of the forest but also a bot programmed with "The Wife's Lament," a text from the Exeter Book describing the suffering of a woman cast out from her home and social circle. Similarly, as students move toward the edge of the sea, they interact with a boat-bound bot which, when prompted, performs the text of "The Wanderer," another Exeter Book lament composed in the persona of an exile. Here, the inclusion of two elegiac poems concerned with the theme of exile provides an opportunity for students to discuss the centrality of "belonging" in Anglo-Saxon culture. Also, as "The Wanderer" and "The Wife's Lament" recreate the experiences of exile (respectively) from male and female perspectives, students visiting these rooms in the museum can discuss how the miseries of exile might change according to the gender of the persona.

The water's edge also provides a link to the "Island Monastery," loosely based on the actual Holy Isle of Lindisfarne, home to Northumberland's seventh-century Saint Cuthbert and birthplace of the magnificently illuminated seventh/eighth-century Lindisfarne Gospels. Just outside the "room" of the monastery, students encounter a high stone cross, similar to the sculptured crosses found at Ruthwell (eighth century) and Gosforth (tenth century), and providing links to images of these sculptures. Like the Ruthwell cross, this virtual sculpture is incised with a shortened version of the poem "The Dream of the Rood," from the tenth-century Vercelli Book. As the long form of this dream-vision poem, a retelling of the Crucifixion from the point of view of the True Cross, ends with a meditation on the soul's journey from this transitory world to the soul's true "eðel" ("homeland") of heaven, this provides a suitable point in the virtual experience for the student to consider his or her "journey" through the natural landscape and final destination at the monastery, and how their world-view might differ from that of the Anglo-Saxon individual. Inside the monastery the students find a scriptorium, a room where they can open chests and scour bookcases to find images from Anglo-Saxon manuscripts (via external links to the British Museum web site) and can read descriptions of the process of creating medieval books and manuscripts.

Several activities are possible at this point: an instructor can prompt discussion about the various texts that students have read in relation to the virtual landscape they have traversed, or can test students' levels of involvement and observation throughout their time in *Middangeard*. A virtual blackboard in the "Scriptorium" provides the texts to numerous Anglo-Saxon riddles from the Exeter Book manuscript—the solutions for which have appeared throughout the landscapes of *Middangeard* in the form of crafted and natural objects. Here, an instructor can prompt students individually or in groups to think about what they have observed in the different rooms and spaces to arrive at answers for the riddles. Other discussion questions posted on the blackboard prompt students to consider the links they may see between literary texts and the "natural" world in which Anglo-Saxons lived, or to think about what these texts might tell us about life inside and on the margins of Anglo-Saxon society. Finally, students can exercise their creative skills and mirror what they've read in class and in *Middangeard* with an activity that asks them to compose a work in the Anglo-Saxon style. Here, a virtual projector provides a lesson on the stylistic and technical characteristics of Anglo-Saxon poetic lines (their use of rhythm, alliteration, apposition, and the metaphorical trick of the kenning) so that students can create their own Anglo-Saxon-esque poetry in Modern English.

Beyond an exploration or recreation of one text, *Middangeard* functions as a point where texts of various genres—the lament, the riddle, the epic, the dream vision—overlap and are anchored to the landscape and to the experience of life in Anglo-Saxon settlements. Moreover, one of the foundational elements of this "world" is its incorporation of links to external sites and resources; for the instructor of *Beowulf* (or any other selection of Old English poetry) it is useful to be able to provide students with the material echoes of this text as discovered in Anglo-Saxon archaeological finds. As Anglo-Saxon texts are removed from modern society by a thousand years (and, the case of American students, an ocean), it is imperative for instructors to find some way of making these literatures accessible, whether that comes from supplementing them with the artwork of that culture or allowing students to explore a similar landscape on their own. I hope that *Middangeard* succeeds in pulling together the various strands of Anglo-Saxon texts—heroic, legendary, agricultural, visionary, and monastic—and presenting these to students in a fresh and contextually rich way.

Moll's World: An Historical Approach to Daniel Defoe's *Moll Flanders*

> Then I repented heartily of all my Life past, but that Repentance yielded me no Satisfaction, no peace, no not in the least, because, *as I said to myself*, it was Repenting after the Power of farther Sinning was taken away: I seem'd not to Mourn that I had committed such Crimes, and for the Fact, as it was an Offence against God and my Neighbour; but I mourn'd that I was to be punish'd for it; I was a Penitent as I thought, not that I had sinn'd, but that I was to suffer, and this took away all the Comfort, and even the hope of my Repentance in my own Thoughts.
>
> *(Defoe, 214)*

Working with a notoriously complex but very appealing eighteenth-century novel, I (Cynthia) began by focusing on a specific challenge posed by the work. One of the most problematic moments of interpretation for students of Daniel Defoe's *The Fortunes and Misfortunes of Moll Flanders* (1722) is the question of the authenticity of Moll's conversion in Newgate Prison. Moll herself is tormented by her motives, as the passage above indicates. However, urging students to recon-cile somehow Moll's remorse for her life of crime with her fear of capital punishment and her personal and material self-interest ignores the way in which the novel builds an ongoing tension between the heroine's moral consciousness and eighteenth-century social and political structures. The passage above is one of many throughout *Moll Flanders* that pits the preservation of the self, in moral, psychological, and material ways, against rigid class, gender, and economic con-ditions. Thus in order to appreciate Moll's experience in Newgate, as well as her prosperity after her release, students should be asked not whether the heroine's conversion is authentic, but what historical and cultural realities make her conversion so complicated. Only an historically informed reading of the novel allows students to distinguish, even if only temporarily, between the emotions elicited by Moll's questionable conversion and the shifting and unreliable social conditions that define her world.

One of my primary goals when teaching *Moll Flanders* and other eighteenth-century novels is to draw students' attention to the complex relationship between text, history, and culture. As demonstrated in the interpretative questions raised by the passage above, an historically informed reading produces a more complex and satisfying experience with the text. Thus I encourage students to read the novels as historical documents, intimately tied to a specific context. Before the class begins reading a novel I assign excerpts from periodicals, diaries, broadsheets, and biographies from the period. These serve as an introduction to the text's primary thematic concerns. As the class discusses the novel, typically over the course of two weeks, they return to the primary documents from the introduction or I might add other short, relevant material to supplement the daily reading assignment. Additionally, the students draw upon these primary documents to complete a research paper that investigates in detail the historical intersections among the novel, history, and culture. The topics for an eighteenth-century novel might include (but are not limited to): female education, marriage laws, the city and country, charitable institutions, fashion, architecture, manners, and trade. The integration of primary contextual materials into class discussion and the students' writing helps locate the novel as a response to, and product of, contemporary concerns.

The Fortunes and Misfortunes of Moll Flanders traces the life of Moll Flanders, from her origins as an orphan (she was born to a convict in Newgate Prison) and her dreams of escaping lower-class poverty, through her adult life as a criminal determined to gain economic and social legitimacy, and ending with her repentance and prosperity in America. When I teach the novel, I focus on the social and cultural conditions that lead the heroine to a life of crime, and the issues to which Defoe was responding, such as penal reform, education, and the debate over the transportation of criminals. References to documents such as the Old Bailey trial transcripts, criminal biographies, and the Ordinary's accounts allow students to understand Moll in relation to eighteenth-century law and justice, and to understand better the conditions, specifically those relating to women, that create her complex attitude toward crime. The way in which students engage with these sources and the period contributes to a sophisticated study of *Moll Flanders* as an eighteenth-century historical document, a study not always effective or possible through a close reading of the novel alone.

Moll's World, the literary virtual world museum I created, offers students an innovative way to explore and understand *Moll Flanders*. Students engage with the historic moment of the novel by taking an active part in building the virtual environment and thus entering into the world that Moll navigates. Building *Moll's World* requires students to draw upon their research and understanding of *Moll Flanders* to construct rooms that highlight the intersections among the novel, history, and culture. Currently, the museum contains some of the documents and information that students will need to build their rooms. Drawing upon the primary documents already in the virtual environment and the ones that I used in class, the students researched an aspect of eighteenth-century life in England and "performed" that life in the virtual world. As they did so they inevitably confronted economic, political, gendered, and historical factors that shaped the heroine and the novel.

Students began constructing the world by working from the particular set of primary documents introduced in an earlier class session. I recommend that instructors make the primary documents readily available to the class, rather than having the students locate the documents themselves, so that students have adequate time to read the novel, decide upon their topic, and analyze the materials relevant for the creation of their virtual world. The instructor can find a number of critical editions of *Moll Flanders* that reprint excerpts of related writings by Defoe and other eighteenth-century writers. Specifically, these editions may include selections from Defoe's *Essay on Projects* (1697), *Conjugal Lewdness; or Matrimonial Whoredom* (1727), and his writings from the *Review* (1704–1714), as well as works by other writers, such as *An Accurate Description of Newgate* (1724), *A Discourse and View of Virginia* (1663), and passages from famous criminal biographies popular during Defoe's era. A number of documents also are available online: the *Proceedings of the Old Bailey Courthouse, 1674–1913* may be found at oldbaileyonline.org; and e-texts as well as resources for eighteenth-century topics such as art, music, and mathematics may be found at *Eighteenth-Century Resources*, edited by Jack Lynch, at ethnicity.rutgers.edu/~jlynch/18th/d.html. And of course, many of these documents can be found via online databases through an institution's library web site and in rare books rooms if the instructor wishes to vary or expand the offerings noted here.

The primary research assignment of the course using my virtual world was the design, construction, and interaction in rooms that represent an engaging museum of significant topics in *Moll Flanders*. Students worked in groups of three to four to research a topic related to *Moll Flanders* and the eighteenth century, but the topics for *Moll's World* can be adapted easily depending upon class size. Based upon enrollment at our university, I expected five to six groups of four to five students. For these groups, broad topics such as criminal transportation and penal law reform, life in Newgate Prison, servitude in england and the colonies, female education and employment, and property and marriage laws offer an overview of the novel's central concerns while providing flexibility for the groups to design their world and assign each group member a sub-topic. Narrowed topics, such as criminal transportation, the design of Newgate Prison, or women and servitude would work well for smaller groups, and additional topics, such as criminal lives, the rise of debt and credit, and on trial at the Old Bailey Courthouse would work for larger classes.

No matter how broad or narrow the topic, however, students were encouraged to emphasize how the topic contributed to an understanding of the novel. When constructing their part of *Moll's World*, each group was charged to consider the relevance of the space's design, how the space would highlight the historical context, and how the class as a whole should consider the space in relation to the novel. As students built these rooms, they decorated them with artwork, objects, supplementary texts, and music. Following this example, other instructors might emphasize that such choices should reflect clearly the way in which visitors will engage with the space. For example, if students are constructing the Old Bailey Courthouse, they might want to include scrolls, books, or art in certain areas, such as "The Bar," Dining Room for Justices, and Session Yard, which when selected by the visitor would provide a type of historical guide to that part of the courthouse. Further, in order to add an understanding of how class and gender intersected in the proceedings, the courthouse design could include a feature that allowed access to certain areas based upon the visitor's "character" while in the virtual world; some spaces would be reserved only for upper-class male judges and lawyers, and some spaces might be crowded with a mix of less respectable witnesses. This feature could also include a way to limit participation in the proceedings based upon class and gender, thus emphasizing the unequal power dynamic that occurred when a female defendant was brought to a court hearing controlled by men. The way in which the students build, design, and lead the class through the room will demonstrate their understanding of the material.

Once the museum is complete, or at least those portions created by the class, students can use the room as the site of discussion. Depending on the teacher's primary goals for the session, students can enter *Moll's World* as themselves or enter as a specific character (or character type) so that their involvement in the virtual world depends upon gender, class, religion, profession, income, age, and/or marital status. Questions may be posed in the rooms themselves via the use of significant objects, or the experience of visiting the room may raise more spontaneous questions from participants. Possible points of discussion when students are in *Moll's World* might include how economic, political, social, and gendered concerns affect the room's design, how each visitor may interact in the room, and the significance of the objects in the room. While in the virtual space, the class can consider important questions related to *Moll Flanders* but also to the eighteenth century overall: How are money and property intimately related to the self in this period? What social circumstances drive Moll and others to a life of crime, and why is it so difficult for Moll to give up this life? How does our understanding of the literary and cultural conventions of sensibility inform the trial scene and Moll's experience in Newgate prison? How does Defoe comment upon penal reform and debates about transportation in his depiction of Moll's experiences in America? The students creating the rooms should be encouraged to develop the discussion topics most relevant to their space.

Instructors interested in exploring the possible uses of *Moll's World* in their classes are invited to visit the world. There are a number of ways in which the world might be useful, depending upon the instructor's goals when teaching *Moll Flanders*. The world will provide introductory information to the novel, Defoe, and the eighteenth century, which could help begin a discussion of *Moll Flanders* or the origins of the English novel, or serve as supplementary material for a discussion of other eighteenth-century texts. The documents posted on the site can provide a research source for the novel, the period, and a special topics course or unit, but also for a study of historicism, feminism, and cultural studies. Further, these documents introduce students to the methods of reading, synthesizing, and discussing primary historical and cultural texts at the same time that they are reading and analyzing a novel influenced by and composed alongside those texts. Instructors also are invited to tour *Moll's World* with their students to learn more about how virtual worlds are imagined. Most importantly, instructors and students should engage in the construction and design of *Moll's World* in order to pose their own questions about the novel and the period, and perhaps imagine and collaborate on how to expand *Moll's World* or create eighteenth-century worlds of their own.

Inismore: The World of the Wild Irish Girl; or, When Footnotes (and Footnotes on Footnotes) Are Not Enough

The virtual world of *Inismore* was conceived originally as a museum space for students—primarily undergraduates, but also graduate students—to address the difficulties in engaging with Sydney Owenson's Romantic-era block-buster, *The Wild Irish Girl* (1806). The novel is fairly short, but richly layered with arcane and truly interdisciplinary interests (archaeology, linguistics, mythology, art history, religion, philosophy, politics, music, etc.), and it is infamous, especially for a novel, for its heavy use of footnotes. So although the plot of star-crossed lovers from warring nations should engage students easily, its self-conscious attempt simultaneously to show Ireland as exotic and to make it newly familiar to its reading audience poses some specific difficulties for those who do not have specialist knowledge of Irish history and culture or are unfamiliar with the characteristic features of late eighteenth- and early nineteenth-century literature. Perhaps because of the complexities of reference in the novel, this fascinating and important work by one of the most interesting Romantic-era women novelists is not often taught. The *Inismore* virtual world has the potential to help bring *The Wild Irish Girl* into its rightful place in the twenty-first-century study of nineteenth-century British literature, and to make the experience of studying the novel more rewarding for students.

My (Chris) initial plan was to imagine a visually (and eventually, aurally) dynamic online project that would enable students to explore a wide variety of supplementary material, picking and choosing at their leisure from what seemed most helpful to them while beginning their study of the novel. Although this virtual museum space is not yet complete, *Inismore* ranges over a wide array of cultural components. One of its most dynamic examples includes images and audio clips of authentic Irish harp performance from the period—a central theme throughout the work—as well as biographical information on famous harpists who are mentioned in the story. It also provides background on central religious and devotional contexts for Irish Catholicism, another key topic that proves contentious for the novel's characters. The third cultural component in this pathway (or "room") of the museum is devoted to Sensibility, a literary and cultural movement whose influence permeates the novel on many levels: from expressions of extreme emotion to strange and idiosyncratic typography and punctuation (much of it used to convey those emotional extremes as directly as possible on the written page), to the more subtle shadings and allusions to other literary works (the novels of Richardson and Sterne, the poetry of Collins and Goldsmith). As Cynthia Klekar notes in her exploratory questions for students working on *Moll's World*, this topic is relevant to Defoe's novel as well, and I imagine that it might offer one of many fruitful connections for those who are teaching a course in which both texts might be featured (history of the novel, literature of the "long eighteenth century," etc.). Different rooms in this area of *Inismore* are devoted to providing examples of literary texts that share some of the literature of Sensibility's unfamiliar attributes, visual images of writers and historical documents themselves (such as title pages from the first editions of some of these older texts), as well as exercises that allow students to explore these contexts further. Research activities play a part here and elsewhere, with specific writing and research exercises geared to the level most appropriate for either undergraduate or graduate students.

As I began to collect and assemble the audio and visual files that I felt were essential for *Inismore*'s multimodal environment, I organized them in fairly conventional ways that made sense to me, and that I hoped would seem intuitive to my students when they first entered the virtual world to explore its resources. My first priority was to ensure a rich visual component, including an array of images that could provide engaging context for a variety of different rooms in the virtual museum. Portraits of the author came to mind immediately, and quite a few were available on the web already. These images were important, not only so that students could envision (and perhaps more fully humanize) our author, but also so that they could see the material ways in which famous painters, engravers, and other illustrators paid tribute to her—sometimes by playing into the self-mythologizing performance of a Wild Irish Girl, which Owenson herself desired, and in other instances by offering less flattering or even critical perspectives of the controversial writer. She was a very public figure for most of her writing life, and these artifacts provide one important means of assessing her changing reception over time. Although I did not offer such an exercise in my class, teachers of the novel might ask students to write short exploratory pieces about these issues, or in a more extended setting, to do some research into the history of the individual artist himself and his relationship to Owenson and to other writers of the era. Her most famous image, René Berthon's portrait in the National Gallery of Ireland, is an exemplary instance of Owenson's favorite mode of self-fashioning: the inspired author sits at a table with quill in hand and pages of writing in front of her, dressed like a Gaelic princess (complete with a cape draped over her chair), staring dreamily off into the distance. Here, the novelist and her most famous heroine seem indistinguishable.

Other images ranged widely from reproductions of the text itself—photos of the first edition, which I took when visiting the rare books archive at Notre Dame—which allowed students to see more clearly what the text as physical object would have looked like to its earliest readers. Such an awareness is especially important for this particular novel, the strangeness of which is heightened by the layout of the text itself, even in contemporary paperback editions: many of the novel's pages are filled with footnotes, and this paratext often overwhelms the narrative itself, vying for the reader's attention in a host of ways. Not only do some footnotes fill entire pages, forcing the reader to shift back and forth from the action of the story itself to the contextual embellishment of the highly learned notes, but some also tell anecdotal tales of their own, stories commanding as much interest as the plot of the novel proper. When students see how this juxtaposition of text and paratext works in the 1806 edition, it dramatizes clearly the innovative character of the work in its own age. Comparing these images to those of a first edition of Austen's (initially anonymous) *Pride and Prejudice*, or another more familiar and more typical Romantic-era novel, would also provide a useful contrast. Owenson's novel emerges as a work of fiction that deliberately and self-consciously intervenes in highly fraught debates about national identity and cultural conflict, themes that might be teased out of an Austen novel with some effort but which are never foregrounded as directly as they are in *The Wild Irish Girl*. Although I did not include such an exercise in class, it would be beneficial to have students research contemporary reviews of Owenson's novel and those of one or more of her contemporaries, comparing her readers' assessments of what was objectionable and what was praiseworthy, and the specific ways in which she stood out amid women writers of her age.

A third category of images central to appreciating the novel consists of different maps of Ireland ranging from the seventeenth to the nineteenth century, which help to more firmly establish a sense of place, one of the novel's foremost concerns. I included maps of Dublin in both 1610 and 1818 to show the significant growth and change over two centuries in Ireland's capital, which was also the seat of power for England's colonial administration. A broader map of Ireland from 1808 provides a full perspective of its geography around the time of the novel's publication, and allows students to trace the route taken by the hero, Horatio, the Wild Irish Girl's eventual suitor. A more detailed map of the west coast of Ireland, where most of the novel's action takes place, helps to put more of the setting in perspective. Drawing on the virtual museum, many exercises could be devised to help students explore the ways that features of Ireland's landscape prove to be key to the novel's action and themes; its geographical proximity to England and France is essential to visualize as well, especially when discussing the violent and unstable political and cultural relations of the period that led to several bloody uprisings, most notably in 1798, and the contentious Act of Union in 1800, events that the novel addresses directly. Ideally, maps could be made into an even more significant component of the museum (although such developments might require a different platform and technical specifications), especially by incorporating a more dynamic and interactive engagement with places of central importance to the plot and routes traveled by characters, perhaps even a Google Earth interface for closer inspection of the contemporary sites described in the novel. Here is an example of ways in which *Inismore* could benefit from some of the strategies deployed successfully in *Middangeard*, although there seem to be fewer currently available resources such as those Ilse Schweitzer VanDonkelaar accessed through the British Library for the construction of her world.

One of the components that I hope to add to the virtual environment is a collection of satirical cartoon images culled from the early nineteenth-century print debate about the Act of Union, images that saturated the popular culture of the day and played an important role in mediating and contesting issues of nationhood as it was filtered through contemporary discourses of gender, as well as what we would today identify as racial and ethnic identity. Although these images often seem to speak clearly and directly to the issues at hand, class discussion and written exercises could profitably explore the broader implications of these satirical images—the most common is that of forced marriage—working to decode what is left unspoken, and also comparing their strategies for political intervention with those of Owenson's novel, especially its famous allegorical conclusion, which imagines a marriage of nations represented in the nuptials of hero and heroine. This neat ending rests uncomfortably for some readers, in part because it comes literally over the dead body of Glorvina's father and also because it follows from the tension of a previous unsettling dynamic—the love triangle established by Horatio and his own father competing for the love of Glorvina. The contemporary cartoons that focus on arranged or, more sinisterly, forced marriage could help more naïve novel readers to consider the sexual politics of the plot's conclusion, and to see much more at stake than simple narrative resolution when comparing the romanticized and the cynical views of marriage and national union that emerge in contrast.

Images are a key part of two other rooms, in fact, those addressing the importance of religion—in this case, representing the three most prominent

Catholic saints, as well as an example of illuminated manuscript—and music, showing multiple images of famous harpists from the eighteenth century as well as examples of major harp styles. More importantly for this latter room, however, each smaller room within it features different pieces of music performed by a classically trained harpist performing on a replica of the Downhill harp, Dennis Hampson's famous instrument that Owenson alludes to in the novel. The author herself played the harp and reveres the tradition of harp playing, especially the (literally mythic) tradition of the bard, the often blind and always visionary artist who was once celebrated by all Gaelic royalty in earlier ages but whose legacy has come to a melancholy end—in Owenson's eyes, much to be regretted—thanks to generations of neglect and, more crucially, to the violent forms of social and cultural change initiated by centuries of colonial domination of Ireland by its English neighbors. The bard serves as a key, ultra-romanticized figure in the novel, blending inspiration, loss, and national identity. Owenson incorporates this rich history in miniature in her footnotes—one of the longest is devoted to Dennis Hampson, who is featured in a room in *Inismore*—and this mix of image and sound files (all of which were fairly easy to locate and to use without raising copyright issues) greatly enriches appreciation of the interdisciplinary inter-texts of the novel.

To return for a moment to the Religion room of the virtual museum, it might be useful to share a set of exercises included here. This topic was one of the most difficult to delimit, because of its scope and complexity. But it is impossible to discuss Irish literature generally, or this work in particular, without attending to the contextual resonance of religious traditions, especially Irish Catholicism. The exercises incorporated in *Inismore* follow basic background information on the three primary saints (Patrick, Bridget, and Columba), and are intended for undergraduates, but might be adapted quite easily to both more and less experienced groups of students.

Concluding Thoughts

Taken together, these three different incarnations of the virtual museum space share the common aims of providing for students a dynamic and engaging point of entry for classic works of British literature that often prove challenging—or in same cases, even alien—for contemporary students encountering them for the first time. Each of us envisioned our museum space somewhat differently, with varying degrees of student collaboration—in the construction of the world itself (as in *Moll's World*), in interactive group activities experienced in real time (as in *Middangeard*), or in more independent exploration of the resources by individual students either inside or outside of class (as in *Inismore*). In each case, however, two principles helped to guide the conceptualization and execution of all three virtual museum spaces: selectively integrating visually (and in some cases, aurally) rich contextual materials that can make the literary works come alive in fresh ways for today's students, and designing accessible pathways to the material—

often with directed activities—that allow for maximum flexibility in different class environments. All of us share the goal of using technology to supplement rather than supplant the literature we teach in the classroom, and we hope that each of these virtual museum spaces enables a wide variety of ways for teachers and students to enrich their experience with these texts and others like them.

EXERCISES

Research Activity 1

Conduct more thorough research on these figures, and determine which (if any) might have deserved both the labels of saint and sinner given what we know about their lives.

- In the narratives of saints' lives, how are the two related? Can we see any parallels between the lives of the saints and the complex lives of the novel's characters?
- What significance might we attribute to the ways in which the characters might be seen to both draw on and to depart from these famous historical models?

Research Activity 2

Explore some recent work by contemporary Irish poets writing in English (or translated into English) and see how many references you can find to these three figures.

- How do they tend to be used in these contemporary settings?
- What role do they play in the works?
- What do they make possible for the poet to imagine or create in his/her poems?
- Are there strikingly different uses of the material in different poets? What might account for such differences?
- Is the identity of the poet an important factor?
- How significant is a sense of history to these works?

These questions and others of your own should help you to craft an argument in a longer analytic paper that examines either (a) the treatment of one saint by several different poets, or (b) the treatment of several different saints by one poet.

11

"THE KINDNESS OF STRANGERS"

Angels in America in a Virtual World

Steve Feffer

At first thought, teaching Tony Kushner's Pulitzer Prize-winning play *Angels in America* through a virtual environment may seem paradoxical to the core themes of the play. After all, *Angels in America*, through its examination of the AIDS crisis and American values, asserts our most fundamental need for humanity and community amid the enormity of change. In *Angels*, Kushner privileges a hierarchy of compassion where being present to share in another's life and community suffering, even when doing so entails harrowing grief and enormous loss, is a more essential act than even a calling from heaven to be a prophet. This sense of presence and community is so powerful it even becomes a thematic concern attending the play's performance. As David Roman suggests in his *Acts of Intervention: Performance, Gay Culture and AIDS*, being present at a performance of the play throughout its 8-hour length makes the audience part of the work's insistence on presence and community, endurance and hope.

> To participate in the marathon performances of a play as demanding as *Angels in America*, as spectator or actor, is to participate in a ritual of endurance (and also of commitment: the marathon performances run the length of a conventional workday and cost more than what many people earn for a day of labor). [. . .] The convergence of the physical experience of watching a performance of *Angels in America* with the feelings produced by *Angels in America* transforms a ritual of endurance into a ritual of hope.
>
> *(Roman, 219–220)*

Yet, presence and community would seem in direct contradiction to a *virtual* environment.

For this reason, when our grant project began to explore virtual platforms, I had reservations about using a virtual environment to teach *Angels in America*; however, I was in the middle of teaching a semester devoted to Kushner's work and decided to experiment with this new technology and explore an alternative approach to such an important play already familiar to many of my playwriting and contemporary drama students. (A recent survey of almost two hundred theatre professionals, academicians, and critics considered *Angels in America* the second most important American play of all time.[1]) Because the play privileges the relationship between presence, space and community, my virtual environment for *Angels in America* considered the play as a series of locations that were both physical and theoretical. In fact, this approach marked the two major spaces that divided the virtual world I created. The physical spaces were locations important to the action of the play: Central Park, which included an interactive map of the park that featured the Bethesda Fountain that figures so prominently as the closing image of the play, as well as the Brambles where Louis cheats on Prior in an act of self-recrimination; Prospect Park, where Harper imagines she has gone to Antarctica; Lower Manhattan, where Louis and Joe work and meet; the Mormon Visitors Center, where Mother Pitt works and Harper seeks refuge, etc., as well as a number of the prominent New York City locations that inform the action.

While the virtual world mapped these physical spaces contemporary to the play's setting, it also allowed inclusion of historical spaces significant to the play: the chamber where Ethel Rosenberg, a figure from the past and who is a character in the play, was executed; the senate hearing room where Roy Cohen, another historical character, sat next to Joseph McCarthy and made his political name. Additionally, in the virtual world the historical spaces could include those that were more epochal or ideological such as the Reagan White House, whose politics and personalities background the play, and the Justice Department where Joe, a closeted gay law clerk and Louis's new partner, has been writing decisions for a conservative judge that negatively affect homosexual cases, such as one where a soldier is dismissed for his sexuality. Indeed, rooms in the virtual environment could be developed to focus on entirely abstract worlds, such as Kushner's image of heaven and its complex theology and cosmology, or Harper's drug-induced image of Antarctica. This use of the virtual environment for exploring physical and imaginary locations enabled my students to visualize more clearly physical locations and put into historical context people, events, and places such as the Rosenbergs or the Reagan White House.

The virtual environment I created also explored both the theatrical and the theoretical spaces that the play inhabits. I was especially interested in using the technology to create virtual locations that could inform students about the theatres and performance theories that delineate Kushner's approach to his *Angel's* material and his larger aesthetic concerns. This was particularly important to this virtual world as modes, forms, and theories of theatre and performance may be harder for the students to grasp than the plays more concrete locations. Kushner has described his aesthetic, especially that used in *Angels in America*, as "The Theatre of Fabulousness" and this second major area of my virtual environment considered the source for this theatrical conceptualization. For Kushner, "The Theatre of Fabulousness" is a stagecraft, style, aesthetic, and politics that conflates the broader queer camp and drag of the Ridiculous Theatre with the epic political theatre of Bertolt Brecht. I found that this space I created in the virtual world became useful to help students understand these two important but different theatrical traditions. For Kushner, "there's fabulous in the sense of an evolutionary advance of being ridiculous, and fabulous in the sense of being fabled, having a history" (Kushner, 1995, 140). Kushner says of this theatre:

> If the great antecedent form of gay theatre was theatre of the ridiculous, then the new theatre . . . all of us who are lesbian and gay and working now in the theatre are creating is something that I'm calling "theatre of the fabulous." [. . .] But one of the things about fabulousness is that there's an issue of investiture, that you become powerful because you believe yourself to be. In a certain sense, the people in the theatre are all fabulous at the moment that Prior, who has become invested by the audience with a moral authority and a kind of prophetic voice, blesses everybody—they're fabulous whether they want to be or not.[2]
>
> *(Kushner, 1998b, 74)*

Thus to this end, Kushner imagines a theatre of extraordinary occurrences, one where the "strings" (such as those that fly the Angel) are meant to show, without compromising the theatre as a place of magic. As he says in his "A Note About the Staging" that prefaces the published version of the play:

> The play benefits from a pared down style of presentation, with minimal scenery and scene shifts done rapidly (no blackouts!) employing the cast as well as stage-hands—which makes for an actor-driven event, as this must be. The moments of magic—all of them—are to be fully realized, as bits of wonderful *theatrical* illusion—which means that it's OK if the wires show, and maybe it's good that they do, but the magic should at the same time be thoroughly amazing.
>
> *(Kushner, 1994, 8, italics in the original)*

My virtual environment became a place where students could foster a visual and corporeal sense of both Ludlum's Ridiculous Theatre and Brechtian epic theatre and what they meant to Kushner and the politics and aesthetics of his work. Thus, off the area designated in my virtual world "Tony Kushner and the Theatre of Fabulousness," where this idea was defined with some quotations from Kushner (such as those above) and images from the productions of the play that illustrated these concepts, there are exits to Brecht's Epic Theatre and Charles Ludlum's Ridiculous Theatre.

Kushner has said that he "always goes back to Brecht" and the impact of Brecht on Kushner's work in general, and *Angels in America* in particular, cannot be overstated.[3] Kushner has made an insistent case that Brecht's specific type of political theatre was important in the evolution of *Angels* and his political aesthetic. As he expressed to Brecht scholar Carl Weber in an interview entitled "I Always Go Back to Brecht":

> Personally, when I go back to Brecht, which I do constantly [. . .] there is an issue of redoing one's commitment [. . .] Through everything in Brecht there is an absolutely serious desire to see the world change *now*, as they say in *Sezuan*: "Now. Now, Now."[4] The urgency of that "Now" is something I go back to Brecht for. So I remind and I chastise myself if I feel that I am slipping because it's very hard to maintain that commitment. He is incredibly important to me as an origin and also a goal.
>
> *(Kushner, 1998b, 123, italics in the original)*

Thus, in this area of the virtual environment, students could go "back to Brecht" (the title of this area) as a theoretical location that outlined Brecht's political and aesthetic concerns, while also simultaneously absorbing Kushner's own artistic and critical connections to Brecht. This space was devoted to Brecht's concept of an epic theatre and it contained key statements from Brecht's "A Short Organum for the Theatre" especially relevant to the play, as well as images from Brechtian productions that connected his work to Kushner and *Angels*. I especially focused on the key elements as described by Brecht in his "A Short Organum for the Theatre" that inform the dramaturgy of the play, such as the distancing or alienation effect, historicization, and social *gestus* as a form of scenic composition. I utilized Brecht's own descriptions of his epic theatrical techniques, such as montage, episodes, dialectics, disruption of the fourth wall, titles, music, and comedy to outline for my students the key components in Brecht's work relevant to the play.[5] I also attempted to provide illustrations of these techniques from productions of Brecht that would have some visual echoes in *Angels*. Furthermore, I provided key statements by Kushner, such as the one above from his interview with Weber, which specified this connection with Brecht.

While the name Brecht, and some of Brecht's work, may be familiar to some students, the work of Charles Ludlum's Ridiculous Theatre—the other key theatrical innovator mentioned by Kushner as one of the cornerstones of his "Theatre of Fabulousness"—is, unfortunately, much less well known.[6] Ludlum's Ridiculous Theatre embraced a queer political aesthetic that featured broad camp and play, and a carnivalesque inversion of social, cultural, and political hierarchy and heteronormativity. It was especially rich in its B-movie reference and bold pastiche of genre styles. As Gregory W. Bredbeck says in his essay "'Free[ing] the Erotic Angels': Performing Liberation in the 1970s and 1990s," "If liberation performance seeks to 'free the erotic angels' of America, nowhere does this impulse find a more fully developed dramaturgy than in the Ridiculous Theatre of Charles Ludlum" (Bredbeck, 276). Thus, it was important in teaching the play to make this more obscure, but highly influential theatre available to students as they approached *Angels*. I constructed this area of the virtual world in much the same manner as I did the Brecht material, and allowed the manifestos of theatre founder Charles Ludlum to describe the theatre's key theatrical tenets and sensibilities as supported by archival texts and images. I then provided text and images from *Angels in America* that echoed Ludlum's work. Some of these connections were merely visual, such as an image of Prior Walter in drag as he reaches up toward the descending Angel. But others referred to more complex theoretical engagements, such as Bredbeck points out between *Angels in America* and Ludlum's *Bluebeard*, perhaps his most famous play, whereby "[t]he copiously hermaphroditic disposition of the Angel recalls *Bluebeard*'s quest for a supreme gender" (ibid., 280). I appreciated the simultaneity that navigation of the virtual world provided in allowing my students to experience the proximity of these diverse theatrical traditions, and make quite corporeal the effect of such varied sources on Kushner's work.

At the center of *Angels in America* stands the great "Angel of History." The Angel serves as both remarkable theatrical-spectacle in its confluence of magic and stagecraft, but also as the philosophical-foundation from which Kushner's play developed. Thus, in my virtual world, the Angel stood at the center of "the lobby" from which all the other rooms were accessed. Once again, the simultaneity that I was able to make present in the world allowed my students to consider the physical nature of the Angel, as well as its philosophical antecedent. As Art Borreca says in "Dramaturging the Dialectic: Brecht, Benjamin and Declan Donnellan's Production of *Angels in America*":

> By employing spectacle in this way [the Angel that is both divine and theatrical construction], *Angels in America* owes a debt to an intellectual and spiritual compatriot of Brecht's, Walter Benjamin. Kushner has stated that the play was inspired in part by the visionary historical materialism of Benjamin's "Theses on the Philosophy of History," especially by this reference to Paul Klee's 1920 painting *Angelus Novus*.
>
> *(Borecca, 248)*

In his interview with Weber, Kushner considers Benjamin's explication of the Klee painting to be "the ground on which Brecht and Benjamin really understood one another. [. . .] It is truly history as the accumulation of catastrophes and calamity" (Kushner, 1998a, 119).[7] In fact, critic David Savran in his influential essay on the play "Ambivalence, Utopia and a Queer Sort of Materialism: How *Angels in America* Reconstructs the Nation" sees Benjamin as central to *Angels*. He notes that *Prior* Walter, the main character of the play, is the "queer commemoration of the Walter that *came before*—Walter Benjamin—whose revolutionary principles he both embodies and displaces insofar as he marks both the presence and absence of Walter Benjamin in this text" (Savran, 18, italics mine).

Because of its centrality to any consideration of the play, Klee's painting *Angelus Novus* and Benjamin's frequently cited consideration of the painting were the first image and text students encountered once they began exploration of my virtual world (Klee's *Angelus Novus* is easily found online). According to Benjamin:

> A Klee painting named *Angelus Novus* shows an angel looking as though he is about to move away from something he is fixedly contemplating. His eyes are staring, his mouth wide open, his wings are spread. This is how one pictures the angel of history. His face is turned toward the past. Where we perceive a chain of events, he sees one single catastrophe, which keeps piling wreckage upon wreckage and hurls it in front of his feet. The angel would like to stay, awaken the dead, and make whole what has been smashed. But a storm is blowing from Paradise; it has got caught in his wings with such violence the angel can no longer close them. This storm irresistibly propels him into the future to which his back is turned, while the pile of debris before him grows skyward. This storm is what we call progress.
>
> *(Benjamin, 257–258)*

I reprinted the Benjamin text in its entirety in my virtual world (as well as here) because of its prominence in critical discussions of the play (especially Kushner's own), including those that may provide little in the way of supporting material to *Angels in America*, such as the introduction to the play in some drama anthologies, among them *The Wadsworth Anthology of Drama, Revised Edition*, edited by W. B. Worthen. This "allegory of history" and its series of paradoxes that Benjamin introduces in his analysis (such as future/past; chain of events/single catastrophe; stasis/progress; utopia/dystopia, etc.) are what critic David Savran calls the "primary generative fiction for *Angels in America*" (Savran, 17).

However, I also see in these contradictions a highly useful way for educators and students to approach this massive work, whether these students are the Advanced Playwriting students that first experimented with my *Angels* virtual world, or students encountering the work for their first time in an undergraduate Studies in Drama course. Influenced by Savran's essay and Benjamin's consideration of Klee, I have frequently begun a classroom discussion of *Angels in America* by asking the students to list all the contradictions or paradoxes that they observe in the play. These have included those that are listed above in the context of the Klee painting, but have also included gay/straight, liberal/conservative, masculine/feminine, etc. (The list is almost endless once one gets started—and, in fact, its enormity becomes a testament to the richness of the play.) I asked the students in the Kushner class to do the same in an interactive manner with their fellow students through the dialoguing function in this "lobby" room of the virtual world. In this manner, a written record was maintained of all the conflicting terms, ideas, positions, characters, etc. that appear in the play. This list continued to grow and expand as students made their way through the world and returned to this originary space of the environment. We then considered the items on the list in the context of differing attitudes in the play, and how we thought various characters might view each of them. In addition, we also considered where Kushner might stand in regards to each conflict. My approach is inspired by Savran, who argues in regards to the play's much-vaunted ambivalence that "despite the fact that this binary opposition generates so much of the play's ideological framework," Kushner clearly imagines a hierarchy where "*Angels* is carefully constructed so that communitarianism, rationalism, progress, etc. will be read as preferable to their alternatives: individualism, indeterminacy, stasis, etc." (ibid., 21–22). This approach also introduced the idea of "dialectics," and the fusion or hybridity that Kushner imagines and stages in *Angels* in regards to many issues, such as gender, identity, sexuality, and spirituality.

This type of listing and interactivity was also utilized in other parts of my virtual environment, especially as I felt that this kind of communal engagement (albeit an online community) seemed more in the communitarian spirit and theme of *Angels in America*. One area that my students particularly enjoyed was in "The Theatre of Fabulousness" section and illustrated the self-conscious movie and genre referencing crucial to the work of Ludlum and the Ridiculous Theatre. Students were asked to leave lines behind in the room that were references to other movies, plays and television shows, such as Prior's from *The Wizard of Oz*, when he emerges from his trip to heaven and says, "I have just had the most remarkable dream. And you were there. And you . . . And you" (Kushner, 1994, 140); or, his reference to *A Street Car Named Desire* during the same scene, when he says, as a thank you to the Mormon mother Hannah Pitt, "I have always depended on the kindness of strangers" (ibid., 141). At times the references are visual as well as verbal, such as Prior's references to the "I'm ready for my close-up, Mr. Demille" scene in *Sunset Boulevard*, during his mutual dream scene with Harper, a scene that is informed by the dialogue, as well as the costume suggestions (ibid., 30); or the "*Very* . . . Steven Spielberg" that is exclaimed by Prior just before the end of *Part One: Millennium Approaches* (ibid., 118). However, this is hardly even a fraction of those available (the Internet Movie Database, www.imdb.com lists close to three dozen), and thus provided great sport for the students—and me.

When I first used this virtual world for the teaching of *Angels in America* in an Advanced Playwriting class immersing themselves in a semester's worth of Kushner's work, the emphasis was decidedly on reading the play for what might be useful to a group of working playwrights. However, when I taught a class on production dramaturgy the following semester, where *Angels* was one of the plays that could be used for a final project, a further potential application for this virtual platform became apparent. In their book *The Process of Dramaturgy: A Handbook*,

Scott Irelan, Anne Fletcher and Julie Felise Dubiner write in their chapter on "Conceptual Frameworks" about the "ways in which the production dramaturg might encourage:

> "Ways of seeing" the relationship between the written text and the eventual live performance event. [. . .] In the long run, detecting or perceiving patterns within the play text—linguistic, aural, visual or otherwise—can not only push the rehearsal process towards a greater sense of coherence but also can enhance the resulting live performance event.
>
> *(Irelan et al., 39)*

As part of their final project, the *Angels* dramaturgy group was asked to consider developing portions of the *Angels* virtual environment that might be useful for dramaturging a production of the play. Certainly the sheer amount of background material that is included in this virtual environment would serve well the research needs of any production of the play. However, I believe that as this technology develops, the potential of this virtual environment for illustrating corporeality and simultaneity, as it charts patterns—much like those Irelan, Fletcher and Dubiner describe in the chapter mentioned above—is great in serving play production through a kind of virtual dramaturgy.

While I still believe that the experience of engaging with *Angels in America* through a virtual environment may be in contradiction with some of the greatest intrinsic values of the play, after working with this emerging technology to help students examine the drama, I found this platform useful for teaching of a number of the most important aspects of the play, especially its use of simultaneity, its emphasis on the relationship between presence, space and community, and its consideration of progress. Furthermore, this *Angels* virtual environment might become a way through interactivity for an extended online classroom community, including those who may enter our virtual world as guests—"the kindness of strangers," as Prior references—to help with the enormous amount of background material necessary for beginning to study—or being part of a production of—*Angels in America*.

Notes

1. John Moore, "Most important American plays: Overall voting," Denverpost.com (February 14, 2011), [www.denverpost.com/theater/ci_14397304?source=email]. Arthur Miller's *Death of a Salesman* was voted as the first most important American play in the same survey.
2. Kushner is referencing here the closing lines of the play where in the epilogue "Bethesda," as set at the Bethesda Fountain in New York's Central Park, Prior Walter, in a direct address to the audience, says, "Bye now. You are fabulous creatures, each and every one. And I bless you: *More Life*. The Great Work Begins" (Kushner, 1994, 148, italics in the original).

3. For additional reading on the influence of Brecht on Kushner and *Angels in America*, see Janelle Reinelt, "Notes on *Angels in America* as American Epic Theatre," and Art Borreca, "Dramaturging the Dialect: Brecht, Benjamin, and Declan Donnellan's Production of *Angels in America*," both in *Approaching the Millennium: Essays on Angels in America*, edited by Deborah R. Geis and Steven F. Kruger (Ann Arbor, MI: University of Michigan Press, 1997), 234–244 and 245–260.
4. Brecht's *The Good Person of Szechwan*, which Kushner has adapted for the stage.
5. For a more detailed description of Brecht's theories and techniques that are described here see "A Short Organum for the Theatre," in Bertolt Brecht, *Brecht on Theatre* (New York: Hill and Wang, 1977), 179–208.
6. For a more detailed discussion by Kushner on the Ridiculous Theatre, see "The Theatre of Fabulousness," Interview with David Savran, in *Essays On Kushner's Angels*, edited by Per Brask (Winnipeg: Blizzard Publishing, 1995), 139–143). For plays and manifestos of the Ridiculous Theatre, see Charles Ludlum, *Ridiculous Theatre, The Scourge of Human Folly: The Essays and Opinions of Charles Ludlum* (New York: Theatre Communications Group, 1993) and *The Complete Plays of Charles Ludlum* (New York: Harper Collins, 1989). For further research on the Ridiculous Theatre, excellent starting places include, David Kaufmann, *Ridiculous! The Theatrical Life and Times of Charles Ludlum* (New York: Applause Books, 2005) and Stefan Brecht, *Queer Theatre* (London: Methuen, 1986).
7. Kushner is speaking specifically here about Benjamin in the context of Brecht's play *Mother Courage and Her Children*.

12

FROM MUDS TO METAVERSES

The Past and Future of Immersive Literary Worlds

Robert Rozema

> The boundary between the inner and outer world breaks down, and the literary work of art, as so often remarked, leads us into a new world.
> *Louise Rosenblatt,* The Reader, the Text, the Poem *(1978, 21)*

My five-year-old son is a video game expert. To be truthful, he is only accomplished at one game—*Lego Star Wars* for the Nintendo Wii—but his mastery of this single game astonishes me. As the title suggests, the game combines the universes of *Star Wars* and Lego: players construct Star Wars characters and play through Lego versions of the entire movie series. It may sound complicated and even improbable, but the first time you duel Lego Darth Vader in the Lego Death Star, you will understand its appeal, even for adults. Most five-year-old boys, like my son Aidan, find the game irresistible.

Like many video games today, *Lego Star Wars* requires more than just quick fingers and good hand–eye coordination. Each of its forty-plus levels presents complex, multilayered puzzles that players must solve in order to advance. There are primary objectives—say, rescuing Princess Leia from the detention block on the Death Star—but also ancillary goals, such as finding hidden objects, accumulating Lego bricks, and beating a time limit. Players with enough bricks may purchase additional game characters and replay levels, or even construct their own *Lego Star Wars* characters for use within the game.

That a five-year-old has solved all of the levels on *Lego Star Wars* is amazing to me, though I am sure his prowess is not atypical. What intrigues me more, however, is the way *Lego Star Wars* permeates his other forms of narrative play. When Aidan plays with his miniature *Star Wars* figures—mostly mine from the 1970s and 1980s—for instance, he uses video game vocabulary from video games: "Dad," he'll say to me, "let's go to the Hoth level with Luke and Han."

In addition to *level*, my son uses *click on* for *select*, as in "just click on the action figure you want to play with, Dad." Our reading of *Star Wars* books is similarly colored by video game play: "I'm Luke Skywalker in this book," Aidan says when we sit down together to read. "Who are you?"

For Aidan, these narrative forms are seamlessly connected. He understands the difference between playing *Lego Star Wars* and reading a *Star Wars* book, but the two experiences are on the same narrative spectrum. He already knows, intuitively, the main argument of this book: that immersive literary worlds can enrich the reading and study of literature, and that literature can inform immersive worlds in meaningful ways. This idea is not new—literary texts and immersive worlds have long been interconnected. This chapter will recount the recent history of that interconnection. The story begins in the late 1970s, in England, with a digital environment called a MUD.

Early Multiplayer Environments: MUDs and MOOs

The first MUD—or Multi-user Dungeon—was designed by in 1979 by Richard Bartle and Roy Trubshaw, two computer science students at Essex University. Bartle and Trubshaw created MUD1, a multiplayer adventure game in which players, connecting over the university computer network, could explore a virtual dungeon, interact with each other, and slay monsters (Haynes and Holmevik, 2001, 2). Unlike *Lego Star Wars*, MUD1 was entirely text-based: players saw written descriptions of rooms, and moving or talking was a matter of inputting the appropriate text commands, most often verb–object imperatives, as in "go south," "take sword," or "kill troll." The computer then displayed a response ("You move south") and a description of the new location ("You are in a spacious cavern") or event ("A giant troll charges at you!"). These textual descriptions may now strike us as quaint, given the stunning high-definition graphics of modern video games.

Still, these early MUDs were compellingly simple. In MUD1, a player advanced by killing mythical monsters and finding treasure, thereby gaining the experience points necessary to move to the next level of the dungeon. If a player persevered, he became a high-ranking wizard, the ultimate goal of the game. In its overall aesthetic and objectives, then, MUD1 relied largely on stock fantasy settings, characters, and plot lines. Not surprisingly, Bartle and Trubshaw admit they were at least partially inspired by *Dungeons and Dragons*, a paper-and-pencil role-playing game loosely based on fantasy fiction. "The main roots were in the imaginations and personalities of their early designers," Bartle claimed in a Gamespy.com interview. "The links between *Dungeons and Dragons* and virtual worlds aren't causal, but they are related: I didn't write MUD1 because I played *Dungeons and Dragons*; rather, I played *Dungeons and Dragons* and wrote MUD1 for the same reason—I like creating worlds" (Jones, para. 8). The fantasy world of MUD1 quickly gained international popularity, as players installed the game on computer networks in Norway, Sweden, Australia, and the United States (Haynes and Holmevik, 2001, 2). The growth of ARPANET, the precursor to the Internet, allowed MUD1 to spread even more quickly.

Soon software companies recognized and capitalized on the connection between fantasy literature and computer gaming. At MIT, researchers developed *Zork*, a fantasy adventure game originally designed for network play. When *Zork* became popular on the MIT network, MIT formed its own company, Infocom, and marketed the game for home computers in 1980. Similar to MUD1, *Zork* required players to explore a dungeon, hunt for treasure, fight trolls with a magic glowing sword, and solve elaborate riddles. *Zork* and its Infocom sequels (*Zork I, Zork II, Zork III, Enchanter, Sorcerer, Wishbringer, Spellbreaker, Beyond Zork, Zork Zero*) came to dominate single-player adventure games in the 1980s (Galley, paras 6–13).

Both MUD1 and the *Zork* games were decidedly plot-driven games. The purpose of playing was well defined, derived from formulaic fantasy fiction and role-playing games: rescue the maiden, slay the dragon, finish the quest. While making for dramatic game play, this narrative structure did limit the range of actions players could perform. A player might successfully "kill troll," for example, but a more creative command like "train troll to fetch the newspaper," was outside the scope of possibility (Murray, 79). Despite these restrictions, however, role-playing MUDs—sometimes called adventure MUDs—flourished in the 1980s. If the abundance of Tolkien adventure MUDs created during this era is any indication, it is safe to say that MUDS are well rooted in fantasy literature.

A different sort of MUD came into being in the late 1980s. In 1989, James Aspnes created TinyMUD at Carnegie-Mellon University. Unlike MUD1 and its descendants, TinyMUD was not based on a fantasy theme. As a result, TinyMUD differed from earlier MUDs in two significant ways. First, TinyMUD focused on social interaction rather than on plot. Instead of killing trolls and discovering treasure, players chatted in virtual coffee shops or engaged in what became known as "Tinysex." Secondly, TinyMUD allowed players to shape the MUD environment itself by adding rooms and other virtual objects, as well as by programming these objects to perform certain functions. Though this required some expertise, a TinyMUD player might create a virtual room for himself, stocking it with couches and chairs for other players to use. In previous MUDS, only game designers and wizards enjoyed these privileges. With its social flavor and creative environment, TinyMUD was enormously popular and by matter of consequence, short-lived. Thousands of players expanded the world until the original server was overwhelmed. TinyMUD survived only one year, but its legacy was more lasting: a new form of multi-user interaction known as the social MUD (Haynes and Holmevik, 2001, 2).

Less tied to fantasy literature than the adventure MUD, the social MUD made multi-user environments more available and attractive to a wider audience. The user population of TinyMUD and similar social MUDS exploded, eventually leading to the creation of LambdaMOO, the most popular social MUD of all time. Developed by Pavel Curtis in 1990 at the Xerox Palo Alto Research Center and Stephen White of Waterloo University, LambdaMOO's chief selling point was its user-friendly, object-oriented programming language that gave players a great deal of creative power. LambdaMOO (for Multi-user Domain, Object Oriented programming) allowed players to build and program virtual objects with only minimal programming knowledge. A LambdaMOO player might design, for example, a virtual cat that wanders from room to room, greeting other players with a friendly meow. To cope with the growth problems of TinyMUD, LambdaMOO players were restricted to a limited quota of memory space to fill with their own virtual creations. Additionally, Curtis created a hierarchy that granted higher-ranking players (wizards, programmers, and builders) more abilities and space than lower-ranking players (players and guests). LambdaMOO eclipsed even TinyMUD in popularity, as thousands of players from around the world logged in to participate in the new electronic community (Haynes and Holmevik, 2001, 3).

As LambdaMOO thrived, it became the subject of academic interest. Increasingly, researchers used LambdaMOO to examine issues such as identity play and social interaction. In *Life on the Screen: Identity in the Age of the Internet* (1995), for example, Sherry Turkle contends that virtual communities such as LambdaMOO allow players to re-identify themselves through electronic discourse. "As players participate," she writes, "they become authors not only of text but of themselves, constructing new selves through social interaction . . . MUDS provide worlds for anonymous social interaction in which one can play a role as close to or as far away from one's 'real self' as one chooses" (Turkle, 12). In this sense, role-playing in social environments like LambdaMOO differs from role-playing in plot-driven MUDS. Instead of assuming a fairly fixed persona (e.g. a dwarf), a social MOO participant, as Turkle notes, is likely to have a more fluid sense of identity, regularly experimenting with age, gender, personality type, and self-description (ibid., 185).

At approximately the same time, a third type of multi-user environment was being developed. If MUD1 can be labeled an adventure MUD and LambdaMOO a social MOO, then this final type might be called an academic MOO. The first such MOO was MediaMOO, created by Amy Bruckman in 1993. A doctoral student at MIT, Bruckman designed MediaMOO as "a place to come meet colleagues in media studies and related fields and brainstorm, to hold colloquia and conferences, and to explore the serious side of this new medium" (MediaMOO par. 1). Like TinyMUD and LambdaMOO before it, MediaMOO flourished, though its chief demographic was far removed from the role-playing aficionados of early MUDs. Its success prompted other institutions to develop their own MOOs for academic, professional, or educational purposes. BioMOO (1993) was created by Weizmann Institute of Science as a virtual meeting place for biologists; Diversity MOO (1993) was designed as a multi-disciplinary educational MOO;

AstroVR (1993) was built to host researchers interested in astrophysics and astronomy (Haynes and Holmevik, 2001, 3).

It bears remembering that these early academic MOOs, like their predecessors, were still entirely text-based. In the years immediately prior to the World Wide Web, MOO participants connected to MOOs via telnet, a text-based protocol for remote computing. Alternatively, MOO users might connect via a software client, a specialized program for accessing MOOs. In either case, the MOO interface was textual, making it necessary to type text commands to navigate and talk in the MOO, build and describe new objects (*digging* in MOO language), and program objects. The learning curve for these text-based environments was therefore steep: in most text-based MOOs, learning the basic commands for moving and speaking meant spending significant time in the MOO or asking more experienced players for assistance. In less friendly MOOs, a novice unfamiliar with basic commands might be labeled a clueless newbie. Creating and programming objects involved more work still, since doing so required a specialized subset of MOO language. Non-programmers can find this language "frustratingly arcane," as Howard Rheingold and others have observed (Rheingold, 165).

Despite these limitations, text-based MOOs held a particular fascination for progressive educators in the composition field, who were experimenting with digital environments as writing spaces. Throughout the early 1990s, a small pocket of composition theorists used MOOs as virtual writing centers, insisting that MOOs empowered marginalized students, established local and global writing communities, promoted collaborative writing, enabled effective peer revision, and supported constructivist pedagogy. Salt Lake Community College, for example, established the "Virtual Writing Center MOO" in 1994, as a space where students could talk with other writers, share their writing with classmates or tutors, collaborate in the construction of the MOO, and even take distance-learning writing classes. Dakota State University developed a similar MOO, the Virtual Trojan Center MOO, which was used for distance education, technical writing, and composition courses (Haas and Gardner, 1–4).

At the University of Missouri Columbia, Eric Crump developed ZooMOO as an online writing center. Reflecting on this experience, Crump suggests "a tool like MUD profoundly changes the landscape of education and how we write our way around the new terrain" (Crump, 177). More specifically, Crump believes that MOO technology can radically reshape how a writing center works. To take advantage of this technology, writing centers must take what Crump calls "an evolutionary leap," and redefine their very purpose. Traditionally, Crump suggests, writing centers have been places where students, oftentimes desperate, seek authoritative advice from expert writers, in hopes of securing a higher grade on a writing assignment. MOOS can certainly accommodate the sort of conversations that typically occur in a traditional writing center. In fact, a MOO may be a better location for discussions about writing, since MOO participants converse by writing. Conversations occur in real time and are remarkably similar to the oral communication that would happen in a writing center. Best of all, MOO discussions can be logged—they are *capturable*, in Crump's language—and transcripts can be given to students for further review. Still, Crump believes that a MOO has greater value. Instead of merely relocating the writing center into cyberspace, the MOO lets a "community of writers" develop and grow. Unlike the traditional writing center, whose purpose is "treat texts" wounded by the red pen of composition instructors, a MOO writing community builds relationships, becoming an egalitarian place "for congregations of writers" (ibid., 185).

Detractors of these writing environments, however, emphasized two chief difficulties. First, the synchronous conversation lauded by Crump and others can be fragmented and hard to follow, particularly when multiple users occupy the same room. It such situations, several conversations can occur simultaneously, making extended, coherent discussion nearly impossible. Second, operating within a text-based MOO is non-intuitive, since users must know a set of cryptic commands to perform the most basic of functions. New users often felt lost or paralyzed in these environments. Making matters more challenging, the help feature on most MOOs requires prior knowledge of MOO vocabulary.

Ultimately, frustrations with text-based MOOs led to the creation of friendlier MOO interfaces in the mid-1990s. If the text-based MOO could be compared to the DOS, the command-line operating system of the late 1980s and early 1990s, then the MOO interfaces that developed in conjunction with the World Wide Web (1994) might be likened to the Windows operating system. Windows provides users with a graphic interface, through which they can directly manipulate files and programs without an extensive understanding of the inner language of the computer. By comparison, several MOO programs designed in the mid-1990s added a Windows-like interface, in the hope of making the MOO environment less daunting for students and educators alike. One example is the Pueblo MOO client, released by Chaco Communications in 1996, which divides the interface into a large reading pane where text descriptions are displayed, a command bar, a clickable exits pane to help with navigation, and a typing pane, where users enter what they want to say. Notably, the reading pane may also include media, such as images or hyperlinks, making the entire interface act like a web browser (Hass and Gardner, 351).

Similar in design to Pueblo, the enCore interface was developed in conjunction with LinguaMOO, a virtual environment created in 1995 at the University of Texas at Dallas. Originally a text-based MOO, LinguaMOO was established for two purposes: first, to serve local instructors and students in the university rhetoric and writing program; second, to host a more global community interested in researching and collaborating on projects focused on the humanities and the electronic media. In light of these goals, LinguaMOO co-founders Cynthia Haynes and Jan Rune Holmevik began work on a more user-friendly interface that would "make it easy for educators to set up and run educational MOOs [and] make it

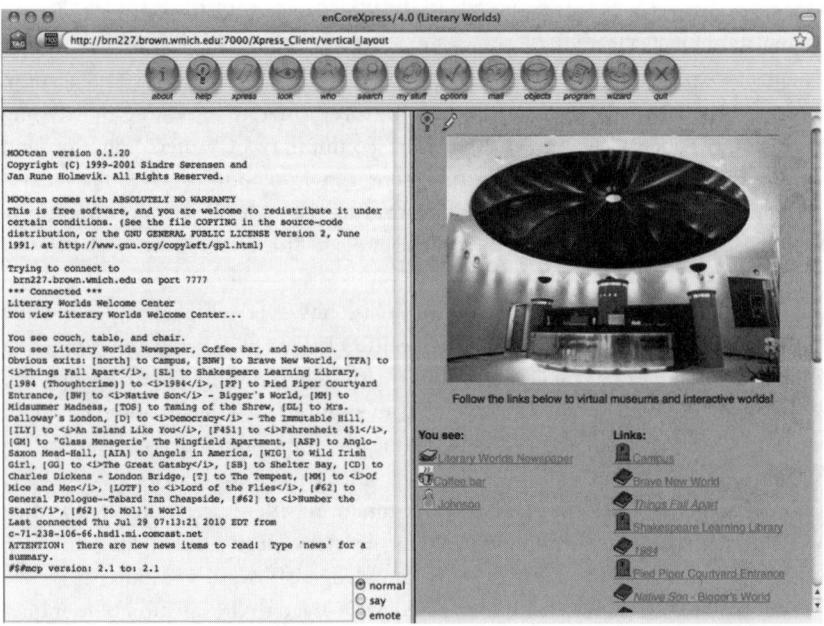

FIGURE 12.1   Literary Worlds Welcome Center

as easy and convenient as possible for users to access and utilize the MOO technology" (Haynes and Holmevik, 2004).

The resulting interface, enCore, debuted in 1998. As shown above, the enCore interface (version 4, released in 2004) splits the screen into two large panels, framed on the top and bottom by two horizontal bars. The left side of the screen represents the traditional text-based MOO, where room descriptions and events are displayed entirely in text. The right side of the screen, however, looks and functions like a web browser. It may include graphics that correspond to the textual description of a room. In this case, the opening screen of the Literary Worlds MOO includes an image of the Welcome Center. The Welcome Center is described in text, on the left side of the screen.

The right side includes navigational links to other rooms in the MOO, including a campus, and multiple story worlds within the MOO: *Brave New World*, *Things Fall Apart*, and *1984* among them. Importantly, these links may also connect to web resources, such as the full electronic text of *Brave New World* or a CNN report on human cloning. Additionally, the right side includes iconic representations of the virtual objects present in the room, including a coffee bar and a newspaper. Users may manipulate each of these objects by clicking on them. Clicking the coffee bar icon, for example, yields instructions on how to drink a virtual cup of coffee. At the top of the screen is a collection of buttons that users may click to perform basic commands, such as viewing other players, creating rooms or objects, or asking for help. The text pane at the bottom of the left screen allows players to talk (say "hello"), emote (scratch head), or issue text commands (drink coffee from bar). Taken as a whole, the split-screen interface and its accompanying command bars provide a more visual, intuitive MOO environment that capitalizes on the resources of the web.

By design, the enCore interface is intended for educational purposes. Teachers may create virtual classrooms and equip them with a variety of helpful instructional tools, such as a recorder that logs MOO conversations, a projector that displays web slide shows, and a VCR that plays transcripts of lectures or study guides. The classroom itself contains virtual versions of desks and blackboards, and may be locked for privacy. Many institutions utilized enCore as an educational tool, since enCore is an open-source program and free to download and install. At one time, many ran academic MOOS using the enCore interface. These included the Old Pueblo MOO at the University of Arizona, the Villa Diodata MOO at the University of Maryland, the Pro-Noun MOO at Purdue University, and the NCTE MOO (LinguaMOO Home). Many of these MOOs defined themselves primarily as writing spaces, virtual versions of the writing centers typically available on campus. Other MOOs were designated more specifically for second language learning. Still other MOOs classifed themselves more broadly as multipurpose educational, professional, or research spaces (LinguaMOO Home).

Even in the heyday of academic MOOs, however, only a handful had literary leanings. This is somewhat surprising, given the MOO's roots in fantasy fiction as well as its capacity to create immersive environments through graphics and other media. In fact, only two MOOs were specifically associated with literary works. The first, the Villa Diodati MOO (aka the Romantic Circles MOO), simulated the Swiss village of Cologny, where Lord Byron owned a home in 1816. Here, according to legend, Byron, Percy Shelley, and Mary Shelley competed against each other in a story-telling contest, a contest that eventually yielded Mary Shelley's *Frankenstein*. Users of the Villa Diodati MOO (now defunct) could stroll through the Swiss village, visiting the school, the village square, the waterfront, or even Maison Chapuis, the cottage rented by the Shelleys in 1816. Each of these locations was represented textually and graphically to immerse players more fully in the literary world—the waterfront had streaming video of Lake Leman. The overall geography of the Villa Diodati was fixed, with no opportunity for users to expand its setting. The MOO also encouraged role-playing: users could "become a *Frankenstein* character," and play a game entitled "In Pursuit of *Frankenstein*." Villa Diodati did offer a variety of resources to aid in critical discussion of Romantic literature. The MOO linked directly to electronic editions of the *Romantic Circles Praxis Series*, a renowned collection of Romanticism scholarship (Villa Diodati MOO Home)

The second literary MOO, cmc MOO (University of Bergen) still hosts the *A Midsummer Night's Dream* Project. The project is intended to replicate "the fictional landscape in Shakespeare's play" and "the Globe theatre and the surrounding streets of Southwark as they were in Shakespeare's time." Users may visit select locations from the play itself, wandering through Titania's Bower and a Wood near Athens. Notably, these settings are closely tied to the language of the play: from a Wood near Athens, for example, users may follow links "over hill," "over dale," "through bush" or "through briar," phrases taken from the Fairy's speech in Act 2.1. At Titania's Bower, lines from Act 2.1 even begin to scroll down the text side of the screen, replicating the scene in real time. These textual elements evidence a close connection between the *Midsummer* Project and the play. Users have no opportunity to role-play as characters, though as Juli Burk argues, the MOO possesses "inherently theatrical elements" (Burk, 233). The *Midsummer* Project does offer users a variety of analytical tools for reading the play, including a hypertext version of the play and links to Shakespeare resources (cmc MOO). At the time of writing, the cmc MOO was still operational.

Both the Villa Diodata and *Midsummer* Project are literary MOOs. Working from these two examples, we might suggest that a literary MOO combines the role-playing aspect of early adventure MOOs, the creative potential of social MOOs, and the educational purposes of academic MOOs. More specifically, a literary MOO replicates the setting of a literary work, allows users to expand and elaborate on that setting, encourages character-based role-playing, and provides a rhetorical space for critical analysis of the literary work.

This book has detailed the development and use of the literary MOO called Literary Worlds, now likely the most trafficked academic MOO on the web. Its authors have illustrated how this kind of immersive environment may be used for literary study. As impressive as the Literary Worlds MOO project is, the MOO platform may not represent the future of immersive literary worlds. Today, most universities have discontinued or abandoned their MOOs, often in favor of newer, graphical environments such as *Second Life*. The remainder of this chapter explores how these environments (often called MUVEs for "Multi-user Virtual Environments") have also tried *with limited success* to replicate rich literary worlds.

The Rise and Fall of the Metaverse

The idea of an alternate, three-dimensional reality that is accessed through a computer network has become a popular meme in recent science fiction and film. The term *metaverse* itself is taken from Neil Stephenson's 1992 cyberpunk novel *Snow Crash*. In the novel, Stephenson depicts an immersive digital environment that is populated by *avatars*—another Stephenson coinage—or virtual representatives of human beings. The metaverse has its own economy, industries, currency, and crime. The hero of the novel, Hiro Protagonist, is a renowned hacker who attempts to locate the source of a mysterious computer virus—Snow Crash—that is infecting avatars in the metaverse and their human controllers in reality.

Just as fantasy fiction shaped the development of early adventure MUDS, science fiction works such as *Snow Crash* have informed the next wave of multi-player environments—rich, graphical environments rendered by high-speed video cards and delivered through broadband Internet connections. The most popular of these environments, *Second Life*, was brought online by Linden Labs in 2003 and now has about 750,000 residents from all over the world. While membership has declined over the past three years, thousands of users still spend time in-world every day, shopping in virtual strip malls, conferencing with business colleagues, socializing with friends or special interest groups, developing their own real estate, patronizing real-world businesses such as Adidas or Disney that have set up shop in *Second Life*, playing in-world games designed by other residents, or frequenting casinos and sex shops.

Unlike many other online worlds that immerse players in already-developed worlds, *Second Life* is almost entirely created by its residents, who buy virtual land and use in-world tools to build houses, vehicles, clothing, and more. This last fact has given rise to an in-world economy, as users buy and sell virtual objects of their own making. For a few, wealth inside of *Second Life* even translated to real-world gains. During the height of its popularity, *Second Life* saw real-world businesses establishing corporate presences in *Second Life*, hoping to attract new customers. Tellingly, most of these businesses have been abandoned in the past two or three years, as interest in *Second Life* waned. But the ability to create and inhabit the virtual world has important educational implications. Many educators have stayed in *Second Life*, using its unique space to develop virtual learning environments.

The most successful in-world educational environment is the New Media Consortium (NMC) Campus. The campus features a large amphitheater where streaming video can be shown on giant screens, plazas, conference rooms, lecture halls, art galleries, teaching spaces, and other accommodations. Both practical and whimsical in design, the campus hosts academic conferences, provides classroom space for NMC members, and gives virtual researchers a place to conduct fieldwork. Today, there are over 3,000 members of the NMC, with most from universities, though non-profit organizations and corporations are represented as well. Members meet regularly on campus to discuss teaching and learning in *Second Life*, to share their expertise, to tour new educational simulations, and to plan for upcoming conferences and events.

The NMC campus is one part of a larger educational community in *Second Life*. Initially, Linden Lab encouraged educators to use *Second Life* for academic purposes. It created a Second Life Campus where university faculty could teach virtual courses free of cost. These courses, taught by professors from a range of institutions, focused on topics uniquely suited to the setting: these include cyber-culture, architecture, new media studies, game design, theater, and more. Over fifty universities developed virtual campuses, including Seton Hall, Massachusetts Institute of Technology, Colorado Tech, the University of Southern California, the University of Pennsylvania, Harvard, and San Diego State University. Many of these campuses are adjacent to the NMC campus, allowing for dialogue and collaboration between institutions. And while some campuses have fallen into disuse as the hype over *Second Life* cooled, the growing body of scholarship on teaching and learning in virtual worlds indicates that these will continue to play a role in higher learning for the foreseeable future (Salmon, 535). Indeed, some colleges are developing their own virtual world platforms or installing an open-source version of *Second Life*, called *OpenSimulator*, on their own servers (Young, 2).

Second Life itself hosts a number of literary worlds that are worth exploration. Many of them may be placed into the categories already established in this text —there are compelling examples of role-play stages, world building, virtual tours, and virtual museums, all based on literary works. Shakespearean worlds within *Second Life* often combine dramatic performance with historical information. At the Globe Theater, for example, users can tour a virtual Globe Theater and watch performances of Shakespearean plays staged by the Metaverse Shakespearean Company. Students of Shakespeare might also visit the neighboring Renaissance Island, where they can walk through a Renaissance-era town and learn more about life in the sixteenth century. At the *Macbeth* simulation, visitors can wander through an eerie landscape while sinister voices whisper key lines from the play.

Other literary environments include virtual museums, where visitors can explore the lives and works of writers. Several virtual museums have been created by the Literature Alive organization, a "non-profit educational group dedicated to creating open access immersive interactive literary experiences in the *Second Life* platform to foster a lifelong love of learning through a lifelong passion for reading" (Ritter-Guth). One such museum is the Edgar Allen Poe House, where users walk through what looks to be a nineteenth-century brick building, stopping to read works by Poe and to examine other Poe resources. Literature Alive has also designed literary environments based on the work of Dante and Chaucer, though these spaces are no longer available in *Second Life*. In these environments, students were meant to experience the setting of a text in a more dramatic, visual, and immersive way.

The most ambitious literary world ever conceived, however, may have been *Arden: The World of William Shakespeare*, a Shakespearean virtual world originally designed in 2006 by Edward Castronova of Indiana University. Castronova envisioned a Shakespearean world, complete with its own in-world economy and cast of characters—rogues, wenches, sailors, princes, clowns, grave-diggers, and all the other inhabitants of Shakespeare's colorful stage. More interested in virtual economies than literary texts, Castronova hoped to build the world (using the Metaverse platform), amass a large number of users, and watch the in-world economy grow—I say, put money in thy purse! The *Arden* project was funded by a sizable grant from the MacArthur Foundation, and like *Second Life*, generated a great deal of hype. But Castronova discovered that the cost of creating *Arden* far exceeded his expectations, and after an incomplete version of the game was released as a plug-in for *NeverWinter Nights* in 2007, the project was put to rest in 2008.

Arden may have failed, but its failure is instructive. While it is enormously expensive to create a convincing multiplayer game, money is not entirely to blame for the downfall of *Arden*. The gameplay itself, as Castranova conceded, was not engaging. "We failed to design a gripping experience," he admitted in an interview with *Wired Magazine* (Baker, 2008). Players were bored by the quests and wanted to battle monsters, not chat with other players about Shakespeare. Castronova has since turned his attention to designing a more game-like version of *Arden*—and exploring existing multiplayer games with literary elements, such as *Lord of the Rings Online*. That Castronova has turned to developing more game-like environments is telling, reflecting larger cultural fascination with video gaming. Once considered the province of teenage boys, video games have gained mainstream acceptance and are now increasingly popular among girls, boys, adults, and even the elderly. It may be that console-based video games, then, best represent the future of immersive literary environments. It is to this future that we now turn.

Gaming and the Future of Literary Worlds

A recent *Pew Internet and American Life* survey found that while only 6 percent of American adults have created avatars for virtual environments such as *Second Life*, the majority of adults (53 percent) play video games. About one-quarter of adults play games on the web, through consoles or computers. Teens, not surprisingly, are even fonder of online gaming, with 76 percent of teens playing games over the Internet (Lenhart). A typical 16-year-old might come home from school, turn on his Xbox, and battle two or three friends—also playing from their homes—in the popular first-person shooter *Halo Reach*.

Notably, most video gaming does not occur in massively multiplayer online games (MMOGs)—the kind of environment that hosts thousands of players simultaneously, such as *EverQuest*, *World of Warcraft*, or, if Castronova realizes his vision, *Arden*. Currently, only about 10 percent of video gamers of all ages have spent time playing MMOGs (Lenhart). This is not to minimize the cultural importance of such games: *World of Warcraft*, a fantasy-based MMOG, has millions of players. In this richly rendered world, players join with others to complete quests. They acquire weapons, wealth, and experience along the way, leveling up as each task is met. Online play also involves challenging other players and guilds—often logged in from the other side of the world—and defeating monsters that inhabit the game world. Most MMOGs are subscription-based: players must buy the software and pay monthly fees, though some MMOGs are now offering free play as interest and membership decline.

Again turning to fiction, we can see MMOGs represented as the future of online gaming: in the young adult novel *For the Win* (2010), for example, Cory Doctorow tells the story of four young gamers who work in digital sweatshops in developing countries. Known as gold farmers, the players use their formidable skills to amass huge wealth inside of MMOGs, and then sell their virtual gold for real money—pawning high-power weapons and armor to new players who are eager to level up without spending hours on the game. In Doctorow's fantasy, the young players unionize in-world in an attempt to gain better working conditions and higher salaries.

As compelling as this fictional world may be, the widespread adoption of MMOGs will likely remain unrealized, as peer-to-peer gaming—the teen playing *Halo* on his Xbox against a select group of friends—continues to grow at a rapid rate. As *Wired Magazine* recently reported, peer-to-peer file transfers, which include console-based gaming, now account for just as much Internet traffic as the World Wide Web (Anderson, 125). To clarify this point: the Internet is really a collection of hardware—a network of computers and data pipelines that are interconnected for information exchange. The web is one piece of software that runs on this hardware. It happens to be highly successful software—so much so that *Internet* and *Web* are used interchangeably. But video game consoles such as Xbox 360 or Sony PS3 also use the very same Internet pipelines to connect players to one another. The majority of console games, in fact, come with *multiplayer* or *online* modes, which typically allow several or even dozens of gamers to compete against one another. This type of gaming has grown so popular, as *Wired* points out, that it is consuming an increasing amount of Internet traffic.

What this means for immersive literary environments can be distilled to the following: until now, literary environments have run on the web. Those described at length in this book run on a specific web application called enCore, itself a combination of a web browser and an earlier Internet application—a text-based network protocol called telnet. As an application, the web has never been particularly good at rendering literary worlds, despite the successes of the Literary Worlds MOO and the emergence of the graphical metaverse. But today and into the future, literary environments will likely exist in video game form, played over the Internet through consoles or, increasingly, mobile devices such as the iPad or iPhone. As a means of accessing a literary environment, then, the web browser may soon be obsolete.

A current example may serve to illustrate the future of literary gaming. First, in 2010, the video game company Electronic Arts released *Dante's Inferno*, a first-person shooter based on the *Divine Comedy*. Developed for the Xbox 360, Sony PS3, and Sony PSP, the game takes players through the nine circles of hell. But where Dante could only observe, and let's face it, gloat over those suffering eternal damnation, players of *Inferno* can eviscerate demons all the way down to Lucifer himself. The high-definition graphics are stunning, rendering the underworld with exquisite and often disturbing detail, and rightly earning the mature rating for intense violence, blood and gore, nudity, and sexual content. And while the game is only loosely based on the epic—I don't remember Dante beheading Cerberus, for instance—there is no denying that playing the game gives students of the poem imagery to draw upon or even critique as they read. Dante, after all, provides plenty of his own explicit imagery:

> Cerberus, cruel monster, fierce and strange,
> Through his wide threefold throat barks as a dog
> Over the multitude immers'd beneath.
> His eyes glare crimson, black his unctuous beard,
> His belly large, and claw'd the hands, with which
> He tears the spirits, flays them, and their limbs
> Piecemeal disparts.

(6: 13–19)

Electronic Arts also offers at least minimal information about the poem on its support site, where players can sample key passages and learn more about the life of Dante. This is likely not enough for traditionalists who abandon all hope when they see the *Divine Comedy* transformed into a gory video game. Indeed, drawing comparisons—or contrasts—between the settings, characters, and plots of the text and the video game may be superficial, even wishful thinking, at a time when gaming is up and reading is down. It may not be enough to say that both games and texts are narratives with their own set of conventions.

A more promising connection between video games and texts may lie in the *experience* of game play itself. As James Gee has long argued, playing video games often involves complex, sophisticated thinking. Gee believes that "Digital games are, at their heart, problem solving spaces that use continual learning and provide pathways to mastery through entertainment and pleasure" (Gee, 2009, 65). Gee is not promoting the educational use of commercial games such as *Grand Theft Auto IV*, but suggesting that deep, serious games might draw on some of the same learning principles embedded within such highly entertaining games. In particular, Gee believes deep games, like commercial games, should do two things well: first, allow the player to learn the rules of the game (and its associated content); and second, motivate the player to keep on playing—and hence, to keep on learning.

Applying these principles, we might imagine, for example, a serious game based on *Lord of the Flies*, in which players must survive on a desert island by managing resources responsibly. Gee observes that effective games have rules that players can manipulate for their own advantage in order to accomplish goals. If one rule of the *Lord of the Flies* game is, for example, that the fire must be kept burning at all times, then a savvy player might assign this task to a rival or an underling, freeing himself for further exploration of the island and longer hunting expeditions. Each player would also have a degree of what Gee calls *microcontrol—*

or the ability to affect a single or multiple elements within the game. In *Lord of the Flies*, this might mean making weaker units (e.g. Piggy and Simon) tend the fire or gather water, while stronger units go hunting or battle rivals. This degree of microcontrol already exists in games like *Age of Empires III*, in which a player delegates different tasks to not two or three elements, but dozens of farmers, builders, hunters, warriors, explorers, and more. The overall effect of microcontrol, Gee explains, is an intimate connection with the virtual world.

Another crucial component of any successful commercial game is that it must create conditions for experiential learning. As Gee explains, experiential learning can only occur if the player is given goals, can interpret her actions in light of these goals, is given immediate feedback, can apply learning to future problems presented by the game, and can learn from other players. In the *Lord of the Flies* simulation, for example, a player might be given the main goal of surviving. The easiest path toward survival, the player might reason, is keeping the signal fire lit and attracting a rescue ship. This might cause the player to delegate a large number of survivors to fire-keeping, a move that eventually leads to the starvation of all of her units, since the few remaining hunters not attending the fire cannot possibly secure enough game to keep everyone alive. During the next round (or the next game), the player wisely divvies up fire-tending and hunting equally. She might also explain her strategy to her fellow player collaborating with her against a computer opponent.

A deep, serious game also offers players particular *affordances* and *effectivities*, according to Gee. An affordance is an in-world element that allows a certain action to be taken. The *Lord of the Flies* island might be populated by wild pigs, for instance, that can be killed and eaten for nourishment. An effectivity is an ability or skill that a player must master in order to take advantage of the affordance. So, only a player who has trained his hunting units (by killing a certain number of birds or snakes) can kill the wild pigs. This in-world condition, in turn, shapes the way the player sees the game: at the outset of the game, he might dedicate a disproportionate number of his units to hunting birds and snakes, hoping to become an experienced hunter more quickly. By consequence, his units populate a portion of the island where snakes and birds are plentiful—far from the signal fire, and far from rescue.

Of course, turning *Lord of the Flies* into a resource-management video game does not ensure that players understand the novel any better than they would without the game, even if the above learning principles are part of the game play experience. In other words, there may not be anything specifically *literary* about the game—unless we take Gee's final point about deep games into account. Every game, Gee suggests, has a *designer story*—the main plot of the game that the developers want all players to experience. But more interestingly, every game also has a *trajectory story*—the actual path the player takes to accomplish the game goals. Good commercial games can be completed in dozens, even hundreds of different ways, and each choice made affects the player and her in-world identity.

If I chose the dark side in *Jedi Knight: Dark Forces*, for example, I can still defeat the final villain of the game, but I will have likely done so with a certain abandon, killing and robbing innocent civilians along the way. To return to *Lord of the Flies*: eliminating my fellow players might guarantee my own survival, but at what cost? If the game allows me to kill off those I am supposed to help, should I make this choice? This kind of moral dilemma—self-interest v. collective good— is at the heart of the novel, and ultimately, any serious game based on the novel would ask players to think about this question. In doing so, they would move from their concrete game-world experience to an abstract plane of thought— just the place where William Golding and English teachers would like them to be (Gee, 2009, 65–77).

Gee has written elsewhere on the idea of the *trajectory story*. In *What Video Games have to Teach us about Learning and Literacy*, he explains that players of video games—first-person games in particular—negotiate three overlapping identities. The real-world identity is the flesh-and-blood player, whose likes and dislikes help to determine the *virtual identity* or *avatar* he develops to represent himself in the game world. The *projective identity* is the final version of the virtual identity— the entity that the real-world player wants his virtual identity to become (Gee, 2003, 50). Each player, then, makes choices in the game, creating a trajectory story that shapes his projective identity.

The parallels to reading are striking. When I read a novel, my real-world self typically identifies strongly with one of the characters. Often the protagonist, this character might be likened to the virtual identity in Gee's schemata. And so, I become Katniss Everdeen—and Katniss becomes a version of me, as my predispositions and life experiences shape my perception of her. At the same time, I have hopes for this character: I want her to act in certain ways, prove herself to be morally responsible, if just a little cheeky. This is my *projective identity* for the character. And strangely, even when I reread a text, knowing exactly how a character acts, I still hope that character will do what I would do. Some part of me begs Macbeth not to kill Duncan; some part of me tells George that he and Lennie are going to be okay this time.

This experience of identifying with characters may be the most promising for serious video games. Can we design literary games that enrich our understanding of character by putting us in similar situations and asking us to make similar choices? Can we design games that help us understand our reading processes more fully, by revealing how our own biases shape our perception of characters and what we wish for them? And can we make these literary games compelling by embedding good learning principles within them?

These questions bring us back to the beginning of the chapter: my five-year-old playing *Lego Star Wars* on the Wii console: immersed in the digital world, he identifies with characters effortlessly and readily blurs the lines between game play and fiction. His experience, I believe, may well represent the future of literary virtual environments.

13

ON THE BUILDING OF WORLDS

Kevin Jepson

"Just start," Dr. Webb said.
"Once the words start appearing on the page it gets easier," he said.
Ha! OK, here goes. . .

When we are immersed in a good book we have a sense, a mental image, of the spaces and characters that exist in the story. The author's text fires our imagination to build such spaces for us. When we really "get into" a book, the plain text on the page can inspire a more powerful "virtual reality" than any computer graphics system yet invented.

Who hasn't wanted to look around behind the action, to explore the worlds in which authors stage their stories?

Personally, I always wanted to roam around in Moria when I first read *Lord of the Rings*. Still do actually. I'm always a bit disappointed when I look at artwork and watch movies based on a favorite author's book, because these works are what others see in their minds, not really what I see! Now, not being a graphic artist myself, there isn't any way that I could generate the images I have in my mind to share with anyone else. Not that I need to particularly, but, if I wanted to discuss or teach a literary work there needs to be some way to bring more to the discussion than simply what others have "said" about it. Literary Worlds can do that.

In some sense, like an artwork or movie, Literary Worlds combines the way text can show us what an author wants us to see, yet with the ability to choose a path around in the space. To be able to look around inside an interpretation of a world an author has created can be a compelling addition to our understanding of a literary work. We can wander in the spaces, role-play as characters, interact with the environments and societies of the books, or delve into the meanings and history of the works themselves. Doing so does not replace the reading of the book, and it is not "spoon fed" to us as a movie is; instead, a literary virtual world is interactive and participatory, augmenting our own internal sense of the world the author has created.

Literary Worlds is based on LambdaMOO, described by its creator, Pavel Curtis, as:

> a network-accessible, multi-user, programmable, interactive system well-suited to the construction of text-based adventure games, conferencing systems, and other collaborative software. Its most common use, however, is as a multi-participant, low-bandwidth (text based) virtual reality.
>
> *(Curtis, 1997)*

Systems based on LambdaMOO are typically called MOOs, which stands for "Multi-user Object Oriented systems." Literary Worlds is thus a MOO, with the addition of a system of web-based components that add many capabilities including: the display of images and sounds, a graphical navigation system, utilities and tools for building virtual spaces, and an interface to the Help system and even internal email. This system, programmed by Jan Rune Holmevick and Cynthia Haynes, is collectively known as the enCore Learning Environment (see the Resources section at the end of the chapter, note 1).

If you have looked through some of the projects built at Literary Worlds, as described elsewhere in this book, you will have seen some exciting ways that this system has been used for the teaching and exploration of literature. Literary Worlds was created as a place in which to conduct such explorations. However the enCore environment can be used for much more than that. It has been used for teaching programming languages (Resources, note 2), role-play gaming, social modeling, group communications, and even a reproduction of the city of Rome where the navigation is all in Latin! (Resources, note 3) The uses to which a system like this can be put are almost unlimited.

The enCore environment is in the public domain so it can be used and modified for free. It uses a fairly simple system, accessible from anywhere on the Internet. In other words, anyone can build in enCore, including those who want to make their own literary worlds and there is *no complex programming required.*

This chapter will help you with the process of building "worlds" and "virtual environments" in a system such as Literary Worlds. It is not a "How To," as in a cookbook full of recipes, nor is it strictly a technical manual that documents the details of how everything works. It should be looked at more as a guide and information source for learning the process of designing and building. First, I will discuss issues to consider if you are interested in designing and creating a space at Literary Worlds, or at other MOOs for that matter. Next, as an example I will illustrate how I created a space within my own world at Literary Worlds.

Finally, I offer information on more advanced topics including using graphics and multimedia, the transcript system, a discussion on the types of users and an introduction to Objects, as well as providing links to references and resources available online.

Before Building

To get the best use out of a system such as Literary Worlds there is a learning curve. Yet, unlike most other computer systems, it is possible to build a virtual space quickly, without any complex programming at all. A useful mental model of this system is that of a series of spaces like the rooms of a house. These spaces are connected by exits and entrances such as doors and hallways. In the early days of text-based multi-user systems, most of which were games, the model was typically that of a cave or dungeon through which the players moved to role-play and explore. There are echoes of this in the titles of the highest level users, still known a "wizards," and normal users, who are still described in the documentation as "players." Even the process of building is still referred to as "digging." The inclusion of multimedia files like sounds or music, links to online resources such as videos, graphics and even games, as well as the richness of web page designs for modern browsers, adds interest and new ways to display information for users. These more modern capabilities are layered on top of a richly interactive text-based system, where players can communicate with others in real time for discussions or role-play.

The enCore Learning Environment is designed for non-technical users to be able to set up and build virtual environments without having to write anything that looks like computer code. Unless you want to that is. In which case whole new possibilities open up using the MOO programming language, also called simply "Moo code," the same language that the entire system is built in. Literary Worlds is still a LambdaMOO-based system, so with a little code work, you can use all the wealth of objects and tools created by thousands of builders, programmers and wizards since LambdaMOO was developed by Pavel Curtis (Xerox Palo Alto Research Center) and Stephen White (Waterloo University), way back in 1996 (Resources, note 4).

Elsewhere in this book seven distinct styles of literary virtual world have been described: intertextual map, virtual tour, role-play stage, alternative reality game, second world, textual riff, and virtual museum. I highly recommend logging in to Literary Worlds as a guest to peruse all of them, when you are thinking about how you would like to build a space of your own. Of course there is no need to build your world entirely by yourself. One of the ways to involve our students is to have them create the spaces as part of a class project. This was the approach taken by Robert Rozema in his world based on Huxley's *Brave New World*.

Assuming you have had a chance to see some of the worlds that others have created, either by reading this book or going to see for yourself at Literary Worlds, there are some design elements to keep in mind when preparing to build spaces of your own. The interface is described in Chapter 1 (see Figure 13.1).

As cool as Literary Worlds is as a place to wander and experience the various worlds already created, it is being used mostly as an educational tool. Building such a space needs some thought as to how you would like your students and other users to interact with the spaces created. Questions to consider:

- What do I want my students or visitors to get out of the space?
- What interactions do I want to encourage? Chat, role-play, discussion, exploration, etc.?
- How important is the graphical information displayed in the right-hand web panel relative to the text information in the left-hand MOO Panel?

Figure 13.1 shows what a user sees when entering my world *Shelter Bay* from the "Welcome Center." There are more blue buttons across the top of the panel than in Figure 1.1 because I have entered the world as my builder character and thus have additional powers (more on that soon). Visitors get a textual description of the space first, with the only graphic a small image indicating whether it is day or night. Since users will tend to concentrate their attention on the graphically rich web panel, to bring more balance to the way users interact with my spaces I have deliberately emphasized text over graphics. Below the

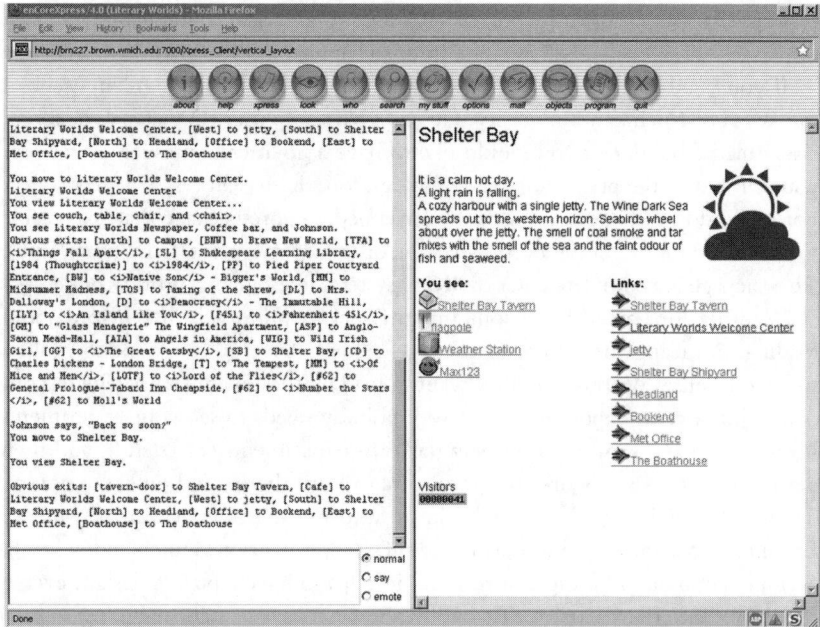

FIGURE 13.1 enCore Builder Interface

description are the two lists: objects on the left, labeled as "You see," and exits on the right, labeled simply as "Links." Because I am trying to show off objects, I have changed some of the object icons from their defaults. This serves to attract the user's attention, but without distracting them from the textual description of the space. When an object is clicked, the flagpole for example, the page displayed has a different emphasis than the space the object is in. The object's page has a prominent graphic as well as the textual description. By clicking a link to an object the user is essentially "looking at" that object. A more prominent graphic rewards the user and serves as an anchor for them to examine it in more detail. This can include reading the information in the MOO panel as well.

Chatting between the players when connected is probably the most common form of interaction and, as you might expect, when many players are chatting at once the text panel fills up and the text begins to scroll off the top. Chatting is not the only form of interaction. Players can interact with the objects in the worlds as well. Some objects can be used as props to enhance interactivity or display information. A number of ready-made educational objects are available, such as classrooms, blackboards, projectors, etc. Other objects can be created to enhance the "atmosphere" of the space.

Designing and Building a Space at Literary Worlds

If you would like to play with the system, to see what it can do and also to experiment with creating a world of your own, then I have a simple bit of advice, the same that I received at the start of this chapter . . . "Just start."

If you want to create a world at Literary Worlds contact Dr. Allen Webb at the Western Michigan University. He can give you a user ID that will be a user class called a builder. If you would like to have a go at creating such a space for yourself, but in the privacy of your own desktop, there is an easy way to do that. For a Windows PC get a copy of the Ewebbed enCore package that is available to download for free at the Barn (www.encore-consortium.org/Barn/news.html). This package is a complete enCore MOO system, like Literary Worlds, but empty and waiting for you to build something. Did I mention it is *free*? (More about loading and using the Ewebbed package below). Even if you want to build a space at Literary Worlds, you may want to load up the Ewebbed package to your own computer to experiment (that way nobody needs to see your experiments if they don't work out). I find being able to experiment, create stuff, and then destroy it if it doesn't work, is a good way to learn the ins and outs of a system. There is an online guide available on how to use the interface of the enCore Learning Environment (www.alamo.edu/sac/english/lirvin/4guide/index.html).

Like any building project in real life, it helps to have a plan, a design, even a rough outline. I have found that one of the best ways to start designing a space is to draw it out on paper. In my case it is often quite literally on the back of an envelope! This doesn't need to be a work of art or an exercise in drafting. Simply getting ideas out, in the form of a map, on paper, can clarify what goes where in the space you want to build. In many ways, such a sketch is the equivalent of a plot outline for a story, or maybe the stage layout for a play.

If you are a new builder, the first thing to do is create a room so you have a place to start building from. The first time you login to the system with your builder ID, you will be taken to a default start room. At Literary Worlds this is the "Literary Worlds Welcome Center"; using the Ewebbed package it is the "enCore Starting Point." There are two ways to create a new space: a graphical tool and the text-based command line. The graphical tool is the easiest to use in some ways, but the command line is more flexible and I'll talk more about that in a bit. If you click on the light bulb "help" icon on the main menu bar you can access the main "help" system, showing the commands and options available to builders. Any place you see a light bulb icon there is help available.

As a builder you cannot really hurt the system by creating things or building rooms, and you can always "recycle," that is destroy, anything you create if it doesn't work the way you want it to.

To create your first room, let's call it "My Room," using the graphical tool, click on the "Objects" icon on the toolbar. This will bring up the "Xpress Object Editor."

This tool can be used to create any of the standard objects available, including rooms. We select "Create New Object" and then "Rooms" from the list on the right-hand side. Select "Generic Room" from the list. Type the name "My Room" into the box. Clicking "Create" will add the new room. You will get a pop-up message confirming the creation of the room and also letting you know that it has helpfully made it your new home and moved you there. That means the next time you login you will be in that room. You can always return to your home from anywhere by typing "home" in the text box. Notice the line that says "Connect my new room to" followed by a drop-down box. If you have existing rooms this box will list them, making it easy to add the exits and entrances between your rooms. These show up as links on the right-hand side of the web panel.

That is all there is to it. You could go on and create all the rooms you need, if you wanted too, from this same screen.

There is, as yet, no text description for the room. You can add in the text description for the new room by selecting the name of the room from the list of objects on the right and choosing "Edit Description" from the drop-down list. This will open a text box into which you can type the description you want to use. You can make a rich textual description of your room that provides visitors with information about its size, what the user notices and senses about it and so on, and/or the "Edit Multi-media Content" option allows you to decorate your room with photographs, graphic images, or even video or sound file links (see below). The "Edit Appearance" option can change the fonts, colors, background image, and the color for the text of the links. Descriptions and decorations to the room can be changed at any time. Click the light bulb icon for help with these options.

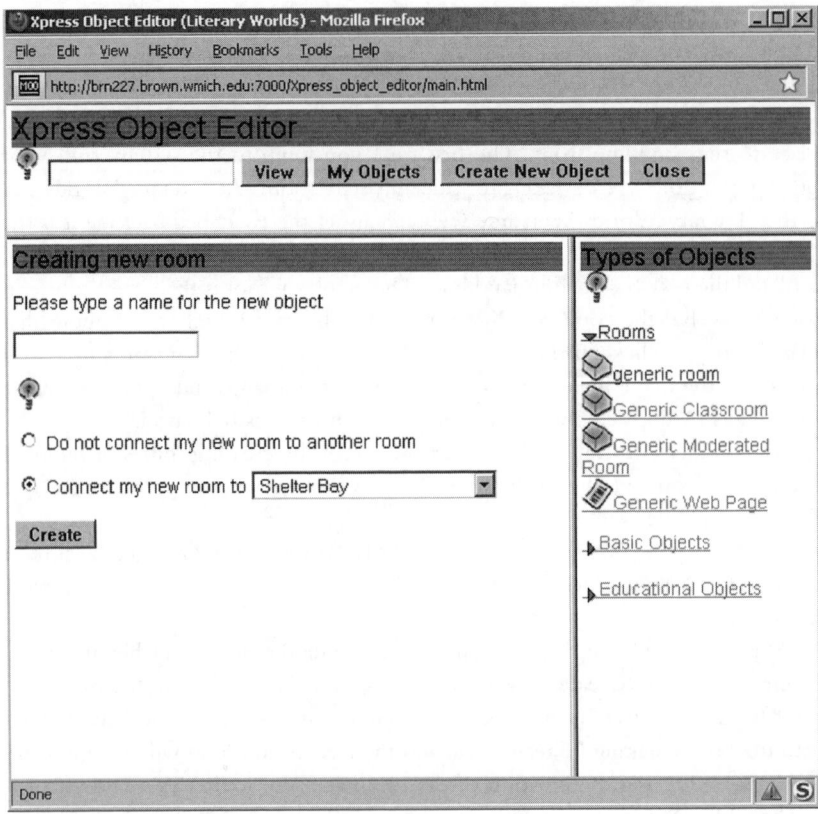

FIGURE 13.2 Xpress Object Editor

An alternative, and perhaps more complicated way, to create rooms is to avoid the Xpress Object Editor and to "dig" them by using the command line (the box on the lower left of the interface). To dig your first room using the command line type "@dig My Room" in the input box on the text panel. The system will respond with a message saying something like, "my room (#186) created." The number in the brackets is the object number of the room. You can then go there by typing "@go #186." If you wanted to make the new room your home, type "@sethome," which will set the new room to be your new starting point when you next login. To create additional exits and entrances between rooms, use the "@dig" command mentioned above. As long as you are the owner or builder of the rooms the procedure is easy. Using the object number of the room, type a command such as "@dig direction to room number." (You can get the number of a room by typing "@examine here" when you are in the room.) When you click the "Look" icon on the toolbar, or type "look" on the command line, the display will refresh and you will see a new exit to the room you created.

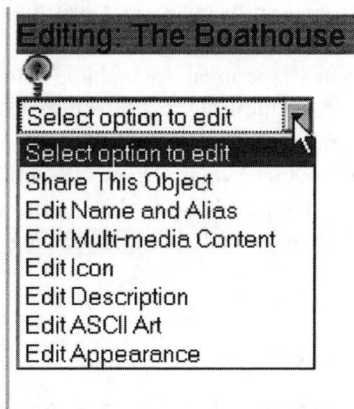

FIGURE 13.3 Edit Appearance

If the room you want to link to is not yours, but is owned by someone else, the system will respond with a message saying you must ask the owner of the room to add the exit. Typically, as a builder at Literary Worlds you will build all your own spaces so this isn't a problem until you want to link with the Welcome Center. Once you want to open your space to guest access, a wizard can add the exit for you. How do you make an object to put in the room? Exactly the same way as you created the room, only instead of selecting a room from the list in the Object Editor choose "Basic Objects" and "Generic Thing." Like a room, an object can include a textual description, images, links to sound and video files, and so on. Special programs can be created for objects, as described in the next section.

When you create an object it will be in your "inventory," that is you will be holding it. You can drop it by typing "drop object name" on the command line. This will move the object into the room with you and it should then show up on the web panel as an object under the "You see" column. You can pick up an object by typing "get object name" on the command line or by clicking the "Take this Object" icon on the web panel.

Building is fun and easy to do, but things don't always go as planned, so being able to clean things up is useful as well. To remove the new room, use the same Object Editor, click "My Objects" and then select the room title from the list of objects on the right-hand side. Then click the "Recycle this Object" button. The system will ask if you *really* want to destroy this object and, if you agree, it will remove it and clean up the exits. Note that there is no way to undo the deletion, so be careful.

If you would like a more detailed example of designing and building a space at Literary Worlds, check out my article at the Barn at encore-consortium. org/Barn/files/docs/Designing_spaces_lw.pdf.

I hope that I have been able to give you a feel for the process of creating spaces at Literary Worlds. Once you have a builder ID, or a copy of the Ewebbed package, I encourage you to experiment by building spaces and creating a world of your own. New ideas for educational and literature-related worlds are always welcome at Literary Worlds.

In the next part of this chapter I will briefly discuss some of the more technical aspects of MOOs such as Literary Worlds. This information is not needed to build worlds, however I hope you will find it useful once you have had a chance to experiment a bit.

Using Images and Multimedia Files

Image and media files give character to your virtual world. Graphics can be added to the description portion of any room or object. You can change the alignment and size of the resulting image by selecting the appropriate option. Keep in mind that the image will be resized to fit the size selected so it is better to resize your image first and make sure it will look like you expect once displayed. The graphics files are actually displayed from links to the file hosted elsewhere than in the MOO itself. Builders at Literary Worlds can be given space to host their graphics and multimedia files, which is convenient. Files can also reside at any web-accessible hosting service. Since the images displayed via these links function as a traditional image on a web page, it is important to keep the files as small as possible to speed up the loading of the page. Multimedia files, such as MP3-based sounds and QuickTime files, can be linked as well. The web panel will trigger your browser to load the appropriate plug-in to display the content of the file. Large sound files and QuickTime files may slow the display. Since Literary Worlds is an educational system, most images can be classed as "fair use," but use appropriate netiquette and obtain permissions as necessary.

Another use of graphics is to change the icons that are displayed for objects listed on the web panel. The default icons are nice, but generic, and eventually every page starts to look the same. Every object has the same icon by default. All containers have the same open box icon, every note has the same piece of paper icon, etc. The "Edit Appearance" option can change the graphic that is associated with the object when displayed on the web panel as a link. These files should be small and similar in size to the default ones and can be hosted anywhere, in the same way as the other graphic files. You can also change the icon associated with your player (avatar) as well.

Creating a Classroom

There is a special class of room designed to enhance the text-based interaction when you have many players online at the same time. This room is a "Generic Classroom." One of the uses of the classroom is as a lecture space. The students sit at desks or tables. They only see chat from people at their desk, but everybody sees text from the instructor. There is a blackboard onto which the instructor can add notes that all the players in the room can see by typing "look blackboard." While none of this is displayed on the web side, as the display does not change, it certainly enhances the control of the text scrolling through the MOO panel. One of the uses for this room is as a staging area prior to a role-play activity. From the Xpress Object Editor select "Generic Classroom." There is help on using the features of a generic classroom available by clicking the light bulb icon.

If you have an existing room and would like to change it to a classroom contact a wizard and they will be able to make that change for you.

Using the Transcript System

The transcript system at Literary Worlds helps teachers to track and record their students' interactions when they are using the system. This is a useful tool, because if your space is more than a few rooms in size it becomes difficult to monitor everybody when you have a full class logged in at once. Transcripts are records of what the players have "said" when chatting during a session, and the transcript also records the paths the students take as they move around the space. At the end of the session a copy of the transcript is emailed to the teacher and the student. The transcript record can be used to assist with evaluating student participation in online sessions. The transcript is also an excellent tool for fine tuning your world. If the students never use a particular room, for example, maybe a description change might be needed to attract their attention.

The easiest way to try out the transcript system is to logon as a "student." This player class is unique to Literary Worlds and is a guest player with the transcript capabilities added. There are thirty student logins available to use at one time.

Typing "Student" as the user ID on the login page will bring up a blank text panel and a black web panel with a message for the player to type "start" on the command line. The system will then request the name of the player, their email address and their instructor's email address. The transcript system will check to make sure the email address entered is a valid format, but doesn't check to make sure it is an actual email address, so it will request confirmation from the player. Once the player confirms that the address(es) are correct the player is moved to the Reception Center from which they can enter any of the worlds.

If your world has defined players that represent specific characters, like the players in *The Village of Umuofia* for example, then a wizard can add the transcript capability to your player.

Player Classes

Most building at Literary Worlds is done by players called "builders," but there are other classes of players at Literary Worlds; wizards, programmers, players' guests, and ghosts.

Wizards are the administrators and master builders at Literary Worlds and other LambdaMOO-based systems. They control the very existence of the system because they are the only ones who can shut it down. There are usually very few of them. Literary Worlds has ten wizards, including me; this is actually an unusually high number for a MOO. Typically a MOO might have only two or three. Wizards at Literary Worlds are a great resource for teachers, builders and programmers and we are usually available, when we are online, for help if needed. (Wizards willing to assist builders and programmers working in Literary Worlds have their contact information linked on the Resources page and in the help available inside Literary Worlds itself.)

Programmers are players who write the code that controls how objects and spaces work inside the virtual environment. This code, stored in programs called "verbs," is written in the language known as MOO code. MOO code is a true programming language and is capable of some pretty complex things. I will briefly discuss some aspects of programming below. Programmers have the ability to create new types of objects as well as modifying the way existing objects behave.

As I said above, most of the spaces at Literary Worlds are created by builders, with the assistance of wizards if code for something special, and cool, is required. Builders can build spaces, traditionally known as "digging." There is a rich set of utilities and tools available to builders for the creation of virtual environments. You will be given a builder-class ID if you decide to build a world at Literary Worlds.

Players are the reason for doing all this. They are the online representations of our students, the actors in our virtual plays, the virtual characters in the online versions of the literary worlds we build. They cannot change or build anything, but they are free to wander, explore and interact with other players. Unlike most purely web-based systems however, they can also interact with objects inside the system. There are many objects that the players can "look at," "pickup," and use that will do things in the spaces. Players are "persistent" in that they continue to exist even when the user has logged off. I recommend that you get a player ID as well as your builder ID. This makes it easier to see what your students will see when they use the system. For some worlds it makes sense to create players that represent characters in the works that the world is based on. These players could have pre-defined descriptions and be placed in specific places within the world. This is very valuable for worlds where role-playing is an important part of the interaction. A wizard can help with the creation of these players for you.

Guests are not always enabled at MOOs, but they are available at Literary Worlds. Guests are temporary players who can explore and interact with the environment much like players, but they are not persistent. They are often used to test drive a new environment before bringing a class to visit, for example.

Finally the lowest level of users in enCore-based systems such as Literary Worlds, which have a web-accessible display, are what I call Ghosts. These are users who are viewing the web displays of our worlds *without* logging into the system. Ghosts cannot interact with the system because all they see are the web pages displayed on the right-hand side. However, it is possible for programmers to detect that their objects and pages are being looked at from the web by a ghost, which has some interesting implications for future work. The "Who is currently online" link on the login page is an example of an object inside the MOO designed to be viewed by ghosts from outside.

Advanced: Objects and Programming

> Objects are, in a sense, the whole point of the MOO programming language. They are used to represent objects in the virtual reality, like people, rooms, exits, and other concrete things.
>
> *Pavel Curtis*

At the start of this chapter I mentioned that MOO stands for a "Multi-user Object Oriented" system. What follows is a brief introduction to objects. While not necessary to build spaces at Literary Worlds, some familiarity with the "Object Oriented" structure that underlies the system is useful in understanding the way the system works. Most of the builders who have created virtual worlds at Literary Worlds have not used or taken advantage of the object oriented system, but those who have are able to create more advanced processes in their world.

Everything in the MOO is an object. Every object has a unique number assigned to it and each object can be referenced by that number. This is important for programmers because many objects can have the same name: there may be hundreds of exit objects named "Out," for example, so being able to work on the exit #186 avoids confusion. For builders, the main reason to worry about the object numbers is when using the Object Editor, to make sure you are changing the description, and other properties, for the right thing. Or, as we saw when using the @dig command, for creating exits and entrances between rooms.

Objects also enforce the separation of "data" and "process." Let's look at a real world object, an apple, and see how reality handles this separation of data and process. Our apple, an object, has certain physical properties (data) such as weight, color, taste, mass, chemical composition, dimensions, etc. It also has properties that place it in space and time, such as latitude/longitude, source, age, height above sea level, etc. An apple also has meta properties such as who owns it, what species it is, how ripe it is, and so forth. To model an apple in the MOO one would want an apple object to have values for some subset of these properties, enough to distinguish our apple object from an orange object, or a rock object for that matter. There are probably some properties of an apple that are unique to that fruit and represent its "appleness." Frankly, none of the ones I listed above are unique to apples. While the values of the properties change depending on whether we are dealing with an apple or an orange, they are common to fruit. Some do not apply at all, and really make no sense, if we are talking about a rock.

If data are the properties of an object then process is about what actions can involve the object. Data is what an object is, process is what an object does. There are two sides to process: actions that an object does, and actions that get done to it. The reason I make that distinction is that much of the processes that involve objects do not care what the object is. If we look at our apple object, for example, it really does not need any uniquely apple processes to distinguish it from an orange or a rock. In the real world our apple object is subject to many processes such as the passage of time, being picked up, being dropped, falling from the tree, being eaten, or rotting on the ground. All of these are actions that the environment does *to* the object, they apply equally to the orange and some also apply to the rock. Again if we were to model an apple in the MOO, we really don't need any specific apple processes added as long as an appropriate process exists in the environment to manipulate the object.

In a MOO like Literary Worlds, the program code that models and keeps track of all the interactions is stored on the objects as small programs called "verbs." These MOO code programs control all the processes and interactions between objects. If every object we modeled had to have its own set of properties and verbs it would quickly become impossible to create anything more than a very small number of objects in a very simple environment. Also, the interaction between all these unique processes would quickly overwhelm the ability of any system to keep track of what is happening to who and with what result. Needless to say, creating useable environments in such a system would be very complex and would require pretty significant programming skills. Luckily the object-oriented nature of MOOs vastly simplifies this.

MOOs are "virtual reality systems," that is, they model physical objects and processes inside a computer-generated, hence "virtual," space. MOOs use a simple logical model of reality, which says that every object is related to everything else and shares common properties with other objects. The more similar two objects are the larger the number of properties they share. There is a kind of logical map that links every object with objects of like kind. The map is a tree that tracks the way objects share properties and processes. The tree is also known as the "Object Hierarchy."

To see how this works let's use our apple as a starting point and examine it from this logical model point of view.

If you think of the properties of an apple listed above, you could probably separate out those that apply to oranges but not rocks. These properties define a logical object that we will call a "generic fruit." Both apples and oranges share most of these properties even if the values might change. Now, if we compare the common properties between a generic fruit and a rock we will find that there are some properties that are common between them too. These common properties define another logical object that we will call simply a "generic object."

Rather than keep track of all the properties for each object, the MOO model says that each branch of the tree "inherits" the properties of the object below it.

So both the rock and generic fruit inherit all the properties of the generic object, and the apple and orange inherit the properties of the generic object *and* those of the generic fruit but *not* those of the rock.

You can see that to create a new object, a banana say, one could look at the properties of the logical nodes of the tree and figure out pretty quickly that such an object needs to be a generic fruit with some modified values for the properties plus any properties that are unique to "banananess" [sic].

So how does process fit into this structure? Here the value of the simplifying logical model really becomes apparent. If one does the same kind of comparison between the logical objects in the tree, only this time comparing processes instead of properties, it becomes apparent that every one of the objects we have defined share processes and that very few are unique to the individual objects. For example we can look at, pick up, throw, drop, smell, taste (?), listen to, kick, etc., any of them! In the MOO an object also inherits the processes (verbs) of the objects below it in the hierarchy. The MOO programmers only have to write the code for these processes on the generic object and it is available for all the child-objects based on it.

This is the key to easily building our worlds without writing any MOO code at all. The code has already been written when the generic objects were created. If we want a container we create a child of the "Generic Container," using the Object Editor or the command line, and we instantly get all the programs needed to open, close, describe, and use this new container. Builders need not worry about the programming at all, as it has already been done.

There are several tools available at the Barn (www.encore-consortium.org/Barn/program.htm) to examine the way the object hierarchy works. The Ewebbed package has these already loaded and I encourage you to load it up and explore if you are interested in how the properties and verbs are linked to the objects. The Ewebbed package also displays the MOO code of the verbs, if you are curious about what the programming actually looks like.

The full set of manuals for working with MOO Code is available from the Program Editor inside Literary Worlds. They can also be downloaded from the Barn (www.encore-consortium.org/Barn/files/docs/lambdamoo/moo-prog-man.zip).

Using the Ewebbed enCore Package

New ideas for educational and literature-related worlds are welcome at Literary Worlds. If you want to create your own MOO universe, you can download the Ewebbed enCore package from The Barn (see Resources) in the Programming section. Screenshots of the Ewebbed system in use are available at the link. The Ewebbed package works on any Windows PC and does not need any complicated installation. You don't need to be an administrator on the PC to load it, which makes it useful for classroom use. Simply unzip the downloaded files onto your desktop and open the "Ewebbed-enCore-V4-a1" folder, double click the "start" file and follow the prompts.

The first thing it asks is whether you want to start the included web server. This is not necessary if you just want to browse the objects and look at the MOO code, but if you want to login to the MOO using the enCore login, as at Literary Worlds, the web server is necessary. The package was compiled to help people who wanted to work with MOO code and is designed as a single user system, but it is also a complete enCore MOO setup that will allow you to play around in the privacy of your own computer. It can be used for small multi-user setups and testing as well, with some simple technical changes to the network settings and the firewall rules on the PC.

There are several options listed once the Ewebbed system is loaded: (1) Open the Object Browser; (2) Start a TKMOO session; (3) Start Xpress and Login; and (4) Close the menu. The first option brings up a web page in your Browser that shows the "Object Hierarchy" on the left and details about the objects, including properties and verbs on the right. This is a very useful tool if you want to see what the code actually looks like. The second option brings up a text-based MOO client called TKMOO and logs you in as a programmer. This is an excellent tool for working in the guts of the MOO. TKMOO has a code editor and object browser that can be used for programming. TKMOO is my primary MOO client when programming. The third option brings up the enCore login screen, called Xpress, which is the normal login screen like the one at Literary Worlds. If the web server has been loaded you can login here using the ID of "Programmer" and the password "newprog" and you have an empty MOO to build stuff in, just like Literary Worlds. All three options can be open at once. To shut the Ewebbed package down simply choose option (4) and then close all the open windows. Note that if you want to keep any building you have done you need to use the TKMOO client and click "Connect" and choose "Localhost Wizard." Then type "@shutdown now" and wait a couple of minutes for the MOO to save the file and close.

Resources

The Barn at encore-consortium.org/Barn/news.html is an ever-growing collection of information on enCore MOOs like Literary Worlds. The Barn has objects, utilities, cheat sheets for coding, links to interesting papers, and the LambdaMOO programming manuals. The Ewebbed enCore package is available for download here as well.

1. www.encore-consortium.org. The enCore Consortium is a direct outgrowth of the enCore MOO Project started in 1997. The enCore Project has made significant progress in making MOO technology available to the average user by providing a modern graphical user interface. Much of the command-line

functionality of text-based MOOs has been translated into a friendlier point-and-click interface common to modern computer applications. One of the enCore Consortium's goals is to continue the development of the enCore program, making MOO functions work more smoothly and powerfully in a web environment.

2. www.euler.vcsu.edu:7000. This is a MOO-based education platform that is devoted to computer science instruction, especially learning programming. It is the creation of Curt Hill with the help of many friends.

3. www.vroma.org. The VRoma Project is first and foremost a community of scholars, both teachers and students, who create online resources for teaching the Latin language and ancient Roman culture. The two major components of the project are its online learning environment (MUVE: Multi-User Virtual Environment), which has received several favorable external reviews, and its collection of Internet resources. The VRoma MUVE requires logging on as a guest or through your personal character and password, but all the web resources are freely accessible on the Internet. Project co-directors: Barbara F. McManus (The College of New Rochelle) and Suzanne Bonefas (Rhodes College); web design: Barbara F. McManus and Daniel Jung (University of Bergen).

4. www.en.wikipedia.org/wiki/LambdaMOO.

CONTRIBUTORS

Cara Arver is the chair of the English Department at Centreville High School in Centreville, Michigan, where she has taught for eleven years. In 2007, she published an article on virtual worlds in the *English Journal*, and she has presented for the Michigan Council of the Teachers of English. She holds an MA degree in English from Western Michigan University.

Jennifer Barns graduated from Western Michigan University in 2009 with a Bachelor's degree in English and History education and the Arabic language. She presented at the Bright Ideas English Education conference in 2006 about her virtual world *The Virtual Tempest*, and plans to continue developing this project. She currently resides in the Detroit area.

Linda Dick's MA in English from Western Michigan University focused on children's literature. She is a published poet and essayist and her chapter on disability portrayal in twentieth-century girls' fiction is included in *Unseen Childhoods* (Bettany Press, 2009). In 2003 she was awarded a Fulbright Scholarship, and spent a month in Senegal, West Africa, studying folklore and oral tradition practices. As an online instructor, she teaches composition and literature at several universities and serves as a writing center tutor.

Meghan Dykema earned her Bachelor's degree in English from Western Michigan University in 2010. While at WMU, she worked as the Assistant Director of the Writing Center and presented at conferences for the International Writing Centers Association, the East Central Writing Centers Association, and the Michigan and National Councils of Teachers of English. She currently lives in Daytona Beach, Florida.

Steve Feffer is an Associate Professor in the English Department and Creative Writing Program at Western Michigan University where he teaches playwriting and contemporary drama. Steve's published plays include *The Wizards of Quiz* (Dramatists Play Service), "Little Airplanes of the Heart" in *Best American Short Plays* (Applause Books) and *Plays from Ensemble Studio Theatre* (Faber and Faber). Additional plays and performance pieces have been published by Heinemann Books and New Issues Press. His writing on theatre and performance has been published in journals, including *Comparative Drama*, *Prooftexts*, and the *Journal of Popular Music Studies*, and in the book *Interrogating America Through Theatre and Performance* (Palgrave/Macmillan).

Joseph Haughey teaches 8th grade English Language Arts at Blythe Middle School in Blythe, California. He is also writing his doctoral dissertation in English Education at Western Michigan University, examining the history of Shakespeare instruction in American schools and colleges. He has taught undergraduate university courses in composition, introductory literature, Shakespeare, and ELA pedagogy.

Kevin Jepson maintains the support web site for the enCore Consortium, is an active wizard at Literary Worlds and other enCore MOOs, and has been a MOO programmer since the late twentieth century. A systems administrator for an oil and gas company, he lives and works in Calgary, Alberta.

Cynthia Klekar is Associate Professor of English and Associate Editor of *Comparative Drama* at Western Michigan University. She is the co-editor of the collection of essays *The Culture of the Gift in Eighteenth-Century England* (Palgrave, 2009). Her essays have appeared in *Eighteenth-Century Studies*, *Philological Quarterly*, *Eighteenth-Century Fiction*, and the *Journal for Early Modern Cultural Studies*.

Todd Kuchta teaches modern British and postcolonial literature in the Department of English at Western Michigan University, where he serves as the Director of Graduate Studies. His book, *Semi-Detached Empire: Suburbia and the Colonization of Britain, 1880 to the Present* (University of Virginia, 2010), draws on postcolonial theory, urban studies, and architectural scholarship to examine the relation between suburbia and imperialism in fiction by H. G. Wells, Arthur Conan Doyle, Joseph Conrad, E. M. Forster, George Orwell, and Hanif Kureishi. He has published articles and book reviews in *Critical Essays on Salman Rushdie*, *The Encyclopedia of the Victorian Era*, *The Journal of British Studies*, *Nineteenth-Century Prose*, *Novel*, *Postmodern Culture*, and *Victorian Studies*. His research interests include imperialism, race, class, and the relationship between narrative and place since the nineteenth century. He is currently researching terrorism in modern British, postcolonial, and contemporary US fiction.

Christopher Nagle is Associate Professor of English and Gender and Women's Studies at Western Michigan University, where he specializes in eighteenth- and nineteenth-century women's writing, British and Irish Romanticism, gender studies, and critical theory. He has been a visiting summer fellow at the University of California, Berkeley and at the University of Notre Dame's Keough-Naughton Institute for Irish Studies and is a research associate of the Somatechnics Research Centre at Macquarie University, Australia. He is the author of *Sexuality and the Culture of Sensibility in the British Romantic Era* (Palgrave, 2007) and his work has appeared in a variety of journals and essay collections. His current projects include a monograph exploring the political engagements of Anglo–Irish Romantic women writers, an edited collection of essays on polyamorous literature, and a study of filmic adaptations of Jane Austen's life and works.

Robert Rozema is an Associate Professor of English (Secondary Education) at Grand Valley State University and a former high school teacher. His scholarship explores web-based applications and their use in secondary English classrooms. He is the co-author of *Literature and the Web: Reading and Responding with New Technologies* (Heinemann, 2008) and has written multiple articles on technology and teaching English.

Gretchen Rumohr-Voskuil, a former secondary teacher, directs the Inquiry and Expression program at Aquinas College. Her Ph.D. in English education from Western Michigan University addresses the history and application of the term "best practice," and she has presented her work at local, state and national conferences. She resides in Grand Rapids, Michigan with her husband and four daughters.

Cheryl Taliaferro is a high school English teacher at the Selwyn College Preparatory School in Denton, Texas. She has presented at conferences for the Texas and National Councils of Teachers of English, the National Reading Conference/Literacy Research Association and published in the volume *Adolescent Literacy, Field-tested: Effective Solutions for Every Classroom* (International Reading Association, 2009). Currently completing a doctorate in reading at the University of North Texas, her dissertation examines high school student responses to a novel set in modern Afghanistan.

Ilse Schweitzer VanDonkelaar holds an MA in medieval studies from the University of York and is a Ph.D. candidate in English at Western Michigan University, specializing in Anglo-Saxon and Old Norse literatures and culture. She has taught at the University of Maryland, Baltimore County and at Western Michigan on topics including early British literature, Norse and Celtic mythologies, and contemporary American nature writing. Her dissertation examines the representation of the natural environment in Anglo-Saxon texts.

Allen Webb is a Professor of English Education and Postcolonial Studies at Western Michigan University. He has written or edited seven books, published thirty articles and given a hundred conference presentations primarily on the subject of teaching literature. He taught English at West Linn High School for six years, at the University of Oregon for five years, and at Western Michigan University for eighteen years. His master degrees and PhD are in English education and comparative literature.

BIBLIOGRAPHY

Achebe, Chinua. *Things Fall Apart*. New York: Norton, 1958.

Anderson, Chris. "The Web is Dead: Long Live the Internet." *Wired Magazine*. September 2010: 123–127.

Baker, Chris. "Trying to Design a Truly Entertaining Game Can Defeat Even a Certified Genius." *Wired Magazine*. March 23, 2008. Available online www.wired.com/gaming/gamingreviews/magazine/16–04/pl_games (accessed September 27, 2010).

Baker, F. W. *Visual literacy*. Available online www.frankwbaker.com/vl_standards. htm (accessed July 30, 2010).

Bakhtin, Mikhail. *The Dialogic Imagination*. Ed. Michael Holquist, trans. Caryl Emerson. Austin, TX: University of Texas Press, 1981.

Barthes, Roland. *S/Z: An Essay*. New York: Farrar, Strauss, Giroux, 1974.

Beach, Richard. *A Teacher's Introduction to Reader-Response Theories*. Urbana, IL: NCTE, 1993.

Beach, Richard, Haertling Thein, Amanda, and Parks, Daryl. *High School Students Competing Social Worlds: Negotiating Allegiances in Response to Multicultural Literature*. New York: Lawrence Erlbaum, 2008.

Beja, Morris. "'The London of Mrs. Dalloway' [map]." *Virginia Woolf Miscellany* 7 (Spring 1977): 4.

Beker, Miroslav. "London as a Principle of Structure in *Mrs. Dalloway*." *Modern Fiction Studies* 18 (1972): 375–385.

Benjamin, Walter. "Theses on the Philosophy of History," in *Illuminations*. Ed. Hannah Arendt, trans. Harry Zohn. New York: Schocken Books, 1969.

Benton, Michael. "Possible Worlds and Narrative Voices," in *Reader Stance and Literary Understanding: Exploring the Theories, Research, and Practice*. Eds. J. Mary and C. Cox. Norwood, NJ: Ablex, 1992.

Berkeley, William. *A Discourse and View of Virginia*. London: William Smith, 1663.

Borreca, Art. "Dramaturging the Dialectic: Brecht, Benjamin, and Declan Donnellan's Production of *Angels in America*," in *Approaching the Millennium: Essays on Angels in America*. Eds. Deborah R. Geis and Steven F. Kruger. Ann Arbor, MI: University of Michigan Press, 1997.

Bowers, C. A. *Let Them Eat Data: How Computers Affect Education, Cultural Diversity, and the Prospects of Ecological Sustainability*. Athens, GA: University of Georgia Press, 2000.

Brecht, Bertolt. "A Short Organum for the Theatre" in *Brecht on Theatre: The Development of an Aesthetic*. New York: Hill and Wang, 1977.

Bredbeck, Gregory W. "'Free[ing] the Erotic Angels:' Performing Liberation in the 1970s and 1990s," in *Approaching the Millennium: Essays on Angels in America*. Eds. Deborah R. Geis and Steven F. Kruger. Ann Arbor, MI: University of Michigan Press, 1997.

Brewster, Dorothy. "*Mrs. Dalloway.*" *Virginia Woolf's London*. London: Allen, 1959.

Bruckman, Amy. "Purpose," a document retrieved by typing "help purpose" at Media MOO (telnet://purple-crayon.media.mit.edu: 8888).

Bruner, J. S. "The Act of Discovery." *Harvard Educational Review* 31 (1961) 1: 21–32.

Burk, Juli. "The Play's the Thing: Theatricality and the MOO Environment" in *High Wire. On the Design, Use, and Theory of Educational MOOs*. Eds. Cynthia Haynes and Jan Rune Holmevik. Ann Arbor, MI: University of Michigan Press, 2001, 232–252.

Burn, Andrew. "From the Tempest to Tomb Raider: Computer Games in English, Media and Drama." *Telemedium* 52 (Spring 2005): 1/2, 50–54.

Carey-Webb, Allen. *Literature and Lives: A Response-based, Cultural Studies Approach to Teaching English*. Urbana, IL: NCTE Press, 2001.

Clarke, Stuart N. "A *Mrs. Dalloway* Walk in London." The Virginia Woolf Society of Great Britain. Available online www.orlando.jp.org/VWSGB/dat/dwalk.html (accessed May 15, 2007).

Cohen, Scott. "The Empire from the Street: Virginia Woolf, Wembley, and Imperial Monuments." *Modern Fiction Studies* 50:1 (2004): 85–109.

College Board. (2010). *English Language and Composition: English Literature and Composition: Course Description*. Available online www.apcentral.collegeboard.com/apc/public/repository/ap-english-course-description.pdf (accessed July 30, 2010).

Common Core Standards for English Language Arts and Literacy in History/Social Studies, Science, and Technical Subjects. Common Core State Standards Initiative. June 2010.

Conrad, Joseph. *Heart of Darkness*. 1899. New York: Norton, 1988.

—— *The Secret Agent*. 1907. New York: Modern Library, 1998.

Crump, Eric. "At Home in the MUD: Writing Centers Learn to Wallow." *High Wired: On the Design, Use and Theory of Educational MOOs*. Eds. Cynthia Haynes and Jan Rune Holmevik, 2nd ed. Ann Arbor, MI: University of Michigan Press, 2001, 177–191.

Curtis, Pavel. LambdaMOO Programmer's Manual. March 1997. Available online www.brn227.brown.wmich.edu/encore/texts/ProgrammersManual.html#SEC1.

Daiches, David, and Flower, John. "A Walking Tour with *Mrs. Dalloway*." *Literary Landscapes of the British Isles: A Narrative Atlas*. New York: Paddington, 1979, 82–89.

Daniel Defoe, *Moll Flanders*. 1722. Ed. Albert J. Rivero. New York: W. W. Norton & Company, 2004.

Dowling, David. "*Mrs. Dalloway:*" *Mapping Streams of Consciousness*. Boston, MA: Twayne, 1991.

Doyle, Arthur Conan. *The Complete Sherlock Holmes*. New York: Doubleday, 1906.

Dressel, J. H. "Personal Response and Social Responsibility: Responses of Middle School Students to Multicultural Literature." *The Reading Teacher* 58: 8 (2005): 750–764.

Eliot, T. S. *The Complete Poems and Plays, 1909–1950*. New York: Harcourt, 1971.

Fanon, Frantz. *The Wretched of the Earth*. New York: Grove Press, 1961.

Feffer, Laura. "Devising Ensemble Plays: At-risk Students Become Living, Performing Authors." *English Journal* 98: 3 (January 2009): 46–51.

Forster, E. M. *Howards End*. 1910. New York: Norton, 1998.

Frye, Northrup. *Anatomy of Criticism: Four Essays*. Princeton, NJ: Princeton University Press, 1957.

Galley, Stu. "The History of *Zork*—The Final (?) Chapter: MIT, MDL, ZIL, ZIP." *The New Zork Times*. July 19, 1995. Available online www.csd. uwo.ca/Infocom/Articles/NZT/zorkhist.html (accessed April 17, 2004).

Gee, James. *What Video Games Have to Teach us about Learning and Literacy*. New York: Palgrave, 2003.

—— "Theories and Mechanisms: Serious Games for Learning." *Serious Games: Mechanisms and Effects*. Eds. Ute Ritterfeld, Michael Cody, and Peter Vorderer. New York: Routledge, 2009.

Glinert, Ed. *The London Compendium: A Street-by-Street Exploration of the Hidden Metropolis*. London: Penguin, 2004.

Golding, William. *Lord of the Flies*. New York: Perigee Books, 1954.

Haas, Mark, and Gardner, Clinton. "MOO in Your Face: Researching, Designing, and Programming a User-friendly Interface." *Computers and Composition* 16: 3 (1999): 341–358.

Hawthorn, Jeremy. *Virginia Woolf's "Mrs. Dalloway:" A Study in Alienation*. London: Sussex University Press, 1975.

Haynes, Cynthia, and Holmevik, Jan Rune. Eds. *High Wired: On the Design, Use, and Theory of Educational MOOs*, 2nd ed. Ann Arbor, MI: The University of Michigan Press, 2001.

—— EnCore Home. University of Texas at Dallas. Available online www.lingua.utdallas.edu/encore (accessed April 17, 2004).

Hoover, Wesley. "The Practice Implications of Constructivism" SED Newsletter 9: 3 (August 1996). Available online www.sedl.org/pubs/sedletter/v09n03/practice.html.

Irelan, Scott, Fletcher, Anne and Dubiner, Julie Felise. *The Process of Dramaturgy: A Handbook*. Newburyport, MA: Focus Publishing, 2010.

Iser, Wolfgang. *The Act of Reading: A Theory of Aesthetic Response*. Baltimore, MD: Johns Hopkins University Press, 1978.

Jackson, Shelley. *Patchwork Girl by Mary/Shelley and Herself*. Watertown, MA: Eastgate Systems. 1995. Available online www.eastgate.com.

Jones, George. "Interview with Richard Bartle." *Gamespy: Gaming's Homepage*. October 27, 2003. Available online www.archive.gamespy.com/dreamers/bartle.

Johnson, Steven. *Interface Culture: How the New Technology Transforms the Way We Create and Communicate*. San Francisco, CA: HarperCollins, 1997.

Kalliney, Peter J. "Strangers in the Park: Woolf, Selvon, and the Traffic in Modernism," in *Cities of Affluence and Anger: A Literary Geography of Modern Englishness*. Charlottesville, VA: University of Virginia Press, 2007, 75–111.

Koehler, Matthew and Mishra, Punya. TPACK Technological Pedagogical Content Knowledge. Available online www.tpack.org/tpck/index.php?title=Main_Page (accessed August 3, 2009).

Kushner, Tony. *Angels in America, Part One: Millennium Approaches*. New York: Theatre Communications Group, 1993.

—— *Angels in America, Part Two: Perestoika*. New York: Theatre Communications Group, 1994.

—— "The Theatre of Fabulousness." Interview with David Savran, in *Essays on Kushner's Angels*." Ed. Per Brask. Winnipeg: Blizzard Publishing, 1995.

—— "I Always Go Back to Brecht." Interview with Carl Weber, in *Tony Kushner in Conversation*. Ed. Robert Vorlicky. Ann Arbor, MI: The University of Michigan Press, 1998a.

—— "Thinking About Fabulousness," Interview With Michael Cunningham, in *Tony Kushner in Conversation*. Ed. Robert Vorlicky. Ann Arbor, MI: The University of Michigan Press, 1998b.

Lancaster, Kurt. *Warlocks and Warpdrive: Contemporary Fantasy Entertainments with Interactive and Virtual Environments*. Jefferson, NC: McFarland & Co., 1999.

Langer, Judith A. *Envisioning Literature: Literary Understanding and Literature Instruction*. New York: Teacher's College, 1995.

Langeley, Batty. *An Accurate Description of Newgate*. London: T. Warner, 1724.

Lee, Harper. *To Kill a Mockingbird*. New York: HarperCollins, 1988.

Lefebvre, Henri. *The Production of Space*. Trans. Donald Nicholson-Smith. Oxford: Blackwell, 1991.

Lenhart, Amanda, Jones, Sydney and Macgill, Alexandra. "Adults and Video Games." *Pew Internet and American Life*. December 7, 2008. Available online www.pewinternet.org/Reports/2008/Adults-and-Video-Games.aspx (accessed September 27, 2010).

Louie, B. "Development of Empathetic Responses with Multicultural Literature." *Journal of Adolescent and Adult Literacy* 48: 7 (2005): 566–578.

Many, Joyce and Cox, Carole. Eds. *Understanding: Exploring the Theories, Research and Practice*. Norwood: Ablex, 1992.

Mishra, Punya. Punya Mishra's Web. www.punya.educ.msu.edu/research/tpck/ (accessed August 4, 2009).

Moore, Tim. *Do Not Pass Go: From the Old Kent Road to Mayfair*. London: Vintage, 2003.

Moretti, Franco. *Atlas of the European Novel 1800–1900*. London: Verso, 1998.

—— *Graphs, Maps, and Trees: Abstract Models for a Literary History*. London: Verso, 2005.

Murray, Janet. *Hamlet on the Holodeck: The Future of Narrative in Cyberspace*. Cambridge, MA: MIT Press, 1997.

NCTE/IRA. *Standards for the English language arts*. Available online www.1.ncte.org/library/files/Store/Books/Sample/StandardsDoc.pdf (accessed July 30, 2010).

Newkirk, T. *Misreading Masculinity: Boys, Literacy, and Popular Culture*. Portsmouth, NH: Heinemann, 2002.

Osberg, Kimberly. "Virtual Reality and Education: A Look at Both Sides of the Sword." Human Interface Technology Laboratory. 1992. Available online www.hitl.washington.edu/publications/r-93–7 (accessed November 3, 2009).

Poole, J. A. "Journey Toward Multiculturalism." *English Journal* 94: 3 (2005): 67–70.

Pope, Rob. *Textual Intervention: Critical and Creative Strategies for Literary Studies*. New York: Routledge, 1994.

Postman, Neil. *Amusing Ourselves to Death: Public Discourse in the Age of Show Business*. New York: Viking, 1986.

"Programming a User-Friendly Interface." North American Web Developers Conference, 1998. University of New Brunswick. Available online www.naweb.unb.ca/proceedings/1998/hass/hass.html (accessed April 17, 2004).

Rheingold, Howard. *The Virtual Community: Homesteading on the Electronic Frontier*. Revised edition. Cambridge, MA: MIT Press, 2000.

Richards, Debbie, Fassbender, Eric, Bilgin, Ayse and Forde Thompson, William. "An Investigation of the Role of Background Music in IVWs for Learning." *ALT-J* 16: 3 (September 2008): 231–244.

Riggio, Milla Cozart. *Teaching Shakespeare Through Performance* (Options for Teaching, 14). New York: MLA Press, 1999.

Ritter-Guth, Beth. Literature Alive Home Page. Available online www.literaturealive. wikispaces.com (accessed September 27, 2010).

Roman, David. *Acts of Intervention: Performance, Gay Culture and AIDS*. Bloomington, IN: Indiana University Press, 1998.

Rosenblatt, L. M. *The Reader, the Text, the Poem: The Transactional Theory of the Literary Work*. Carbondale, IL: Southern Illinois University, 1978.

—— *Literature as Exploration*. New York: Modern Language Association, 1995.

Rozema, Robert. "Falling into Story: Teaching Reading in the Literary MOO." *English Journal* 93: 1 (2003): 33–38.

—— *Electronic Literacy: Teaching Reading and Literature in a Digital Age*. Doctoral Dissertation, Western Michigan University, 2004.

—— *Literature and the Web: Reading and Responding with New Technologies*. With Allen Webb. Portsmouth, NH: Heinemann, 2008.

Ryder, Martin. "The Cyborg and the Noble Savage: Ethic in the War on Information Poverty." 2008. Available online www.carbon.cudenver.edu/~mryder/savage.html# def_constructivism (accessed July 3, 2009).

Salmon, Gilly. "The Future for (Second) Life and Learning." *British Journal of Educational Technology* 40: 3 (2009): 526–38.

Savran, David. "Ambivalence, Utopia and a Queer Sort of Materialism: How *Angels in America* Reconstructs the Nation," in *Approaching the Millennium: Essays on Angels in America*. Eds. Deborah R. Geis and Steven F. Kruger. Ann Arbor, MI: University of Michigan Press, 1997.

Smith, M. W. and Wilhelm, J. D. *Reading Don't Fix No Chevys: Literacy in the Lives of Young Men*. Portsmouth, NH: Heineman, 2002.

Soja, Edward W. *Thirdspace: Journeys to Los Angeles and Other Real-and-Imagined Places*. Cambridge, MA: Blackwell, 1996.

Spivak, Gyatri. *The Postcolonial Critic: Interviews, Strategies, Dialogues*. Ed. Sarah Haraysm. New York: Routledge, 1990.

Squier, Susan M. "The Carnival and Funeral of Mrs. Dalloway's London." *Virginia Woolf and London: The Sexual Politics of the City*. Chapel Hill, NC: University of North Carolina Press, 1985, 91–121.

Steinbeck, John. *Of Mice and Men*. New York: Penguin Books, 1993.

Stern, Tiffany. *Rehearsal from Shakespeare to Sheridan*. Oxford: Oxford University Press, 2008.

Stoll, Clifford. *Silicon Snake Oil: Second Thoughts on the Information Highway*. New York: Doubleday, 1995.

Sutherland, John. "Clarissa's Invisible Taxi," in *The Literary Detective: 100 Puzzles in Classic Fiction*. Oxford: Oxford University Press, 2000, 461–70.

Thacker, Andrew. *Moving Through Modernity: Space and Geography in Modernism*. Manchester: Manchester University Press, 2003.

Todorov, Tzvetan. *The Conquest of America: The Question of the Other*. New York: Harper & Row, 1984.

Turkle, Sherry. *Life on the Screen: Identity in the Age of the Internet*. New York: Simon & Schuster, 1995.

Villa Diodati MOO. Created by Steve Jones, Carole F. Meyers, Mark Ledden, Ron Broglio. University of Maryland. Available online www.rc.umd.edu:7000 (accessed April 17, 2004).

Weinreb, Ben, and Hibbert, Christopher, Eds. *The London Encyclopedia*. London: Macmillan, 1983.

Wells, H. G. *Tono-Bungay*. 1909. New York: Oxford University Press, 1997.

Wilhelm, Jeff. *You Gotta Be the Book: Teaching Engaged and Reflective Reading with Adolescents*. New York: Teachers College, 1997.

Wilson, Jean Moorcraft. *Virginia Woolf, Life and London: A Biography of Place*. New York: Norton, 1988.

Wood, Andelys. "Walking the Web in the Lost London of Mrs. Dalloway." *Mosaic* 36: 2 (2003): 19–32.

Wolff, Janet. "The Invisible *Flâneuse*: Women and the Literature of Modernity," in *Modernism*. Ed. Michael H. Whitworth. Malden, MA: Blackwell, 2007, 199–213.

Wolfreys, Julien. *The J. Hillis Miller Reader*. Stanford, CA: Stanford University Press, 2005.

Woolf, Virginia. *The Diary of Virginia Woolf*. Ed. Anne Olivier Bell. 5 vols. New York: Harcourt, 1977–1984.

—— *Mrs. Dalloway*. 1925. San Diego, CA: Harcourt, 1981.

Wren, Robert M. "*Things Fall Apart* in Its Time and Place." Critical Edition of *Things Fall Apart* by Chinua Achebe. Ed. Fancis Abiola Irele. New York: Norton, 2009, 528–534.

Young, Jeffrey R. "After Frustrations in Second Life, Colleges Look to New Virtual Worlds." *Chronicle of Higher Education* (February 14, 2010).

Zwerdling, Alex. "*Mrs. Dalloway* and the Social System," in *Virginia Woolf and the Real World*. Berkeley, CA: University of California Press, 1986, 120–143.

INDEX

Note: Page number in *italics* represent tables and figures.